Multimedia Systems and Applications

MULTIMEDIA SYSTEMS AND APPLICATIONS

edited by

R.A. Earnshaw
University of Leeds, UK

and

J.A. Vince
Thomson Training and Simulation, UK

ACADEMIC PRESS
Harcourt Brace & Company, Publishers
London   San Diego   New York
Boston   Sydney   Tokyo   Toronto

ACADEMIC PRESS LIMITED
24–28 Oval Road
LONDON NW1 7DX

U.S. Edition Published by
ACADEMIC PRESS INC.
San Diego, CA 92101

This book is printed on acid free paper

A catalogue record for this book is available from the British Library

ISBN 0–12–227740–6

Typeset by Phoenix Photosetting, Lordswood, Chatham, Kent
Printed in Great Britain by The Bath Press, Avon

Contents

Colour plates are located between pp. 110 and 111.

Contributors

J.L. Alty
LUTCHI Research Centre, University of Loughborough,
Loughborough LE11 3TU, UK

C. Beardon
Faculty of Art, Design and Humanities, University of Brighton,
Grand Parade, Brighton BN2 2JY, UK

J. Bergan
LUTCHI Research Centre, University of Loughborough,
Loughborough LE11 3TU, UK

D. Clark
i-Media Ltd, 1 Addington Road, London N4 4RP, UK

J. Dickens
Simon Olswang & Co., 1 Great Cumberland Place, London W1H 7AL,
UK

C. Dormann
Rediffusion Simulation Research Centre, University of Brighton,
Grand Parade, Brighton BN2 2JY, UK

D. Fischer
Coventy School of Art and Design, Coventry University,
Priory Street, Coventry CV1 5FB, UK

W. Hall
Department of Electronics and Computer Science,
University of Southampton, Southampton, SO9 5NH, UK

M.A. Harrison
Computer Science Division (EECS), University of California,
Berkeley, CA 94720, USA

C. Machover
Machover Associates Corp., 152A Longview Avenue, White Plains,
NY 10605, USA

S. McEwan
Dorling Kindersley Multimedia, 36–38 West Street, Cambridge Circus,
London WC2H 9NA, UK

W.M. Newman
Rank Xerox UK Ltd, Cambridge Europarc, 61 Regent Street,
Cambridge CB2 1AB, UK

S. Nowak
Hodos Ltd, New Caledonian Wharf, Odessa Street, London SE16 1LU,
UK

C. Richards
Coventry School of Art and Design, Coventry University, Priory Street,
Coventry CV1 5FB, UK

A. Schepens
DOW (Benelux), Terneuzen, The Netherlands

M. Sherwood-Edwards
Olswang, 90 Long Acre, London WC2E 9TT, UK

H. Sloan
Consultant, The Square House, Latchmoor Grove, Jerrards Cross,
Bucks SL9 8LN, UK

M. Wilson
Informatics Department, Rutherford Appleton Laboratory, Chilton,
Didcot, Oxon OX11 0QX, UK

S. Worden
Faculty of Art, Design and Humanities, University of Brighton,
Grand Parade, Brighton BN2 2JY, UK

About the editors

Rae Earnshaw is Head of Computer Graphics at the University of Leeds. He has been a Visiting Professor at Illinois Institute of Technology, Chicago, USA, Northwestern Polytechnical University, China, and George Washington University, Washington DC, USA. He was a Director of the NATO Advanced Study Institute on "Fundamental Algorithms for Computer Graphics" held in Ilkley, England, in 1985, a Co-Chair of the BCS/ACM International Summer Institute on "State of the Art in Computer Graphics" held in Scotland in 1986, and a Director of of the NATO Advanced Study Institute on "Theoretical Foundations of Computer Graphics and CAD" held in Italy in 1987. He is a member of ACM, IEEE, CGS, EG, and a Fellow of the British Computer Society.

His interests are graphics algorithms, human–computer interface issues, scientific visualization, graphics standards, workstations and display technology, multimedia, CAD/CAM, graphics system building, and education issues.

Dr Earnshaw has written and edited 18 books on graphics algorithms, computer graphics, visualization, and associated topics, and published a number of papers in these areas.

Dr Earnshaw Chairs the Scientific Visualization Group at the University of Leeds, is a member of the Editorial Board of *The Visual Computer*, Vice-President of the Computer Graphics Society, and Chair of the British Computer Society Computer Graphics and Displays Group.

John Vince is Chief Scientist at Thomson Training & Simulation Ltd. He holds an M.Tech in computer science and a Ph.D. in computer graphics from Brunel University, UK. Prior to taking up an industrial appointment, he had been with Middlesex University for 16 years, where he taught computer graphics and computer animation. During this time he established a successful computer animation unit which undertook a wide variety of animations for television and film special effects. His PICASO and PRISM computer graphics systems were used for this work and for teaching computer graphics to students and professional graphic designers. He has written six books: *A Dictionary of Computer Graphics, Computer Graphics for Graphic Designers, The Language of Computer Graphics, 3D Computer Animation, Computer Graphics, Virtual Reality Systems*, and was co-editor of *Interacting with Virtual Environments*.

His interests are in graphics algorithms, real-time image generators, computer graphics technology, display technology, mathematics for computer graphics, virtual environment systems, and teaching issues in computer animation.

He has given many presentations on all aspects of computer graphics and computer animation, and has become an active member of the virtual environment community. He is a fellow of the British Computer Society and a Visiting Professor at the University of Brighton.

Acknowledgements

Many people have supplied information on their uses and applications of multimedia. Many designers and implementors have supplied details of their software and its applications. We express our thanks and appreciation to all those who have contributed.

DISCLAIMER

The views expressed by the contributors of information on products is believed to be accurate and given in good faith. However, authors and publisher do not hold themselves responsible for the views expressed in this volume in connection with vendor products or public domain products. In addition, the authors and publisher do not hold themselves responsible for the accuracy or otherwise of data extracted from vendor specifications.

COPYRIGHT MATERIAL

Some slides are reproduced by permission of their originators and these are noted in the text. Some materials are reproduced by permission of other publishers and societies.

ADDRESSES OF EDITORS

Dr Rae A. Earnshaw
Head of Graphics
University of Leeds
Leeds LS2 9JT
United Kingdom
Email: R.A.Earnshaw@leeds.ac.uk

Prof. John A. Vince
Chief Scientist
Thomson Training & Simulation Ltd
Gatwick Road
Crawley
West Sussex RH10 2RL
United Kingdom

Foreword

From the mid-1940s, visionaries and futurists have been predicting a convergence of technologies leading to an era in which information of all types is easy to store, retrieve, modify and present. The "memex" of Vandevar Bush, the "docuverse" of Ted Nelson, the "Information Age" forecast by the Fifth Generation Project, and the Information Superhighway all promise us a "Multimedia Age". As the economic impact of such a world becomes clear, the predictions for the future become more marketing oriented and strident. How much is real? Where do we really stand?

The technological progress is quite real. We do have more powerful and cheaper computers. The line between PCs and workstations has blurred. The cost of internal memory is lower and there have been substantial improvements in secondary storage as well. Advances in display devices have offered improved resolution in television screens, computer displays, and printers and scanners. At the same time, there are reductions in cost and footprint size. Color and stereo audio technology are now available at reasonable prices. Networking connectivity has been achieved by tens of millions of users. The combination of networks and large databases is providing access through the internet to all forms of information. Simple viewers like Mosaic provide free access to graphical information and (hyper) text, but animations and video are lacking for the moment.

Video remains an area in which convergence has been less clear. The television industry started to follow the lead of the major manufacturers toward HDTV but the rapid advances in digital TV seems to be more promising. Progress seems likely to be delayed in the U.S. by a squabble between TV networks over spectrum allocations which may be lost if a digital standard rather than HDTV is chosen.

The CD-ROM has become a standard method of distribution. While well-suited for audio, it has many defects as a video or multimedia storage vehicle. Refinements such as double speed or "quad speed" are now available. A new format has just been introduced which will allow double-sided recording and a single CD. These devices should effectively replace VCRs for playback.

Multimedia is more than a collection of traditional technologies. The key is the software which allows us to manage the individual media types and to blend them into multimedia applications. Specifically, this means graphical user interfaces, authoring systems, editors, special effects technology, and so on. Here we find good products in the commercial domain which are getting faster, cheaper, and better. Some of the newer products use new data representations that achieve significant gains in productivity. A concrete example is the FITS technology used in the "Live Picture" system.

But there is so much more progress that needs to be made. For example, it has been estimated that it takes one hundred hours of authoring time to produce one hour of industrial quality computer-based instruction. Authoring must be made more efficient and it must work in a truly cross-platform manner. It is possible to use the techniques of artificial intelligence and virtual reality to produce more realistic and exciting interactions.

What are the fundamental applications? Education, training, corporate presentations, informational kiosks are known to all. Another exciting area involves live remote cooperative media-rich applications. There are medical applications involving on-line conferencing and on-line discussion about medical diagnosis by distant experts examining X-rays or other scanned images. Such remote medical conferencing is especially critical when an injured party is in an isolated location such as a ship or in an underdeveloped area.

The emergence of multimedia technology raises societal issues like intellectual property, privacy, and secure commercial transactions. A multimedia author may need a broker to secure all the releases and license to use clips, music and art in a presentation. Juries may need to decide if an image which resembles a licensed one has been inspired by it or was created from the original and digitally altered or "morphed".

In some sense, the age of Multimedia has arrived. We have developed many of the technologies dreamed of by the futurists. The tools for integrating these are not yet ideal but better and more powerful tools are becoming available affordable prices. And there is no shortage of research and commercial opportunities.

Michael A. Harrison
Berkeley, USA

Introduction

For centuries the printed word has been a vital medium for sustaining the transfer of knowledge and information from one generation to another. Books and manuscripts have been used to document the rise and fall of entire civilizations, and they have provided a medium where typographers and artists have created some of the most precious artefacts of our creative endeavours. Even in a society immersed in non-stop television, ubiquitous background music and questionable videos, the printed word has retained a unique position as a natural and vital medium for communication.

Books and journals preserve a record. It can be objective or subjective, but as an externalization and description it can give an account of what was said, done, or discovered. Above all it is criticizable. This is is one of the primary virtues of the written record, as has been argued by Sir Karl Popper. It becomes the benchmark against which other conclusions, opinions, or discoveries can be measured.

It is difficult to quantify the total pleasure that can be derived from a book: on the one hand, it has the power to immerse our minds in historical and imagniary scenarios, and on the other, it can be a desirable crafted object. Paper weight and quality, binding, page layout, illustrations, even its unique aroma, contribute to a book's physical intensity. making it a pleasure to hold, as well as to read and own.

Books have evolved considerably over the centuries, both in the way they are manufactured and in how they are designed. Text has been embellished by decorative and illuminated fonts, and complemented by beautiful illustrations. Even the "pop-up" folded 3D models have been used as an exotic form of illustration. More recently, interactive books have enabled readers to navigate different routes through their texts.

How far books will continue to evolve is difficult to predict, but hopefully they will continue to be enjoyed by readers of all ages and in all disciplines. In the meantime, however, the digital computer continues to find success in application areas never anticipated by its inventors. A technology that was intended to be the servant of mathematicians and scientists has become a medium for journalists, artists, designers, musicians and teachers alike.

The digital domain gives us high-speed, error-free transmission, security through encryption and the integrated encoding of text, images, animations, and sound. Digital technology allows this data to be stored compactly, accessed randomly, edited, merged, copied, and reorganized at incredible speeds. However, the computer's ability to control different media sources simultaneously is only one aspect of today's multimedia revolution. For the first time in centuries we have discovered a domain that challenges the way we organize and interact with text, images, and sound. What is more, it is available on low-cost personal computers and accessible to virtually everyone.

Combine computer technology and networking technology and the desk-top PC then becomes a window on to the world of electronic information. The user can browse through information banks held on data systems world-wide. The renovated ceiling of the Sistene Chapel in the Vatican Museum in Rome can be brought on to the desk-top PC. Almost instantaneous transfer of multimedia information is now possible, allowing the possibility of modifying the original database so that it is always up to date, and the linking of different items of information to allow the user to assimilate it more easily or to explore new avenues of interest.

Like an embryonic technology, multimedia is developing at an incredible rate. Hardware and software products may have a short life, but new and imaginative multimedia packages appear with increasing regularity. However, in spite of this change, the enthusiasm for multimedia applications continues as its true potential emerges.

The true success of multimedia systems is not really about computers and technology but the ability to simulate and interact with real and imaginary media-based worlds. It is going to take time to research and understand the ramifications of this shift in the way we relate to information.

This book brings together a collection of international contributions on multimedia systems and applications, and looks in more detail at some of the current issues in the research and development of multimedia and applications which exploit it. Part I on Systems looks at technology, interfaces and techniques; Part II on Applications looks at simulation, education, publishing and multimedia futures.

David Clark explores some of the possibilities that arise when systems for the delivery of interactive multimedia are considered. Different types of data are requird for interactive media, and appropriate ways are needed for storing and accessing them.

Michael Wilson describes methodologues for enhancing multimedia interfaces with intelligence, so that they can interface more naturally to the user's needs and requirements in different application domains. Commercial products are increasingly including automated graphical design and input checking heuristics (e.g. for spreadsheets) and it is expected that there will be increasing interest in this important area. With these technologies, interfaces move from being purely multimedia towards multimodality.

Interface design is the theme of the chapter by J. Alty, J. Bergan and A. Schepens, which outlines the methodology used for designing and implementing the PROMISE multimedia system for use in studies of a chemical plant. Results of the study are reported.

Michael Harrison reviews the essential elements of hypermedia. Twelve crieria or rules of hypermedia systems are outlined. It is proposed that any robust, or industrial strength system must meet these criteria if it is to realize the full potential of hypermedia.

Wendy Hall summarizes the current work on hypermedia tools for

multimedia information management, and the need to integrate specialist multimedia processing tools with standard application packages.
Open hypermedia systems can be used as means to this goal. An example is Microcosm.

William Newman presents an analysis and evaluation of multimedia
systems and maintains that successful design of multimedia systems
depends on the availability of methods for analyzing and evaluating the
designs. Better methods are needed, organised around the solution life-
cycle in reall application environments.

The second part of the volume presents a range of applications where
multimedia technology is being exploited.

Stefan Nowak looks at multimedia in simulation and training; Clive
Richards and Detlev Fischer examine the presentation of time in interac-
tive animated systems diagrams; aspects of the exploitation of mutlime-
dia in educational environments are presented by Rae Earnshaw, and
Colin Beardon. Applications in publication and the exploitation of CD-
ROM technology are summarized by Howard Sloan and Stewart McEwan.
Julian Dickens and Mark Sherwood-Edwards outline some of the copy-
right issues from a legal perspective.

Finally Carl Machover looks at the future and anticipates the growth in
demand and application areas.

What of the future? Clearly we are seeing a growth in the exploitation
of CD-ROM for published materials. However, it is unlikely that digital
media will replace the printed medium in the near future. Although
many publishers are evaluating the new media, it is mostly in conjunction with existing media or to take advantage of the opportunity to present new kinds of information (e.g. moving images, sound, indexing etc.),
or to produce it quickly.

Multimedia is perceived to be a technology. In fact it is the utilization
of technology to encompass developments and deliverables in the area of
media. Text, pictures, animation, sound, and images can now all be
stored, modified, and accessed via computer technology, often at low
cost. It is these developments which are driving the migration of mass
services and utilities to the desk-top and which are fuelling the initiatives
outlined in the Follett Report on Libraries. Technology is a given, and
will be all-pervasive. What is not so easy, and which requires skill, is the
utilization of the technology in optimum ways for different kinds of
information, often in integrated form. Thus technology is best exploited
by those with expertise in media, whether it be images, sound, or television. To fail to do so will result in poor systems with low usability and
providing low quality information.

John Vince
Rae Earnshaw

PART 1

Systems: Technology

1 Defining the multimedia engine

David R. Clark

1.1. SEPARATING DESIGN FROM DELIVERY

The processes of design and delivery of interactive media programmes are quite different (Clark, 1989). This difference arises from the fact that during the design process the tasks all relate to the creation of a related set of interactions from a more-or-less *ad hoc* set of ingredients; the process is heuristic, subject to revision and re-creation. The delivery process, on the other hand, is the execution of a set of pre-defined tasks as induced by the user, where the tasks are pre-defined by the design process. As a consequence of this difference, many of the elements essential to the design process are not relevant to the delivery system. The practical consequence of this is that the engines for design and delivery must be quite different if each is to accomplish its tasks efficiently.

Whenever you see a programme being delivered on the same system on which it was designed, you can be sure that this state of affairs does not favour the users, especially if they have had to purchase the machine.

1.2. THE DELIVERY ENGINE

As the commercial success of any system will depend on its reception by end users, the most important aspect of interactive media is the delivery system. There will be many more of these than there will be of design systems, since the metaphor is that of publishing, where a small cadre of experts collaborate to produce objects which can be reproduced for distribution. It is the facilities of the delivery system that will determine the success of any programme, provided only that these can be bought sufficiently cheaply.

1.2.1. Cheapness

The fundamental factor in the acceptance of a new technology is its price/performance ratio. One of the places where this ratio is weighted heavily in favour of price is education and training, because there is no accepted opinion that the techniques so far employed are effective. The sensitivity to price is also a feature of the consumer market, and as these are the only volume segments of the market, the inescapable conclusion is that the absolute cost of a delivery system is of profound importance. All design constraints must be considered in the light of a possible mass market: this leads to some unexpected conclusions.

(a)   Consumer-driven market

In a consumer-driven market, it is the *expectations* of the consumer that are all important: unfortunately, those expectations are often ill-founded, have been created by fiction and the popular press; they are an unreliable and capricious lead to follow. The oceans of drivel about "virtual reality" sloshing to and fro today are a perfect example of the difficulty of conducting a rational debate on the future of interactive systems. Nevertheless, some attempts must be made to gauge the possible foci of interest that will determine the acceptance of a new delivery system.

My starting-point is that whatever else they provide, interactive media must have "TV" as a subset. This is not a comfortable conclusion, as today's technology is stretched to deliver high quality moving images with synchronized stereo sound at an affordable price: a TV plus a video recorder represents one of the more expensive personal luxury purchases for most families. To approach the quality available at the point of creation requires equipment costing some £1500. (Systems capable of producing the finest quality cost upwards of £20 000.)

(b)   Entertainment plus ...

The advent of the possibility of interacting with the images and participating in the course of action of the program has engendered much speculation and not a little experimentation in the use of such interactive systems for education and training. In order to provide the economic base for such applications, however, there will have to be a consumer market employing the same techniques. There is no appropriate model in the entertainment industry. The games machines, such as Sega and Nintendo, are far too formulaic and restricted in visual scope to form a worthwhile basis for programmes whose natural mode is "televisual". The demands of full-screen full-motion images with lip-synchronized sound are too great, even without the extra load of looking ahead to prepare for instant transitions to one of a number of alternative continuations. There must be a significant advance in the technical competence of a consumer hardware if the promise held out by the new interactive media is to be fulfilled.

(c)   The standard device

One way of accelerating a developing market is to provide several outlets for the same piece of hardware. In the case of the new interactive media, a good strategy is to work towards the universal delivery engine, the basic ingredients of which can be incorporated into machine tools to deliver set-up, maintenance and operation instructions, classrooms to deliver interactive learning programmes and the home to offer both entertainment and private self-improvement, whether for hobbies or more overtly educational pursuits. In each case the basic engine can be configured by appropriate add-ins to refine the capabilities to the particular tasks. This chapter will try to define some of those capabilities and indicate how such local configuration could take place.

1.2.2.   Multimode storage

There is a craze at the moment to put all data into digital form. This is not necessarily a winning strategy, since the sole virtue of digital coding, its resistance to corruption by noise, is not always an advantage, and its vices, the effects of sampling and quantization and the proliferation of bits, are often deleterious in the extreme. Uniformity is not a virtue in itself, *pace* the whole of the natural world, and great efficiencies and economies can be obtained by matching the needs of the data to the requirements of the systems designed to store and manipulate them. Interactive media systems have three distinct types of data that pose completely different requirements: pictures, sounds and control structures.

(a)   Data types

These three types of data are distinguished primarily by their fidelity criteria. To a high degree of approximation, control structures must be conveyed perfectly. They are intrinsically digital since their target is a digital control system. By comparison with sounds and pictures, their data volume is minute. Exactly the reverse is the case for sounds and pictures: they are inherently analogue and in digital terms their data volumes are immense.

Pictures.   The more we study the way in which we apprehend the world through our eyes, the more complicated the matter becomes. The process of "seeing" is not well understood, and is the subject of much controversial research. One day we may have good theoretical guidance on the best way to structure mechanical systems so as to make the best of the eye–brain combination that is to decode their output. For the moment, the most useful information is to be gained from examining the performance of the eye (and ear) as transducers. It is convenient to divide the picture stimuli into two groups: images and graphics.

1.   *Images* are all those pictures which result from a mechanical mapping of the external world into two dimensions. The generic is a photograph, which has been imaged by the camera onto the

film. The essence here is that there is an attempt to make a mapping of the external world – every point in the image corresponds to a point in the object. (The converse is, of course, not true.) The attempt may be frustrated by noise of one kind or another, but the fidelity criterion refers to an external entity.

2.   *Graphics*, on the other hand, are the remainder of the class "Pictures" and derive from an act of drawing. Here the fidelity criterion is entirely subjective. In digital representation, graphics may be of two types: bitmaps or procedures. The latter are of interest in that the picture composed of many procedural entities retains the implied meaning pertaining to the constituents, whereas the bitmap contains no components to which such meaning can be attached. Images are, of necessity, bitmaps. The digital representation of procedural entities is very efficient and their realization depends on drawing rules that admit of precise and efficient definition. Bitmaps have no generalized properties of this kind and their efficient storage and display is content-dependent.

Sounds.   The importance of sound in the creation of context is often overlooked, but the demise of the silent film with the advent of added sound should never be forgotten. There are two broad types of sound in relation to pictures, distinguished by the necessary connection or otherwise between them and events seen or implied by the picture.

1.   Sound events which have objective correlatives in the picture, such as speech and moving lips or the slam of a visible door, are called *sync* sounds. Failed correlation is most off-putting, and proper conjunction is a most effective part of the film-maker's art. As we shall see, achieving this correlation imposes heavy demands on some types of delivery strategy.

2.   Those sounds which add to the meaning and effectiveness of a scene but do not have objective correlatives in the picture have the film-maker's term *wild* sound. Unfortunately, their starts and finishes are just as tightly confined to the rhythm of the pictures as are the synchronized sounds, so this lack of a precise visual cue does not significantly alleviate the problems posed by the delivery of sync sound.

Control.   The user never sees or hears the control information – it is destined solely for the machine, and so quite different rules apply to its fidelity. In fact, this aspect of interactive systems is the least problematical, and will remain so. One possible avenue that is yet to be explored, however, is the use of musical instrument digital interface (MIDI) structures for the management and synchronization of interactive media data types. At present there is no industry standard for the synchronization of pictures that has a resolution fine enough to reflect the timescales of sound. (Timecode's finest operational division is $1/25$ s; musical articulation produces changes at least ten times faster.)

1.2.3. Particular channels

The different types of data, and the need to deliver them in precise temporal relationships, argues for keeping them in separate channels wherever possible. This is the practice universally followed in film, video and most channels associated with broadcasting (the exception being the transmission of sound in the synchronizing intervals of a video picture on some internal transmission lines). Whilst this reflects the widespread use of frequency division multiplexing (FDM) of analogue transmission channels, it is fair to say that the modern trend is towards time division multiplexing (TDM) even for video signals. This trend has been favoured by digital time-compression techniques, and looks to provide significant advantages in the analogue domain. However, TDM in a single channel can create a potentially catastrophic bottleneck when the delivery of interactive moving pictures with synchronized sound is required (as exemplified by the CD-I system).

(a) Data density

The most important feature of interactive media presentations is their dependence on pictures. The demands of pictures are formidable, and the current state of technology requires that special-purpose engines be constructed if the full versatility demanded by conventional picture-making is to be maintained (Clark, 1994). A simple example suffices. The clockspeed of a contemporary high-end PC is about 50 MHz. The fundamental clockspeed of composite video is 4.43 MHz (PAL) and the pixel rate for a PAL raster is 14.77×10^6 per second. This is why all video operations have to be handled by dedicated hardware, and the ability of the PC always represents a bottleneck. One screen of legal CCIR video (not the smaller RS170 value appropriate to the USA) is spanned by 768×575 square pixels; if the information is stored in 2 bytes, as is common practice in the broadcast industry (CCIR 601), this requires 0.883 Mbyte of data. Any decrease in this value represents an unnecessary loss of information.

Sound is about two hundred times less data-dense as pictures for the same perceived fidelity. The byte rate from an audio CD is 0.176 Mbyte/s compared with approximately 33 Mbyte/s for RGB video.

(b) Latency

The need to store and retrieve large volumes of data to support interactive media displays has led to various methods being adopted, the earliest being analogue FM carrier modulation (videotape and laservision), the more recent being various digital compression strategies (Run Length, Huffman, JPEG, MPEG encoding). All these schemes impose a latency period between the request for the information and its availability for display. In the laserdisc system there are two factors which affect this latency: the natural period of the video signal (1/25 s) and the search time of the engine. This ranges from zero for adjacent pictures to about 1 s for a skip over an intervening 50 000 pictures. This system is far-and-away the fastest access medium for worthwhile numbers of pictures.

The latency in the digital codings arises both from a search time and a decompression time. The decompression times are data dependent and decompression can only begin when all the compressed block is available to the processor. The consequences of this unpredictability of the arrival time of valid data are serious for interactive media programmes.

(c)   Versatility

In interactive systems the emphasis must be on the support for alternative outcomes. This is a far more severe problem than playing out an interrupted video stream. Not only must any sound be delivered at the moment appropriate to events in the picture, but that stream of events must be capable of diversion to an alternative stream of equivalent complexity within the natural interval of the event flow. A "cut" must be instantaneous, even if it is to a new event stream. There is no reason why film-makers and storytellers should be subject to more constraints on their style in the new interactive media than they are in the conventional linear media from which the new world will derive most of its grammar (Clark, 1991). Unfortunately, this puts a very high premium on zero latency and effectively rules out any of the contemporary digital solutions.

(d)   Veracity

The acceptability of pictures and sounds is a very subjective matter. A good guiding principle seems to be that the "camera" should be the weakest link in the chain, in the sense that the initial step should impose the fidelity criteria. Unfortunately, this has not been the course followed in the broadcast media, where it is the final display element, the domestic TV, which has until recently been the most serious limiter of performance. The most potent results from the advances in electronics technology are now to be found in the field of display device design; it is no longer the case that the final display need be the single most deleterious stage. Currently the pressure to reduce fidelity derives from the demands of the transmission channel, but as it is by no means clear that the most worthwhile uses of the new interactive media will involve long serial transmission channels, it is inappropriate to impose these constraints on the emerging systems.

There are two opposing factors which constrain the level of fidelity required in a system: the level of prior knowledge of the pictures and sounds to be displayed and the *a priori* attitude to the likely veracity of the events. The more expert the viewer, the lower the fidelity required to extract worthwhile information – for example, even the poor quality of the radiographs in everyday hospital use is sufficient for the expert eye to disambiguate the cracked bone from the negative scratch; similarly, if the expectation is that the image is to be believed, then it will be until a contradiction arises. It is here that the interpolated digital reconstructions are at their most dangerous, since the expectation is that every point in the picture corresponds to a real point in the imaged object, whereas this will only be true for certain key frames, the majority being interpolants whose content is not derived from the real world at all.

The principal conclusion to be drawn from this is that the more inexpert the viewer, the higher must be the fidelity of the pictures. Systems for learning about the "real world" must be capable of portraying it no less accurately than cameras can record it.

1.2.4.   Forms of storage

Just as the types of data differ in their intrinsic requirements, so the forms of their storage will differ. The discussion of fixed and removable storage of different latency is a familiar topic in conventional desktop computation, but it is given added weight when the demands of pictures and sounds are included.

(a)   Fixed

The division of storage into immediately accessible space with a latency no greater than CPU access time and more remote storage, whether on disc or other means, is standard practice and the different handling strategies are reflected in the operating system. They share, however, an immutable common rule – there is never enough memory. The point of exhaustion of RAM is reached almost instantly when working with images. One only has to consider the requirements imposed on an application that works on images and which must support "undo". There must be room to keep the version to which to revert without undue delay.

Display.   "Undo" is just one of the actions which impinge on the use of display memory. The main task of display memory is to provide digital samples for conversion to the analogue signal needed to drive the display. The 4×3 aspect ratio of the screen and the precise rules for the rasterization to suit the refresh rate of the display are not easily mapped onto routinely manufacturable chips, and it is only comparatively recently that the full CCIR raster can be supported by a digital mapping. The interleaving of writing to arbitrary cells of the display memory with the regular reading of the memory to support the display raster sets a limit on the rate at which the screen may be updated, and the current interlacing of two half-resolution fields per video frame also gives rise to "interlace flicker" if computer-generated pixels occur in isolation in one or other of the fields of a video frame.

Computation.   From the point of view of computing, processing an image requires that the "record" size be far larger that conventional processing units. The techniques now available for the alteration of an image, such as convolution with kernels of various forms to give different filterings, require unacceptably large amounts of time which programmed for von Neumann engines. All these image processing tasks are far better achieved by special-purpose engines which can use the ordered elements of picture memory in a processing pipeline. This is an extension of the idea of special engines for the computation-intensive tasks in computer graphics.

(b)   Removable

The reasonable expectation of delivery systems designed to work with pictures is that those pictures will be provided by others. This is most naturally achieved by removable storage systems. Although there are magnetic and magneto-optical read/write removable cartridge systems, the trend is to read-only and WORM laser systems. The advantage of these systems is that some already have a video version for pictures and sounds, as well as incorporating digital data.

Laser read/write.   Even before the advent of the Philips patents for the encoding of video and audio as "pits and islands" on a reflective surface to be scanned by a laser spot, there were other patents to encode information on a disc reversibly. The release of the read/write laserdisc into the consumer domain is a purely commercial decision, based on the recovery of investment in the now obsolescent videotape technology. The ROM and WORM laser systems already offer very useful properties for interactive media delivery systems.

Laserdisc (LD).   As all laserdisc systems read in a spiral which starts at the inner radius, they have no necessary size short of the maximum diameter determined by rotational stability. Conventionally, they are made with 3.5, 5, 8 and 12 inch diameters. The FDM carrier system holds one analogue composite video signal and a separate signal which can either be two analogue audio signals (LaserVision) or a single CD-audio signal (LaserDisc). (The NTSC version can fit in both the analogue and digital signals in addition to the vision signal, since the bandwidth of NTSC video is smaller than that of PAL.) Since the picture and sound (and/or digital data) signals are held in parallel, the questions of synchrony between pictures and sounds are not problematic, this manner of storage offers great advantages for interactive media delivery systems.

LD-ROM.   After a number of false starts, the manufacture of discs which contain all three types of data in their appropriate form is now routine. The ways in which these types can be traded off against each other in laserdisc is shown in Figure 1.1.
    The internal (shaded) volume is the standard set for the largest diameter disc, and the outer limits are those available by using the vision signal for either digital data or digital sound. If the multiplexed analogue components (MAC) (Morcom and Drury, 1983) encoding scheme is used for each video line, then it is very easy to store all types of data **in the**

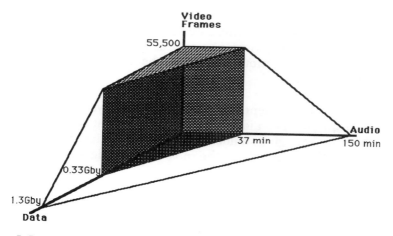

Figure 1.1   Ways in which laserdisc data capacities can be traded off.

vision signal. Remember that all this information is held in a single FM carrier represented by the pits and islands on the disc spiral.

Compact disc (CD).   The CD format has attracted a great deal of attention in recent years and has now been stretched far beyond its design specification. A clear demonstration of this is the tendency to spin the disc faster than the standard set for the format in its original audio design requirements in order to make it usable as a digital data store. It is worth remembering that the CD format was designed for the very specific purpose of holding an accurate record of the audio signal. The performance of the ear sets the value of the sampling frequency and the sampling depth (Carasso *et al.*, 1982). Taken together, these define the digital data rate of 176 kbyte/s; the total capacity of 660 Mbyte comes from the need to hold at least one hour of music. Attempting to use this single serial channel for other things than high-quality music has not been a good idea.

CD-ROM.   The first of the extra uses for CD-DA format was for digital data of a conventional computer kind. Unfortunately, the system has the intrinsic drawback of being a constant linear velocity (CLV) device – the angular rotational velocity is continually adjusted to maintain a constant linear velocity under the detector. In its original audio form, this was the ideal solution, since the data could be presumed to come sequentially for the great majority of the accesses – this is the intrinsic property of music! The same cannot be the case for data in general, so the CD-system cannot be efficient as a random-access data store. One case where this CLV constraint need not be serious in principle is where the data form a large coherent block – a picture for example. Unfortunately, this advantage is negated by the data rate, which, at 150 kbyte/s, is too slow in comparison with the data rate appropriate to the delivery of pictures: the digital data rate which provides an equivalent bandwidth to LaserVision for moving pictures is a factor of 60 times greater that the CD rate.

Trying to interleave pictures, sound and control information into a data stream designed specifically for sound only is a folly, and, although interesting demonstrations have been created in such systems as CD-I, the design constraints which this interleaving imposes on any general implementation are, in my view, so severe as to relegate such systems to marginal activities; for serious activities, the effort required does not yield worthwhile returns.

Smartcards.   The rapid development of solid state storage systems, as exemplified by smartcards, offers an ideal way of providing fast access removable storage. There are emerging standards for this convenient way of packaging ROM and RAM, but perhaps the most exciting developments lie in putting processing power on such cards.

As memory.   Smartcards are the best way of providing information to interactive media delivery systems. As they require no moving parts, their reliability is very high, and their capacity is commensurate with the requirements for the delivery of interactive programs. The generation of a "run-time kernel" from the authoring program necessarily results in a great reduction in both the size of the operating code and the data structure. Reductions from 3.5 Mbyte of "creation" code to 8 kbyte of "delivery" code and from 1.5 Mbyte to 56 kbyte of data code are typical in the i-Media system. As these types of card can be both read/write and read only, all the variations on protection and audit trailing can be incorporated as required by the particular application.

As processor.   One of the potentially most exciting developments in the field of smartcards is their use as combined processor and memory cards. It is not hard to envisage a box containing display memory, LD drive, video digitizer and input device control, all waiting to be configured by the addition of a particular processor plugged into the smartcard socket. As the creation and delivery of interactive media becomes a more mature field, we can look to such re-configurable systems forming the basis for every delivery platform.

1.2.5.   Separate processing

In the ideal delivery system there will be a number of separate processing tasks, each managed by an appropriate subsystem, since the model of a single von Neumann engine system is inadequate to the simultaneous nature of many of the tasks to be undertaken. In systems such as CD-I and 3DO there are separate subsystems to handle sound and image storage and display, but the process of subdivision has still some way to go before a sufficient degree of autonomy is reached for the various processes.

(a)   Programmable framestore(s)

The current generation of delivery systems do not support run-time picture composition. This is a major failing, since the ability to compare two arbitrary images is central to many tasks with an educational component. There are many examples of the serial presentation of still pictures or movie sequences, but it must be possible to allow the user to define an arbitrary segment of a picture, store a scaled copy of it in the display memory and add to this display other arbitrary segments of other input images, the resulting composite being available for interactive response. Such tasks as this require a programmable framestore. Given programmable memory of this kind, an easy extension is to enable rapid convolution of large images should image-processing features be required.

One immediate benefit that a framestore gives to laser vision systems is the ability to decouple the display from the drive. At present the picture from an LD system is delivered direct from the rotating disc. One consequence of this is that there has to be an interruption on the steady flow of pictures if the reading head has to jump more than a few frames. A picture store obviated this problem, and has been incorporated into some videodisc players for many years. A second advantage of the existence of a picture store is that it decouples the sound and picture channels, making "sound-over-still" possible. Now that framestores and real-time digitizers are off-the-shelf items, there is no reason why they cannot be incorporated into delivery systems routinely.

(b)   Graphics generation

The ability to generate procedural graphic images, the simplest example being good-looking text from scalable fonts, is essential for the next generation of interactive media delivery machines. This area is very well understood from the past decade of advances in computer graphics and presents no problems for the contemporary hardware designer who has grown up with the likes of QuickDraw. The management of colour is also well-understood and presents no serious problems. Moreover, now that real-time video digitizing is available in silicon, the versatile compositing of video and graphics is routine on dedicated machines and is ready for migration to simpler delivery engines.

(c)   Look-ahead

The essence of interactive, as opposed to linear, programmes is their ability to switch smoothly from one stream of picture and sound presentation to another. At any point in the interative programme a (small) number of alternatives will be appropriate for selection, and only one of these can, of necessity, be an immediate physical continuation from the storage system. The next major development in interactive systems that must be incorporated into the delivery system is the ability to "look ahead" and pre-load the appropriate alternatives to enable arbitrarily smooth transitions. As all the necessary information is available in the delivery program, this is not a complex task; it is more a matter of the correct organization of hardware and a degree of autonomous activity.

(d)   Navigation

There are still many unsolved problems in the definition of navigation in interactive programmes. The very use of the word "navigation" is itself problematic – the word presumes an external referent, e.g. "north", that is true and determinable at all points in the domain. No such external referent can be defined for an interactive media programme, and, as many of the existing programmes so amply demonstrate, it is all too easy to get lost in hyperspace. The exploration of metaphors for conceptual organization is a contemporary research activity and, at present, there are no clear signposts to the likely outcome. The current fad for icons, mice and the other paraphernalia of the GUI must surely be a transitory phase, but, in general terms we can predict that whatever the outcome, it will have its mechanical expression in an autonomous sub-system.

(e)   Audio processing

There may be several streams of audio to be managed and combined for output in an interactive media programme, for example the sound track from the pictures, some stored sounds relating to interface activity – beeps etc., pre-loaded soundtrack to be played out over still images and – possibly – real-time input of speech (or music) by the user. All these entities must be stored digitally at an appropriately sampled and quantized degree, and managed by a dedicated audio sub-system.

1.2.6.   Connectivity

The diversity in the optimum forms in which the various types of data are managed internally must be mirrored in the ways in which information can be supplied to or received from the delivery engine. Whilst by definition the delivery system will be self-contained, once the programme material has been inserted on whatever medium – optical disc or smartcard – is chosen, there will have to be output to a screen and speakers and input from some user-driven device. There are arguments in favour of network connection for delivery systems, but these are more economic than technical: in the last analysis it is better to have one's own copy of whatever information is required rather than to have to use an umbilicus to a master store, just as the chained book in the library gave way to universal ownership with the advent of the paperback.

(a)   Input

It may be that the use to which the delivery engine is to be put involves taking signals from another source. For example, a body scanner is designed to produce images on a screen, and the maintenance/instruction/help system for such a machine must have access to its output and connection to its input in order to deliver the appropriate responses. In the domestic situation the engine may be connected to an incoming signal from aerial, cable or dish and may require outgoing connection via the telephone line or cable return path. It may need to function as a Minitel terminal and receive digital data from a telephone or cable system.

Video formats.   The requirement imposed on broadcasters in the USA by the FCC to keep the same channel bandwidth as currently allocated to NTSC for any new digital video service is proving harder to meet than when that same restriction was imposed on the extension of the monochrome channel to colour in the 1950s. Digital services are more than a decade away for the transmission of continuous HDTV sequences and unforecastably far away for interactive programmes. Furthermore, the improvement in the coding schemes for analogue video which are still taking place will keep analogue systems in the forefront of technology for several years.

Analogue pictures.   Analogue video can be distributed in many ways, the most common being as a modulated carrier. This RF distribution is used by terrestrial, cable and satellite broadcasters, and the signal has to be demodulated from the carrier to extract base-band video and audio. This demodulation is accomplished by the tuner, which may also have to reconstitute the baseband signal if it has been encrypted. At present the baseband video is an FDM system in which the two chrominance signals formed by a co-ordinate rotation in RGB space are modulated onto a sub-carrier which is chosen to interleave its power spectrum with the harmonics of the luminance signal. Referred to as *composite video*, this single signal can be recorded or further decoded to provide the R, G and B signals for the display. Composite video is now rather long in the tooth as a system and is being replaced by variants in which the components (Y, U and V) are kept separate, either by TDM or by using separate channels. All modern broadcast technology uses some version of this so-called *component video*. The key feature of analogue video systems is that they are carefully optimized to the performance of the human visual system and attempt, at an appropriately fine temporal resolution, to provide one-to-one correspondence with the external world.

Digital pictures.   The three signals leaving the camera head and driving the display device are intrinsically analogue. In between, it is necessary to code them for transmission, processing and storage. In cases where resistance to noise is at a premium, it may be advantageous to code the signals in digital form. To do this the signals must be sampled and quantized, and this leads either to huge volumes of data or to compression algorithms which corrupt irretrievably the original signal. For broadcasting purposes, in which repeated recording is sometimes required in the production process, the resistance to noise degradation and the control of the increase in effective contrast which is the usual concomitant of copying, are of considerable value. Special-purpose engines of considerable cost and complexity are presently required for this task. The problem is that the sampling and quantization introduce unpleasant artefacts (e.g. "staircasing" of smooth lines near the horizontal and vertical) if the correct filtering processes are not carried out, and blurred pictures if that filtering is carried out badly.

In order to reduce the total quantity of data which is required accurately to represent an analogue picture, various strategies have been proposed, the most promising of which is to remove some of the high frequency (detail) information in the original signal on the grounds that it will not be displayed at the end of the line anyway. This is the philosophy behind JPEG, the public-domain encoding strategy for still pictures, and MPEG, and the soon-to-be-agreed standard for moving images. Because these coding schemes are intrinsically lossy, the damage to the original cannot be undone. Furthermore, as this process takes place in the (real part of the) Fourier domain of the picture, decoding requires the full complement of harmonic components before any part of the image can be reconstituted. This imposes a latency on decoding which can be minimized at the cost of making the encoding process more difficult. At present there is a factor of 60 overhead on real time in the coding of CD-I moving images of limited decoded quality.

Control data.   The delivery device must accept input from the user and there may be a case for its accepting data from a remote source. There is a trend to the use of IR remote control in domestic use, but this may not always be a good system in the workplace or classroom, where a wired channel is more appropriate. While keypresses are the most common form of user action, there is a growing number of applications which use barcode input, and standards are emerging for the specification of particular functionalities across different hardware manufacturers.

Some means of sending and receiving small quantities of data to and from a remote site will be necessary if the delivery system is to be used in a time-critical application, or if data accumulated in the course of using a programme (an audit trail) need to be processed rapidly at a central site. All that is needed here is a modem, and such devices and their software are ideal candidates for delivery on smartcards.

(b) Output

The primary output of a delivery system is sounds and pictures. At present, analogue audio is quite sufficient for sounds, since the speakers provided for desktop systems cannot reproduce the signal derived from the CD-DA data stream. As the delivery system will have CD-DA as a complete subset, it is sensible to include the standard optical data connection currently used for hi-fi. If this data path is accessible to other separate processors, it will offer an upgrade path when digital long-haul transmission becomes viable.

The greatest diversity of output formats is currently for pictures, and the target display device must be able to accept the picture output signal. It is easiest to classify the possible types by the number of separate channels they require.

Video formats (Quantel, 1990).   Analogue video is unique in that it contains picture and synchronizing information in separable form: the problem of data framing in digital decoding is absent; this is why the signal is so robust in long-haul transmission. The display device requires four signals: the three brightness signals for R, G and B, and the line and field synchronizing pulses. These can be delivered in a number of ways, according to the coding scheme.

RGB.   This is either a four-wire or a three-wire set of signals, depending on whether the sync signal is added to one of the brightness signals (usually green). The bandwidth of these brightness channels is 6 MHz for video.

Component.   The R, G, B and sync signals can be combined in a number of ways, but all of these combinations begin with the transformation by matrix rotation of the {RGB} triple to a set of axes that take the performance of the eye into account. This new space, {YUV} can be band-limited asymmetrically, since U and V, the chrominance components, need carry only 1/10th of the information of the luminance, Y. The traditional way of delivering these components in a broadcast channel is composite video, a one-wire channel.

One-wire: composite video is an FDM combination of Y, U and V. It has a number of drawbacks in that luminance and chrominance can be confused, as in the coloured fringes on closely-spaced monochrome variations, and the need for comb filtering of the chrominance sub-carrier so as not to lose the high-frequency luminance detail. The two coding strategies for combining the components into composite video in this way are NTSC and PAL. There is a digital standard for sampling this format (D2).

A number of manufacturers are using TDM to combine the components. These methods are variations on the multiplexed analogue components (MAC) proposals developed by Graham Crowther for Marconi in the 1970s, and they are based on the time compression of the components so that all may fit in one line period. Near-broadcast or better performance can be achieved with compression ratios such as Y:U:V::5/7:1/7:1/7. The resulting analogue signal can be recorded and transmitted.

A system which requires the storage of the chrominance from line to line is SECAM. In this method only U or V is transmitted on a carrier with Y, and U and V are transmitted on alternate lines of the field. Like composite video, this system is in decline.

Two-wire: the chrominance components can be modulated onto a carrier and provided separately, thereby avoiding most of the problems of composite video. This system is now referred to as S-VHS, and is widely used in domestic formats.

Three-wire: in the professional context, the component video signal is stored as a two-channel system on tape but moved between machines as a three-wire system, with a separate channel for each component.

Data formats   These matters have been covered in the section on the input to the delivery system.

(c)   Mobile telecoms

As one of the possible consumer uses for an interactive media delivery system is in-car travel information, it seems appropriate to think of information transfer via some form of mobile telecoms link. Again, this is just the sort of sub-system which can be delivered on a smartcard.

1.2.7.   User interface

This is perhaps the most problematic aspect of today's interactive media programmes. The fashion for mouse-driven systems in desktop computers is spilling over into other areas, but it is not clear that an icon-and-pointer system is anything other than prettification for interactive systems of any worthwhile complexity.

There is no doubt that "point-and-click" strategies are appropriate for intrinsically pictorial information. The trouble is that when the image has arrived as a bitmap, there is no *a priori* way of discovering the "meaning" of any particular area of bits. That information has to be "authored" into the image before the "hot-spots" technique can be used. This is an immense problem for any reasonable set of images, like, for example, the Bio-Sci II videodisc, with its 30 000 images of the natural world. When the hot-spots are graphics, rather than images, it is easy to recognize them from a pointer position, since their convex hull is part of their description.

As we gain experience in the presentation of information in pictorial form, it becomes clearer that a 2-D representation is too restrictive for systems of worthwhile complexity. However, the use of a 3-D space, whilst attractive in theory, presents almost insurmountable problems for the interface designer. Experiments with data gloves and other ways of delivering 3-D positioning information show that there is a long way to go before such systems can be routinely integrated into practical interactive systems.

Perhaps the most promising avenue is via soft keys, so that the absolute number of elements can be kept to a minimum and the function of each key is indicated on that key whilst that particular mode is active. Such systems form the essence of such graphical systems as the Quantel Paintbox, and derive from stylus-driven CAD systems of the 1970s. David Hon of IXION showed a mechanical soft-key system in 1987.

1.3.   POSSIBLE ARCHITECTURE

Figure 1.2 shows in block form the major components that will be required in the interactive media delivery system of the next decade. The essential features are that the bulk of the information to be displayed will come from a LaserDisc drive (**A**), and its data paths will be treated separately. The pictures in analogue form can either be digitized in real time

(**B**) or fed to the display (**H**) via a video mixer on the end of the D/A converter (**G**) which manages the output of the programmable framestore (**E**). Audio follows a similar route, and is buffered in a digital store (**F**).

The system is given its specific capabilities by individual smartcards loaded in the module (**D**), and the address management, routing and other general housekeeping, including data transfer to the external world (**J**) and the user interface (**I**, **K**), is handled by the central management unit (**C**).

Digital information from the laserdisc has its own path to the central unit, where it is available to the individual processors on the smartcards.

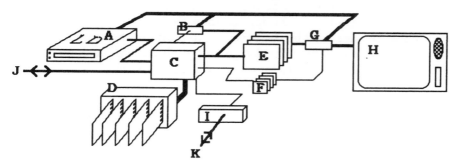

Figure 1.2   Major components of an interactive media delivery system of the next decade.

1.4.   CONCLUSIONS

The marriage between television and computation is not yet a happy one. Power having swung from the picture-makers with little understanding of computation to programmers with little understanding for the logic and grammar of pictures, the balance of influence has not yet reached a new point of stability. It is worth remembering that this point of stability will not be on a line between the two current extremes. The new discipline of interactive media will share parts of the current components but will bring elements of its own, forming the apex of a triangle with TV and computing as its base.

This new discipline will need new instruments with which to express its ideas. The tools from TV and computation are not appropriate, and their use is currently holding back the development of the new world of interactive media.

Central to these ideas is the separation of the processes of design and delivery of interactive programmes. As these processes are logically distinct, the engines which support them will also be different; furthermore, the nature of the delivery engine is the greatest single determinant in the wholesale adoption of the new media.

As moving pictures are central to the new interactive media, their management and delivery is of cardinal importance. At present, and for the next decade at least, low-cost, high-fidelity digital solutions are not viable. Meanwhile, low-cost, high-fidelity, high-capacity analogue systems are a commercial reality, and can be efficiently integrated into digital systems.

The individual configuration of a system is most easily set by providing a CPU, memory and program on a smartcard. A number of different cards can be added to build up the appropriate overall configuration. The infrastructure for this distributed computing is managed by a resident processor and operating system. Careful design of this infrastructure will enable such systems to develop in step with advances in both analogue and digital technology.

The existence of a low-cost delivery system which can be configured at will to suit a range of different applications, from the home to the classroom and workplace, will be the best way to promote the rapid uptake of interactive media systems. The design and production of such an engine should be the highest priority for our emerging industry.

REFERENCES

Carasso, M. G., Peek, J. B. H. and Sinjou, J. P. (1982). The compact disc digital audio system. *Philips Technical Review*, **40**(6), 151–164.

Clark, D. R. (1989). Separating out the design and development of IV from its delivery. In Tucker, R. (ed.) *Interactive Media: the Human Issues*, pp. 56–62. Kogan Page, London.

Clark, D. R. (1991). The demise of multimedia. *IEEE Computers and Graphics and Applications*, **11**, 75–80.

Clark, D. R. (1994). Constraints imposed by programme content on the design, delivery and use of interactive media presentations. *Computers and Digital Techniques*, **141**(2), 85–92.

Morcom, R. and Drury, G. (1983). MAC – the video coding system for DBS. *Journal of the British Kinematic Screen and Television Society (BKSTS)*, **65**(11), 602–611.

Quantel (1990), *The Digital Fact Book*, 5th Edn. Quantel, 31 Turnpike Road, Newbury, Berks RG13 2NE.

About the author

David R. Clark is Visiting Professor in the Department of Electronic Media at the University of Middlesex and also teaches and researches at the University of Portsmouth in the Department of Design and Media. He also works for i-Media, an operation providing cost-effective solutions to customers' requirements for interactive systems. His Ph.D. was in Explosion Theory, and after 10 years as a research chemist, he took up film-making and joined the University of London Audio-Visual Centre, starting as a trainee producer and leaving as its Director in 1991. His textbook *Understanding Interactive Media* is due to appear in 1995.

PART 1

Systems: Interfaces

2 Enhancing multimedia interfaces with intelligence

Michael Wilson

2.1. INTRODUCTION

Current interest in multimedia follows the lead offered by large software developers. First generation personal computer applications such as word processors and spreadsheets are now established, and for software manufacturers to grow they mzust find new applications. Fighting for market share is not sufficient to sustain profit and growth. Either they expand the market for the devices on which their applications run by introducing them to the home and integrating them with television, video, CD and other home entertainment systems, or they find new applications in their established office markets (Templeton, 1993). Networked and groupware versions of established office products are a temporary growth area, but when this is saturated a new area must be opened or growth will cease. Similarly hardware manufacturers must foster a need by the user for more CPU cycles, greater memory and disk space, or else they too will find their market saturated.

The accepted solution to opening the home market at the same time as increasing both new software applications and hardware demands is multimedia. Digital sound and video consume orders of magnitude more disk space, network bandwidth and CPU time than conventional data types. They also appear compatible with the main TV, cable, film and music industries entertainment output. The provision of multimedia facilities appears to support a new form of publishing. There was no benefit in publishing digital versions of Jane Austen novels as linear electronic text at inflated prices compared to books. The publication of the text of Shakespeare plays in conjunction with video of an acted performance, the sounds of respected actors speaking the lines, pictures of contemporary life and theatres, and historical commentary all interconnected, appears to meet the need not only to experience the play but understand its original context, and in doing so it appears to offer a richer experience (Cotton and Oliver, 1993). This interconnection of media and the provision of links between disparate sources of information follows the vision of Vannivar Bush (Bush, 1945) and Ted Nelson (Nelson, 1988) which are the most commonly cited stimuli to hypermedia.

MULTIMEDIA SYSTEMS AND APPLICATIONS
ISBN 0-12-227740-6

A contrasting vision is provided by Arthur C. Clarke in *2001* of an anthropomorphic computer HAL (Clarke, 1968), which not only provides data, but presents it to the user as appropriate to the user's task, when required. It is this second view which is explored in this chapter. Not only the provision of access to data, but the provision of information. Information theory distinguishes passive data from information which has the defining property that it can be used to change the course of human action (Pierce, 1980). There is a vast amount of data available; locating that which is relevant to a user's task and presenting those aspects of it which convey the crucial information is not a trivial task (Card *et al.*, 1991). Indeed the recent history of artificial intelligence following the HAL vision of computing has been fraught with excessive predictions and frustrated ambition.

In parallel with the recent rise of multimedia computer output has been a growth in novel input devices. Pen-based handwriting recognition, speech input of commands, speech to text, CAD-interpreted hand-drawn diagrams and Jot pen standards are supported by personal digital assistants (PDAs) and recent workstations. Half of the small personal computers sold are expected to include both voice and pen interfaces by 1998 (Crane and Rtischev, 1993). This combination of input and output media has led to research in not only multimedia, but also multimodal computer systems which use multiple input and output channels, as well as context information and data abstractions to provide co-operative interaction with users.

This chapter discusses current research in introducing intelligence into the analysis of the input to computer systems and the generation of output from abstract representations in multimodal systems. Although neither the interaction mechanisms of handwriting or speech recognition, nor the context-based dialogue control required by such systems even approach marketable standards (even a 99% recognition rate would fail on six letters in this paragraph with the result that one word per line would have to be re-entered), they are providing a direction for future developments.

After discussing the definition of multimodal systems an example system, MMI^2 will be described to illustrate their function and practical limitations. Then a multimedia presentation system closer to practical marketability, but including components from such multimodal systems, will be described to illustrate more realistic intermediate developments – MIPS (multimedia information presentation system). The purpose of this chapter is firstly to inspire faith in the objectives of multimodal systems, and secondly to show that practical progress can be made in the market towards them by introducing some features from them into simpler multimedia architectures. The use of limited heuristics for automated graphics generation and text correction are already being used as unique selling points to distinguish the existing spreadsheet and word processing applications which are market leaders so that they can provide more functionality than competitors. Further elements of multimodal systems will have to be introduced into multimedia systems as the market develops, for similar reasons.

2.2.   MULTIMODAL AND MULTIMEDIA SYSTEMS

This section describes a framework for classifying multimodal and multimedia systems using different input and output modes, and showing the other variations which arise from their use. The distinction between multimedia and multimodal interfaces is not obvious. Some authors regard multimedia as different presentation media and multimodality as different user input modes. Others make a distinction between the simple media which convey a message (e.g. video, sound, image) and the human sensory modalities which perceive it (e.g. auditory, visual, tactile). In contrast, multimedia is sometimes used to indicate an audiovisual presentation as in television or films; sometimes it excludes these and only refers to interactive multimedia which can be browsed, such as hypertext containing video and images as well as text; or sometimes these are also excluded as being insufficiently rich in their interaction, so that only the interaction by users with simulations of objects which can be manipulated as they would be in the world, in a manner closer to virtual reality, is considered to constitute multimedia. The term multimedia in a different community is even a label for the use of many mass media such as radio, magazines, books, television.

An important distinction during development is that multimodal systems are designed to be co-operative interfaces which actively choose the most effective and efficient presentation mechanisms for a user; whereas multimedia systems present the information in the medium which the author has provided. The sense of co-operativity intended here follows Grice's (1975) co-operativity principle: "Make your contribution as is required, at the stages at which it occurs, by the accepted purpose or direction of the talk exchange in which you are engaged". From this it follows that both participants in a co-operative interaction have a common immediate aim and the contributions of the participants will dovetail.

The contrast intended here between a multimedia and a multimodal system is best explained within the MSM framework proposed by Coutaz *et al.* (1993) as a design space for multi-sensory motor systems. This framework is presented from the computer system designer's perspective and differentiates some obvious features of multimedia while adding those which distinguish multimodality. The framework is represented as a six dimensional space in which systems can be described, so that they are not points, but occupy a sub-space (see Figure 2.1).

Three of these dimensions are easily understood in the context of most multimedia systems. Firstly, channel direction is the direction of information passing either from the user to the system or from the system to the user. Secondly, for each direction there can be one or more channels along that direction. Therefore a conventional telephone would allow one channel using audio to pass along each direction from one user to another. A video phone would allow two channels along each direction, with sound and vision passing between each end. Both the conventional and video phone would allow synchronous communication between both users at the physical level. Conventional television would allow two channels of audio and video, but only in one direction. This introduces

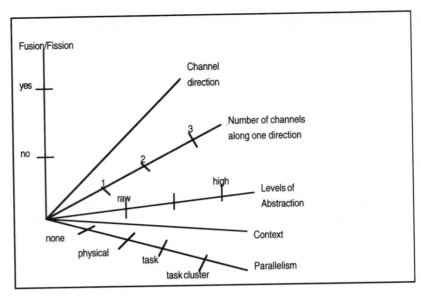

Figure 2.1.   The MSM framework: a 6–D space to characterize multi-sensory-motor interactive systems. (After Coutaz *et al.*, 1993.)

the third conventional multimedia dimension of parallelism; the video phone would be parallel at the physical level, allowing both audio and video simultaneously and synchronized. A low bandwidth communication channel may only allow sound at one time and video at another at the physical level. However, this may support parallel synchronized use of both media at the task level if the user does not notice the results of the division at the physical level. Similarly, input systems may allow only one mode to be used at a time (e.g. speech or pen) at the physical or task levels. More complex forms of parallelism can be introduced than purely at the physical signal level by supporting structured tasks or task clusters in parallel.

Although these three conventional dimensions appear clearly defined from the system's perspective, the exact definition of a mode and its correspondence with a physical channel are not entirely clear. There are those who regard "natural language" as a single interaction modality whether it is typed, hand-written or spoken (e.g. Cohen, 1992), whereas there is considerable research showing that spoken and keyboard interaction differ in many ways (e.g. Chapanis *et al* , 1977; Cohen, 1984; Oviatt and Cohen, 1991; Rubin, 1980). If someone is using a device such as MMI[2] which can input and output a subset of natural language, the user has to develop a clear mental model of the scope of language which can be used with the device. If the output from the system can be through either a form of canned text or through language generated from a deep logical representation, then the canned text will contain more complex language than the generator can produce. If the generator and the comprehension system have the same complexity, then the output from the generator should be used as the basis for the model of what can be input to the comprehension system by the user, and not the canned text. Therefore, to support a clear mental model in users, the output from the generator and the canned text should be separated so that users regard them as different, and only use the appropriate one as the basis for their models. Therefore the generated and canned text subsets of natural language should be treated differently and either presented in different windows or by different voices. These could both be presented as text on the screen for the visual channel, or passed through a text to speech synthesizer for output through the auditory channel. Whether they should be regarded as different modes or not is still unclear.

Similar examples are available when using freehand graphics input to a system which is then interpreted and presented back to the user as an object-based image, and direct-object based graphics with direct manipulation. Should these also be regarded as separate modes while they are both on the same channel? Should pen-based gesture be seen as a different mode from direct manipulation of graphics? Various studies are currently being carried out to investigate these issues of the definition of modes more completely (e.g. Bernsen, 1993).

When using a video phone it is possible to send instructions by both speech and image, and to refer in speech to items displayed visually. This process includes the speaker dividing their intended message between two channels – audio and video – and synchronising references between them. This process of the speaker dividing the message is termed the *fission* of the intended message. The complementary function of *fusion* is performed by the listener who will interpret the video and audio signals and fuse them together to construct a single comprehended message. In the example of a video phone, the speaker and listener will perform these functions, the device will perform neither. For a device to perform actions based on inputs from two or more different modes such as Bolt's (1980) "Put-that-there" system, the device must perform the fusion. In Bolt's system a naval commander could view a map of ships in an area of sea, and command the system to put-that-there while pointing at a ship and then a location. The system would have to fuse the gesture and voice input into a single message in order to perform the action of moving the ship, and then presenting the result on the display. This example performs fusion, but since output is only graphical it does not perform fission. Another example system which performs fission without fusion would be the COMET system (Feiner and McKeown, 1991) which provides explanations of how to fix and use radio sets for soldiers. In this a soldier can select questions about radios from a menu, the answers to these are constructed by the system which then decides on the best channel to present the information. In most cases the information in the message is presented to the user in a combination of images and text; the images showing where on the radio objects are, with salient components highlighted, and the text explaining the actions to be taken on the objects (simple actions such as the clockwise turning of a knob are also represented by conventional images such as arrows). The COMET system performs fission of a message between presentation modes, but does not perform fusion of input since all input is from menus.

Fission and fusion are represented on a single scale on the MSM framework so that if both or either is performed the "yes", rather than "no" value would be used. These could be divided onto separate dimensions if the distinction between these two were required to be drawn more clearly.

The video phone system only supports the transmission of raw audio and video information. This may be digitized and compressed, but it is not abstracted into any form of meaning representation. On the fifth scale of the level of abstraction then, such devices would be scored as transmitting raw information. An audio phone system which included an on-line language translation system would be required to abstract above the raw digital signal level and recognize words, relate these to meaning and employ higher levels of abstraction to support the translation. For an example of a voice-operated device such as an isolated word speech based command interface to a washing machine, the device would have to abstract to a level of word meaning in order to recognize the meaning of the single commands. This would be a higher level of abstraction than merely storing the raw signal. The Put-that-there system must abstract both gesture and voice input to a higher level than the raw signals, in order to fuse the two meanings together and resolve references between them, to produce a single interpretation of the meaning of the speaker. Similarly, the COMET system must abstract to a high meaning bearing level of representation in order to construct its answers to questions. These must later be translated down to low level raw signals in order to present the answers to the user. Therefore the use of higher levels of abstractions is required to support fission or fusion of information in different modes.

The sixth dimension in the MSM framework is that of context. As there are different levels of abstraction which can be considered, so there are different contexts. The preceding dialogue provides a context in which the targets of references in the current utterance can be found. This context must be maintained to resolve anaphora (references to ideas previously mentioned in the textual dialogue) and deixis (references to objects outside the text part of the dialogue presented in images or other modes). There is a context provided by users themselves, since they have different preferences for the way graphics are presented, whether information should be presented as tables containing exact numbers or as business graphics which provide an overview of the information, or emphasize contrasts, differences or trends. Each user has a different knowledge of the facilities offered by the system and how to use it; they also have different knowledge of the task domain, with different misconceptions of it which require explanations to be tailored to them in order to indicate and correct these misconceptions. There is also the context of the task the user is performing which will influence the structure of the dialogue, when the system provides the user with the initiative and when it takes it for itself. The dialogue context, user models, and task plans each provide contextual information which can be used to interpret input and to tailor output when it is represented in the appropriate abstraction. MMI^2 contains explicit representations of each of these three contexts (in the dialogue context expert, user modelling expert and informal domain expert respectively) which can be drawn on by the modes during comprehension and generation, and by the communication planning components of the system.

2.2.1.   Why multiple modes?

The justifications for using multiple output media to present information are given elsewhere in this book. The motivation for trying to use multiple input modes rather than relying on direct manipulation or command languages alone is that individual modes have different strengths and weaknesses as illustrated in Table 2.1 (after Cohen, 1992).

The objective of using multiple input modes is to allow the user to utilize the strengths of each mode while providing mechanisms for overcoming the weaknesses of each. In conjunction with multiple output media the use of the corresponding input media will provide maximum engagement with the information. The identified weaknesses of direct manipulation are all overcome by the strengths of natural language. However, natural language introduces new weaknesses which have to be overcome by the development method of the system, particularly in assessing the coverage of natural language required by a task and the presentation of this to users so that they can develop clear mental models of it (e.g. Fraser, 1993; Karlgren, 1993; Veronis, 1991; Wrigley, 1993). These issues are normally addressed by using Wizard of Oz studies at an early stage in the development method to state the natural language requirements (Nickerson, 1977; Dählback *et al.*, 1993).

Despite these problems with their concommitant costs, there are considerable advantages in natural language, which justify its use. One is its ability to carry complex quantification on both commands and queries as illustrated in the dialogue with the MMI^2 system below:

A1.   User: Which machines do not have disks?
A2.   System: cmr1 cmr4.
A3.   User: Add a small disk to every machine that does not have a disk.

Table 2.1.   Complementary interface technologies: direct manipulation and natural language.

	Direct manipulation	Natural language

Strengths	1. Intuitive
	2. Consistent look and feel
	3. Options apparent
	4. Fail safe
	5. Feedback
	6. Point, act
	7. Direct engagement with semantic object
	8. Acting in "here and now"
		1. Intuitive
		2. Description including
		    (a) quantification
		    (b) negation
		    (c) temporal Information
		3. Context
		4. Anaphora
		5. Delayed action possible

Weaknesses	1. Description including
	    (a) quantification
	    (b) negation
	    (c) temporal Information
	2. Anaphora
	3. Operations on large sets of objects
	4. Delayed actions difficult
		1. Coverage is opaque
		2. "Overkill" for short or frequent queries
		3. Difficulty in establishing and navigating context
		4. Anaphora is problematic
		5. Error prone
		6. Ambiguous

A4.   System: OK.
A5.   User: Which machines do not have disks?
A6.   System: None.
A7.   User: Does every machine have a disk?
A8.   System: Yes, cmr1, cmr2, cmr3, cmr4.
A9.   User: Does every machine have a small disk?
A10. System: No.

Another is its ability to express and resolve complex references as in the example below. In the above example the user issues a command in utterance A3 which uses complex quantification including a universal quantifier and negation which would be very hard to express through direct manipulation or in an artificial command language. In the second MMI^2 dialogue fragment utterance B9 refers to the disk on the server brought into focus as a component part of the machine referred to by its functional role as a server in utterance B7 rather than simply the last disk explicitly mentioned in utterance B5.

B1.   User: Add a 375Mb Disk to the server.
B2.   System: OK.
B3.   User: Add a small disk to cmr3.
B4.   System: OK.
B5.   User: What is the cost of the disk?
B6.   System: 1909 Sterling.
B7.   User: What is the cost of the server?
B8.   System: 4114 Sterling.
B9.   User: What is the type of the disk?
B10. System: 375 Mb Disk.

2.2.2.   MMI^2 – a multimodal interface for man-machine interaction with knowledge based systems

To illustrate the architecture and knowledge required by multimodal interfaces which support not only multiple channels in both directions and parallelism, but also semantic abstractions, fission and fusion, and the use of rich contexts, an example system will be described. Although other demonstrators such as COMET (Feiner and McKeown, 1991) are more impressive in generating combined multimedia, they do not include advanced co-operative dialogue or input modes. The MMI^2 system was developed with the purpose of demonstrating the architecture and development method required to produce large scale co-operative interfaces to KBS (Binot *et al.*, 1990). The first demonstration task used in this system is that of designing local area computer networks for institutions such as hospitals or universities (Figure 2.2 shows a screen from this system). A second demonstrator task was used to evaluate the generality of the architecture and the portability of the knowledge: the monitoring of wide area computer network performance (Plate 1 (colour section) shows a screen from this system). The overall architecture of the MMI^2 system is shown in Figure 2.3.

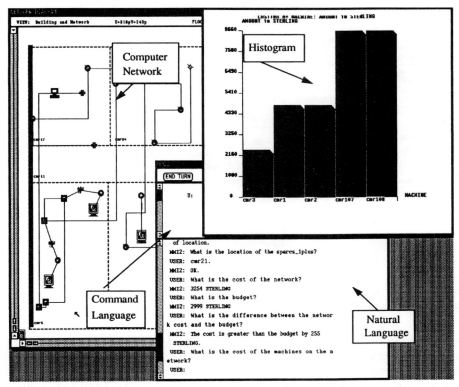

Figure 2.2. An example screen from the first MMI² demonstrator showing different interaction modes with the underlying application.

The architecture of the MMI² system can be viewed as three layers: the mode layer, the dialogue management layer and the application layer. Each mode in the mode layer of MMI² has a generator to produce the mode's output from the system generated meaning representation and a parser to produce the meaning representation from user input. The modes supported are English, French and Spanish natural languages, command language, non-speech audio, graphics for displaying CAD diagrams which support direct manipulation and freehand mouse drawn input, and business graphics (charts, tables, pie charts, hierarchies) with direct manipulation by the user on them. Pen-based gesture (as used in PDAs) on both these and the text modes. The natural language modes use conventional natural language processing techniques, the graphics mode uses explicit knowledge about the design of graphic presentations to produce effective and efficient presentations (Chappel and Wilson, 1993; after Mackinlay, 1986). Therefore several channels are clearly used in both directions between the system and the user. These channels can be used in parallel and are synchronized to support both fission and fusion, with synchronization of system output to multiple modes being managed by the Interface Expert.

As described within the MSM framework, the freedom provided to users by multimodal systems firstly relies upon the use of an abstract meaning representation common to all information sent to or received by each mode. The representation used for this must be able to express all

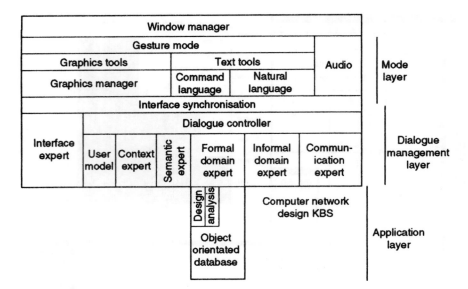

Figure 2.3. Architecture of the MMI² Multimodal man–machine interface for knowledge-based systems.

such information in order to allow the choice of the most appropriate mode for output and to fuse the input from different modes. In MMI² the language is called the common meaning representation (CMR). This language is used to pass between the mode and dialogue management layers of the architecture, allowing a clear interface where different modes can realize (generate images, language, etc.) any CMR description.

The CMR is used to support the fission and fusion of information between modes and to supply a common dialogue context through which to resolve references made within and between modes. Each CMR packet contains one or more CMR_acts, along with the status, mode and time for those acts. Each CMR_act represents an utterance in a discourse (e.g. sentence within a paragraph or speaker's turn of natural language). Each CMR_act contains an utterance type, one or more CMR-expressions, and a slot for mistakes. Each CMR-expression represents a possible interpretation of an ambiguous utterance. Each CMR-expression then contains annotations, a logical formula, and syntactic information. The status field is only used for internal error checking and the time field to co-ordinate input and output at the interface. The mode field identifies the mode through which the packet was received as user input, or the one for which it is destined as system output. The role of the utterance type is to define what processing, what functional interface call, should be used (either to retrieve an answer, to determine the truth of a formula, to assert the formula in the application, or to retract the formula from the application). The annotations and syntactic information are used to convey details of the gender, number of objects mentioned and other features for natural language processing. The formula includes a typed first order logic with relativized quantification and second order relation symbols, as well as the promiscuous reification of objects and events (after Hobbs, 1985). Table 2.2 shows an example of the CMR (1) for a user's input of selecting

Table 2.2.   Three CMR examples resulting from a graphical selection of a shaft (1) , the text utterance "Is using thin cable possible in this shaft?" (2) , and their fusion (3).

```
(1) CMR(
[
 CMR_act_analysis(
             u_type(phrase([var(x1)]),none),
             [
             CMR_exp(
                     [],
                     identity(var(x1),const(cmr_Shaft0)),
                     nil)],
             nil)],
ok,
Graphics,
time(56,53,23,11,6,1991))

(2) CMR(
[
 CMR_act_analysis(
             u_type(polar,question_mark),
             [
             CMR_exp(
                     [
                     anno(x1,[name(using-thin-cable),singular,definite]),
                     anno(x2,[singular,definite,neuter])],
                     description(desc(E,x1,USING,
                             identity(var(x1),const('using-thin-cable'))),
                     description(desc(E,x2,SHAFT,true),
                     description(desc(E,x3,IS_POSSIBLE,true),
                     conj(
                             [
                             atom(ARG1,[var(x3),var(x1)]),
                             atom(ARG2,[var(x3),var(x2)]])])))),
                     nil)],
             nil)]
ok,
English,
time(56,53,23,11,6,1991))

(3) CMR(
[
 CMR_act_analysis(
             u_type(polar,question_mark),
             [
             CMR_exp(
                     [
                     anno(x1,[name(using-thin-cable),singular,definite]),
                     anno(x2,[singular,definite,neuter])],
                     description(desc(E,x1,USING,
                             identity(var(x1),const('using-thin-cable'))),
                     description(desc(E,x2,SHAFT,( identity(var(x2),const(cmr_Shaft0))))),
                     description(desc(E,x3,IS_POSSIBLE,true),
                     conj(
                             [
                             atom(ARG1,[var(x3),var(x1)]),
                             atom(ARG2,[var(x3),var(x2)]])])))),
                     nil)]
             nil)]
ok,
English,
time(56,53,23,11,6,1991))
```

an object on the screen and (2) for asking a question about it. Example (3) shows the CMR which results from the resolution of the referent in the question (in 2) to the object selected in the packet without unresolved references (in 1).

CMR is inefficient at encoding bulky media for presentation since it contains the logical information to be presented. The image, video or sound rendition is then selected by the mode to present this information. In the first demonstrator the exact geographical building structure at the level of walls as well as the logical structure of computer networks was encoded in this representation (as shown in Figure 2.2), with a resulting slowing in performance. In the second demonstrator, map information (as shown in Plate 1 colour section) was not encoded in CMR, merely the logical label of the overall map.

Within the MMI^2 system it is reasonable to consider three levels of abstraction on that dimension of the MSM framework. There is the raw input which is typed, or presented through mouse movements as gestures, manipulations or menu selections. Above this there is the CMR which is common to all modes expressing the logical context of communication actions. Thirdly, there is a higher level of abstraction used to plan communication in terms of communication forces (Cohen *et al.*, 1990). At this level, communication acts are labelled as providing such things as apologies, problem reports, justifications, or requests. These follow the philosophy of communication acts which are common to intentions that can be expressed in any mode proposed by Maybury (1991) following the notion of communication as an action-based endeavour, originally proposed by Austin (1962). In addition to these three levels of abstraction there are clearly other local abstractions within the overall system: within the gesture mode, strokes are combined into multi-stroke gestures; within the natural language modes, there are syntactic abstractions; within the graphics mode, pixels are placed together into icons to represent objects, or into lines and surfaces. However, each of these abstractions is specific to a mode, and they are used as steps to relate communications in each mode itself to the meaning representation which is common to all modes. Therefore considering the three levels of abstraction mentioned above provides a clearer view of the operation of the overall system.

The second necessity for a co-operative multimodal system is that there is a common reference context for all objects. MMI^2 contains a Context Expert that stores all objects referred to in the CMR representations of the dialogue which pass between the mode layer and the Dialogue Controller, and it provides the Dialogue Controller with candidates to resolve diexis and anaphora (e.g. Cohen *et al.*, 1990). Therefore each mode can refer to objects mentioned in other modes where the references will be resolved by the Context Expert as illustrated in Table 2.2. For example, the user can combine text input and mouse pointing (e.g. "Is using thin cable possible in ⟨mouse select⟩ this shaft?") and the system can combine graphical output with text (e.g. "What is the type of ⟨system highlight cable⟩ this cable?").

The range of contexts used in MMI^2 to interpret user input and generate system output is larger than just the dialogue context. Two other domains of knowledge are represented as contexts: the context of the user, and the context of the task being performed. The user model contains a model of the beliefs of the user (Chappel *et al.*, 1992). It monitors all messages passing between the mode and dialogue management layers in CMR and extracts from them beliefs which the user holds (both correctly and incorrectly with respect to the knowledge stored in the KBS in MMI^2, which is assumed to be correct), and the intentions of the user. This user model then acts as a server to other parts of the system which require knowledge of the user, such as the graphics manager for planning effective graphics communication, the natural language generators for generating text, and the communications and informal domain experts for planning multi-modal fission.

The informal domain expert contains plans of tasks the user may wish to perform. These provide a context in which to evaluate informally the user commands and queries, and a model of the position of the user in a task can be drawn on when the Communication Planning Expert is generating system output. When the user asks "What is the cost of the network?", the cost of each item in the network must be known. If some items are underspecified for pricing (e.g. a cable has been classed as a generic cable rather than a particular one for which a sales price is listed) such unmet preconditions to the calculation of the price will be determined by the informal domain expert. A second example could be if the user issues a command to "Add a computer to the network?"; in this case the unmet preconditions would be the exact type and location of the machine (e.g. a Sun Sparc2 in Room36). In both these cases the informal domain expert plans provide the context to identify the unmet preconditions that would be passed to the communication planning expert which would in turn continue a co-operative dialogue with the user to meet the objective of their plan by asking for the required information. The dialogue which arises from the use of the task context can be deeply nested since many preconditions may have to be met, but it is clearly directed to the aim of the user which has been identified in the task plan, and thereby conforms to Grice's cooperativity principle.

The communication planning module generates large CMR structures which can be passed to the modes for output to the user. The response the communication planner would make to this example illustrates the use of the third and highest level of abstraction mentioned above: that of communication actions. The reply to the request to "Add a computer to the network?" might be one of the following (as rendered by the English mode):

1.   I am sorry.
2.   The location and the type of workstation CMR98 are underspecified.
3.   Adding a workstation requires the specification of the location and type.
4.   What is the type of the workstation CMR98?

These four replies would be associated with the communication actions of Apology, Problem Report, Justification and Request respectively. If the problem had already arisen recently in the dialogue context and the same output produced then the dialogue context would show this and the justification would be omitted. Similarly, if the problem appeared frequently, the apology may be replaced by an exclamation. The context of the user model could also be drawn on to elaborate the justification if it showed that the user was unclear about the types of workstation which were possible answers, so that a list would be provided. This example shows how the task context is used in the informal context expert to trigger co-operative dialogue, and both the context of the user model and the dialogue context are used to modify the system output.

This example of communication planning produces output purely for natural language modes, and does not illustrate multimedia output. The output generated can be directed at different modes depending on which is most effective at conveying the intended class of information. Table 2.3 shows the relation between different information types and their presentation from the COMET system which is similar to the heuristic rules used in MMI[2].

As mentioned above, the informal domain expert supports the interpretation of user input CMR packets against tasks plans. Obviously these do not answer most questions or perform most commands represented in CMR packets. Indeed, no commands are performed as a result of this informal evaluation which merely checks that they can be performed at the time they are issued. The main application program contains expert systems which perform the design of computer networks and store those designs in an object-oriented database. It also contains analysis experts which can analyse the stored design for its potential extensibility and other properties of interest to the application user. To perform the design, analyses, assert building components or design requirements in the database, requires formal evaluation against the database or experts. To answer queries about the objects in the building or on the network requires formal interpretation against this database. This application is accessed through the formal domain expert which provides a functional interface which includes three operations: Assert, Retract and Goal, to update the knowledge bases, retract information from them, and ask questions of them. This is similar to the level of operation provided in other knowledge-based systems (e.g. Guha and Lenat, 1990). For each application domain predicate defined as permitted in CMR within the semantic expert there is an interface in the formal domain expert which maps it to the application itself to support the main operation of the system.

Table 2.3. The relation between different information types and their presentation (after Feiner and McKeown, 1991)

Information Types	Presentation Style
Location Information Physical Attributes	Graphics Only
Simple Actions Compound actions	Text and Graphics
Conditionals	Text for connectives text and graphics for actions
Abstract Actions	Text Only

MMI^2 does not include a broad knowledge base of common-sense knowledge (e.g. Guha and Lenat, 1990) but it must include more than just the limited domain knowledge for the demonstrator application for designing computer networks. The interface expert contains information about the interface itself. This is available to answer questions about the interface and its capabilities, but also for the evaluation of predicates in the CMR about the interface. For example, if the user commands the system to "draw a bar chart of the cost of computers on the network" then concepts such as bar chart are not network design concepts, but interface concepts; thus their evaluation is against the domain of the interface rather than network design. The third domain for formal evaluation is that of the user model which is also available for the evaluation or interpretation of predicates in CMR about the user (e.g. to answer questions such has "Who am I?"). All three domains are accessed through the same functional interface which supports the formal evaluation of CMR predicates by the dialogue controller and support the re-use of the modules outside the single application task of local area network design used in the first demonstrator as shown by the development of a second demonstrator in the area of wide area network management.

2.2.3. Advantages of multimodality

The MMI^2 system described illustrates the architecture required for a multimodal system which supports co-operative dialogue. There are potential modes such as the use of machine vision understanding systems to interpret body posture and facial expression to provide additional data to determine the intended pragmatics of utterances which it does not use; neither does it include continuous output media such as video or sound. Both of these have been considered within the general architectural design and should be compatible with it, with the meaning representation used, and with the view of interaction proposed in the MSM framework.

Such interactive systems as MMI^2 may seem a long way from current multimedia systems but they do provide several advantages. Firstly, users can maximize expressiveness by choosing the appropriate input mode: natural language for complex quantification and reference use, freehand drawing for inputting building designs, and pen-like gestures for editing, or direct manipulation to move objects in the CAD displays. Secondly, the system supports the fusion of multimodal input and the fission of output through the use of a single abstract meaning representation, as well as the use of a single dialogue context to resolve intra- and inter-modal referents. Thirdly, the use of the dialogue context, user model, and task model support co-operative dialogue where the user and system have the same aim, while system output is tailored to the user at the point they are in the task and dialogue. Fourthly, the most effective and efficient output mode can be selected for system expression through the use of heuristic communication rules, and the rendition of the abstract meaning representation is generated by further heuristic information design rules within the individual modes (automated graphics design rules or natural language generation system). These four advantages of multi-modality arise from the three additional features in the MSM framework (fusion/fission, levels of abstraction towards meaning and context) beyond the three found in conventional multimedia systems (channel direction, number of channels along direction and parallelism).

2.2.4. Limitations of multimodality

Unfortunately there is a price to pay for the added expressiveness which arises from the multimodal approach. There are serious problems in the use of natural language comprehension modes because of the difficulty with specifying the requirements for a fluent and robust system (Stede, 1993). The conventional techniques for developing natural language interfaces (as used in MMI[2]) are very data dependent where the data is col-lected through Wizard of Oz experiments on potential users in the pro-posed task. This results in the implementation not of an English natural language interface, but one which understands the limited subset of the English lexicon, grammar, semantics and pragmatics which are exhibited during that data collection. The engineering issues associated with natu-ral language comprehension are a major current research topic, but at pre-sent the development methods do not provide users with a clear mental model of the sublanguage which can be used (Veronis, 1991; Wrigley, 1993).

The second major limitation arises from the abstract meaning repre-sentation itself as a medium for encoding graphics and continuous media. Although the CMR has been shown to be sufficiently expressive to repre-sent the information conveyed through the modes it is inefficient. For CAD displays of buildings and networks this information included the location of walls, rooms, cables and machines relative to each other. The lines and icons to represent these were generated in the graphics mode. For complex diagrams these representations could be 100,000 lines of CMR logical formulae. For large bodies of text or continuous media to be retrieved these representations would become even larger and less effi-cient. The CMR is also non-standard, with the result that information must be translated into it for presentation. Further research is required to improve the efficiency whilst maintaining the expressiveness of the meaning representation language. The third problem with developing commercial products incorporating the context models included in MMI[2] to represent the user, task and domain is the effort required to encode them and link the interface to the underlying application. The fourth lim-itation in applying the approach is in the generality of the output genera-tion rule sets. Although the concept appears to have been proved, further focused projects are required to refine the generation rules along with the context sensitive reference resolution rules.

Complete multimodal systems such as MMI[2] are currently only research demonstrators which can produce potent illustrations of multi-modal interaction, but are not even robust enough for real user evaluation. However, many components shown in this system are being brought to the marketplace where there is seen to be a need for them. Gesture interfaces of the form used in MMI^2 have now been incorporated in PDAs for recognizing symbols, even if they are not practically sophisticated enough to interpret cursive writing sufficiently reliably yet. The freehand input of building drawings and their automatic interpretation into objects used in MMI^2 has also been incorporated in many PDAs. Several companies are developing speech input command systems which will fuse their input with that from gesture mode using principles developed in MMI^2. Many spreadsheet developers are including business graphics creation rule sets to generate bar charts, pie charts and graphs automatically from spreadsheet data using rules similar to those used in the MMI^2 graphics manager. Constrained natural language query systems for databases incorporate technologies which are a subset of those used in the MMI^2 natural language input mode, and many of these are starting to incorporate graphical interface tools to help complement natural language, combining modes again using principles seen in MMI^2. It is not practical to move from current application architectures to logic-based, dialogue-centred systems such as MMI^2 in one step. It is necessary to isolate out those aspects which can be combined into more conventional designs to add functionality to them in order to create dynamically presentations which are tailored to the user, task and dialogue context as those in MMI^2 are.

2.2.5. MIPS – a multimedia information retrieval and presentation system

The first problem in the implementation of the multimodal approach identified above was the use of natural language as an input mode. If this is replaced with a less free input mode such as menu-based form completion the problem of clarity in users' mental models of the limitations on input will be overcome. If the task is limited in potential complexity from a design task to an information retrieval task then the expressiveness required in the dialogue will be commensurately reduced. However, if the dialogue is restricted in this way, then the expressiveness permitted the user is also reduced, but although dialogue will be more predictable, it can still include complex subdialogues.

The second problem identified was the use of the CMR to encode graphics and continuous media for system output. In MMI^2 the logical representation in the CMR carried the identity and relationship of objects to be presented to users. For generated natural language output these representations can be very large. Equally the CMR is a non-standard representation and retrieved information would have to be translated into it. In an information retrieval task it is unreasonable to assume that all the retrieved data will already be written in such a logical language, rather it will be in text or media formats. Queries for information retrieval are normally made in a logical representation (e.g. languages such as SQL) which can be extended to convey both details about the expected media sought (e.g. a video of New York harbour rather than a textual guide to it) and about the pragmatics of the retrieval process itself (e.g. a cost and time above which the retrieval would not be desired). The major problem comes with the returned data format. Existing databases use many different formats.

To allow any operations on the returned data these would have to be converted to a single format, or a group of formats understood by output modes. Equally, for large amounts of retrieved data which were to be stored (or cached) locally to allow users to browse them, the media would have to be linked together to support the user's task of browsing. Current hypertext systems are closed individual products where the reader can choose routes through a pre-written web but they support links between data on the basis of logical structure and allow the incorporation of different media. Unfortunately, both the content and the link design have usually been completed by the author. A step towards opening up such systems is provided by the Microcosm system (Davis *et al.*, 1993; Hall, Chapter 5 this volume) which separates the link structure from the data assets presented in the hypertext, thereby allowing users to link pre-existing documents, images and other media items to a web. Since media items are independent they can also be stored in the formats of common presentation tools, providing users with a more consistent system image between the hypertext and other tools on a system. This changes the hyperdocument from being purely an artifact created by an author to one which can be part of an open information system where assets can be re-used in many documents. The next stage in opening up hypertext documents is to represent the link structures themselves in an interchangeable language. This would allow a set of data assets and the link structure to be portable across different presentation and link authoring platforms. This standardization of open link representation is available in the ISO HyTime standard for hypermedia time-based data (Newcombe *et al.*, 1991; ISO, 1992). These two advances of opening hypertext by separating assets from links and then using standardized representations for both assets and link webs support the portability of hypertext. By employing a HyTime web to represent the logical structure of returned data in the form of links, with the data assets themselves represented in their original stored formats a more efficient portable representation would be achieved for data to be browsed or presented than the CMR used in MMI^2. This arrangement would allow the representation of raw multimedia data, with a logical representation of both queries and the link structure of returned data. A conceptual representation of these logical labels would be required in a domain context model in a knowledge-based system (KBS), although this would not be required throughout an architecture. Similarly, the highest level used in MMI^2 (the communication act level) could also be represented for limited reasoning about communication planning in the form of information presentation design although this too would not be required to be transmitted throughout an architecture, as indeed it was not in MMI^2 where it was limited to the Communication Planning Expert.

While overcoming the problems introduced into multimodal systems by a common meaning representation of both user input and system output, by using a task of reduced dialogue complexity, extended logical query languages for user input and a standard hypermedia language which separates data and structure for output, we have also maintained the functionality of fission/fusion and multiple channels in both directions from the multimodal approach. However, we also wish to maintain the advantages provided by the use of context for tailoring output and generating it from communication rules. To do this we must maintain contextual models of the domain, task, user and dialogue which can be used to constrain query processing, the linking of returned data into hypertext webs and the presentation of those webs to users, through the use of communication rules which guide the linking and presentation of returned data. MIPS demonstrates this more practical approach to multimedia presentation while drawing on some intelligent communication heuristics.

It is currently possible with commercial products on a PC to retrieve information from SQL servers, data-bases and documents across a network, whether that information is text, relational tables, images, sound or video. That information can be presented through tools in a commercial windowing system to users for them to read, or cut-and-paste into multimedia documents.

Unfortunately, the range of different data sources which can be used is limited; the queries to produce the information must be specified for each of the data sources and not as a single query to retrieve the information from each of them; and the tools to present the information will each occupy a different window on the screen and use proprietary presentation styles which differ from each other depending on the source format of the information.

The second currently available form of presenting multimedia information is by authoring it in a proprietary tool into a discrete document or hypermedia network which the user can then browse through. However, the user has no access to documents outside the hypermedia network and is tied to a proprietary representation format.

MIPS seeks to combine the best of these two approaches and thereby to overcome the problems of each. MIPS is a presentation tool which includes an access mechanism to distributed heterogeneous data sources. Therefore the access to databases and document stores is provided. It includes a conceptual model of the domain covered by the data sources encoded in a KBS which supports a single query tool that can be used to recode a query for each relevant data source from a single user query. This allows data to be retrieved on a topic from all available data sources as a result of a single query rather than requiring individual queries to each data source. The data that is returned from the different data sources will not be presented in different windows for each source, but the data will be combined together into a single relational table, or into a single hypermedia document for presentation. The information will not have to be presented in the stored presentation style since all information will be tailored by a knowledge-based information design system which will tailor it to the needs of individual tasks and users.

When the information is retrieved it can be included in an existing hypermedia web which will be grown with new information. The growing of this web with new information requires a clear description of the semantics of the information which is provided by the conceptual model of the query in the domain. It also requires skill in designing the web additions which are created by the information design system using the conceptual model of the query.

The hypermedia web itself does not have to be tied to an individual producer's proprietary representation since the data (which is the content), and the structure of the web are separated from each other. The data can be stored in any format for which presentation mechanisms are provided, or for which there are available translators to the formats of available presentation mechanisms. This not only frees the data from format constraints but allows it to be used in many hypermedia documents, or by completely different applications. Even the definition of the structure of the web itself does not have to be stored in a proprietary representation, since the format used is that of the ISO HyTime standard which is based on SGML and not one created solely for the system.

There are not currently many HyTime products on the market, but ten years ago when SGML first became a standard there were not many SGML products available. It is expected that in the same way that many government agencies and large companies now use SGML based products to support the interchange of text, large organizations will adopt HyTime to support hypermedia. This will motivate software developers to produce HyTime authoring and presentation systems based on the standard.

The architecture of MIPS is shown in Figure 2.4. Although its objective is to support the retrieval of information from heterogeneous distributed databases and to use communication rules implemented in a KBS to organize these and present them, this system must be more market focused than MMI^2 and therefore must address intermediate market needs too. Any hypermedia product at present must be able to support the conventional publishing life cycle of authoring, distribution and reading without adding intelligence in itself. Therefore MIPS must be capable of this too, and be able to present pre-written hypermedia documents without any queries. To do this, presentation tools, a presentation manager to control the browsing of the web structure and the delivery of data assets to those tools, and a storage mechanism for the hypermedia web are required. The shaded area in Figure 2.4, shows the architecture required for these functions: presentation tools, a presentation manager, and a HyTime Engine to provide fast access to the object-oriented database containing the web link structure.

Once the querying facility is added, it can be used in two ways. Firstly, users can issue queries through the formatted menu interface provided by the query tool. Secondly, authors of hypertext application documents can include pre-written queries in those so that they provide the most up to date information (for example, a table of airline flight costs in a hypertext published tourist brochure can be updated from a remote database when that node is viewed rather than relying on the information provided at the time of authoring). In order to connect the hypermedia tool to existing heterogeneous databases, a selection and retrieval tool to select the appropriate database as the target for a query, and to format the query for that database is required. Once the query is formatted it must be dispatched to the remote or local database through a communications module, and the returned data must be passed back to the selection and retrieval tool. This must be incorporated into the HyTime web representation by a Web Builder, so that the node can be presented. Again, in Figure 2.4, the modules to provide this functionality are also shown: Selection and Retrieval Tool, Communications Module and Web Builder. The functionality to support the access of heterogeneous remote data sources will not be discussed in this chapter, although it is presented in Behrendt *et al.* (1993).

To support the dynamic construction of screens in response to user queries at run time rather than pre-written queries produced by an author requires a Query Tool for the user to express queries in (also shown in Figure 2.4). In order to perform the selection of the appropriate database from the heterogeneous set available the system must know what databases are available, what information they represent, what format queries and returned data use, and other information about cost, access time and other non-functional requirements in order to optimize the query. This information is stored in the KBS which supports the Query Tool and Selection and Retrieval Tool in the construction of queries. Similarly, the returned data must be constructed into a node, which must be linked to other nodes, and then presented on the screen using the most

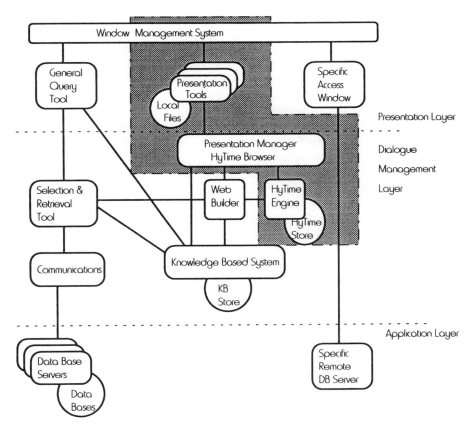

Figure 2.4. Architecture of the MIPS multimedia presentation system.

effective and efficient presentation mechanisms available for that class of data. Again, rules about information design to support this task are stored in the KBS which supports the Web Builder in constructing the node, and the Presentation Manager in selecting the most efficient presentation tools to render a presentation mechanism.

As with the MMI^2 system, the architecture is clearly divided into three layers responsible for the presentation of information, the dialogue management and the application itself. The application in this view of MIPS is the conjunction of local and remote databases. This clear division is a little confused by the existence of two permanent stores in the dialogue management layer – the HyTime store and the Knowledge Base; and one in the presentation layer – the files of local data assets for presentation. Given current hardware, the size of video and sound data files, and the speed of transferring them, it is necessary to keep large data assets as close as possible to the presentation tools to provide the speed and quality of presentation demanded by users. MIPS is designed to be run as a client server system with several client machines running presentation tools, with one server responsible for the database access. Therefore to keep data assets close to the presentation tools they are stored on the client machine on which they run, although they can be regarded as data assets cached from those held in databases. The dominant dialogue control mechanism is the web structure itself which restricts the links available to users within the web. Although the hyperdocument may be considered as the application; that is, an application divided between assets and web, the sole role of the web is to control dialogue. This is therefore represented within the dialogue management layer. The KBS store contains knowledge used by the KBS to select databases, and design nodes and presentations. These functions are comparable with the informal domain expertise and communication planning functions in the MMI^2 system and for the purpose of the main application function are also dialogue management functions so their placement in the dialogue management layer is appropriate.

One of the objectives of MIPS is to improve the portability and interoperability of hypermedia systems. Portability is addressed by using existing data formats and presentation tools, and by using a standard representation for the web. To promote interoperability knowledge about the applications with which it must operate has been included in the dialogue management layer, within the KBS: about databases to which it is connected, and about presentation tools available at the local site. Also knowledge has been included about the presentation of data assets, and the construction of nodes, links and presentations, so that data can be integrated into the hyperdocument web. There are several discrete bodies of knowledge that have been included within the KBS, but unlike the MMI^2 architecture where the knowledge is distributed around the system most of it itself a KBS written in Prolog, in MIPS all this knowledge is placed in a single KBS separated from the rest of the architecture. This allows the KBS to act as a server to the rest of the system and for a core presentation-only system to operate without it. However, this does not constrain the complexity of the KBS itself which is now internally modularized.

There are four domains of knowledge which the KBS must know about to perform its functions. Firstly, it must contain knowledge about database access in general and the optimization of queries. Secondly it must understand the principles of information design in order to construct nodes, links and screens. Thirdly, it must understand the language of the application domain, since actual queries to databases in an application will use this information, and the actual data to be presented in an application will be in terms of this information. Fourthly, it must have knowledge of the actual presentation tools present at a site and the rules for choosing these for a presentation mechanism. These four domains of knowledge interact so that there is general knowledge about database access and information design, then layered upon this there is knowledge specific to the application domain. The knowledge which was spread through the communication planner, graphics manager and interface expert of MMI^2, here all resides in information design and presentation knowledge. What were the domain experts in MMI^2 here become knowledge about the domain of database access and the application domain. In order for the KBS to perform its functions, other knowledge which was present in MMI^2 must also be included here. In order to design information it is again necessary to represent the dialogue context, and to classify the user in a user model. Similarly, to permit any portability of the KBS it is necessary to divide four domains of knowledge between task models which describe the functions to be performed in an application domain platform, and then layer application domain knowledge on top of this in a conventional KBS domain model.

These various layers of knowledge required to automate presentation design must be acquired, and cannot all come from an application builder or author who is not a knowledge engineer. General knowledge about database access and information design exist within the basic MIPS KBS. There is also a core ontology of terms defined which are used in the MIPS document type definition (DTD) for HyTime documents produced for MIPS. On top of this it is necessary for the application builder to extend the ontology for the application domain through a simple tool designed for this purpose. The domain specific rules for database selection and information design can also be entered by the application builder (author) since only a very limited set of these beyond the ontology are required (e.g. constraints on some transitive inferences such as "travel from A to B, via how many intermediate places"). It is necessary to extend the directory of remote databases available for an application, and indicate the schema of these using terms in the ontology, but this is a form completion exercise and does not require knowledge acquisition. The application builder will also specify the simple user modelling structure by choosing categories of features which can be associated with different user groups in the ontology. The application builder will therefore be required to enter some information into the KBS, but form interfaces are provided to limit the complexity of this operation. These must be evaluated before the system could be viable, and they will undoubtedly have to be changed, but the present system is intended to address this potential problem of overloading the application builder. Once an application has been written in a domain (e.g. Greek tourism) very small additions would be required for further applications. Therefore the knowledge can be seen as one general layer, a second for the application domain and a third for each specific application. The application builder would obviously have to author the HyTime web for an application as well as entering the KBS knowledge. It is probable that some data assets would also have to be created for an application, although these could already exist or be the responsibility of database providers.

Once the application has been created it must be installed at each site. Another layer of customization is required here to state which actual databases are connected to it, which actual presentation tools are present at the site and which actual user groups are potential users. The preferences of the user groups can also be tailored to the site. This provides a fourth layer of customization to the user site. The fifth layer of customization available is to each independent user who can customize their own user model to include their own preferences for database access variables (cost, time etc.), presentation tools to be used, language etc. These can be defaults for users at a site, or can be set explicitly by users willing to devote the effort to this task. The sixth level of customization available is to an individual session's dialogue context. This is automatically performed by the KBS which keeps track of the context throughout use and automatically updates the user model of a user on the basis of usage.

These six layers of the customization process provide the knowledge on which the system can base its retrieval and information design judgements and tailor them to individual users so that they appear intelligent. To perform these customization steps three different groups of users have been distinguished: application builders who develop the application, site managers who configure the application to a site, and end users who configure the system to their own preferences. Other groups of individuals could also be involved such as specialist asset generation teams (including film directors, graphic artists etc.), remote site database managers, or even domain modellers.

In this application both the problems of heterogeneous database access and those of information design must be addressed. A major worry in the automation of these two areas is the need for general knowledge and ontologies. Stated boldly, the generation of general knowledge systems is a long term goal of the artificial intelligence community and should not be regarded as a solved problem. Within the limited application supported by MIPS, and with the deliberate exclusion of any natural language input, it is hoped that these issues have been sufficiently constrained so as not to be onerous to application builders. If this is proven not to be so in evaluation, the approach should not be rejected immediately. Artificial intelligence workers such as Guha and Lenat (1990) are developing exactly the form of general knowledge base which could be used to support heterogeneous database access (Lenat and Guha, 1991) and may provide a general basis for the link creation part of the information design process in MIPS applications.

MIPS supports the retrieval of any information stored in data sources. One practical limitation on this is the communication of large media (i.e. video, sound) over computer networks. If this is not practical in real time then the system is only useful for retrieving less bulky media. This is an immediate problem, but even now there are local uses for this technology if not over wide area networks. A second problem with the retrieval of such media is the indexing of it in databases. There are currently no clear standards for the storage of multimedia data, nor for querying it. Querying may seem a strange point to raise, but if a video display is being automatically composed, it could also be automatically edited. That is, a ten minute video of a scene could have a shot extracted from it, or a series of shots which could be put together into a three minute sequence. If the video were indexed using techniques such as that proposed by Burrill *et al.* (1994), then it could have an index attached to each scene and shot, not only with the identity of characters, locations and actions in it, but also video attributes such as whether it was an establishing shot, close-up, pan etc. Such indexing on semantic content and video attributes would support the retrieval and composition of sequences according to rules of video direction. This is one example of the forms of presentation design which could be developed for multimedia systems using a MIPS architecture as the starting point, although it has not been developed yet.

MIPS is a demonstrator which is considerably simpler than MMI^2. Within the MSM framework of Coutaz *et al.* described above, it supports only one channel from the user to the system, since all user input is through keyboard or mouse selection, but it uses visual and auditory channels for presenting information to the user. It does not support the fusion of user input, but since it can produce several media in reply to a query, it could be said to support fission. It has been designed as a multimedia rather than a multimodal system which does not support advanced user input dialogue, so this judgement is not surprising. Similarly, parallelism is only supported in system output at the physical level, and could only be said to be supported in user input at the task level if queries are pending the return of data while a user continues to browse the hyperdocument. The abstraction of the dialogue supported is more problematic. Outside the KBS there is no abstraction of navigation commands to the web, and little abstraction in data source queries. Within the KBS there is some abstraction of the query to the user's task level but this is mainly to support the use of contexts. The MIPS KBS is designed to accommodate the context of the task, user and dialogue in designing presentations for returned data and linking these into the web. It is this use of contexts in presentation generation which is the contribution of any intelligence in this system. The system has not yet been implemented to a stage which will support evaluation so it cannot be judged whether this is enough. However, an evaluation will take place in Greece of an application in the tourist domain in order to answer this question.

2.3. CONCLUSIONS

Current multimedia systems present text, images, sounds and video as static objects. The organization of these objects is determined by the author, and the reader has a comparatively passive role. In order to involve multimedia in more applications it must become more active, and the representations used must include meaning which can be manipulated in more complex dialogue structures. The technology currently used to support multimedia presentation does not incorporate any analysis of the signals; any discussion of human–computer communication modalities inherently involves, at some level, the machine's determination of the content of messages, and its need to communicate the content of its own messages. Multimodal systems use different media for input and output, and rely on abstract representations of the information in order to control the dialogue and application. An example multimodal system was described – MMI^2. Such systems are far from the current market, but they provide the basis for determining the theory of multimodal communication which is required to be stated in detail if multimedia presentations are to be automatically created.

A second, less advanced multimedia system (MIPS) has been described which is an improvement on current hypertext, and which includes some intelligence to support the dynamic creation of multimedia documents from retrieved data. This illustrates a second route towards the introduction of intelligent multimedia through open systems which interact with existing data sources. Although this system does not include the advanced dialogue of a multimodal system, its use of context information to create presentations dynamically, and the local use of conceptual and communication act levels of abstraction within the information design rules of the KBS may incorporate the most robust aspects of the more exotic system in a way which can be included in commercially supported products.

It is arguable that neither of these systems portrays intelligence as the chapter title suggests. This conclusion is either drawn because of a conviction that it is a misnomer to term any system intelligent, or because there are few examples presented that show the systems in operation. If the first is true, the term is used suggestively rather than with any psychological conviction. If the second is the case, on several occasions when MMI^2 has been demonstrated to computer professionals they have refused to believe that it was interpreting the user's input or generating its own output. They claimed that there was either somebody behind the curtain, or the demonstration was so well prepared that the system could not stray outside it. It is this impression of disbelief in those who see the systems which leads to their being called intelligent. Their developers do not make any greater claim.

This chapter has not described various rule sets for dialogue context, user or task modelling, for generating output in different modes nor for selecting media, but references have been provided to sources of this information for those who wish to acquire it. These rule sets for designing system output are still active areas of research, but some are being incorporated into existing major software products to provide them an edge in the current market. The heuristics described in this chapter may not currently be available in multimedia products, but they illustrate what may well be available in the future, since the market appears to be demanding the use of these techniques.

ACKNOWLEDGEMENTS

The research reported in this paper was partly funded by CEC Esprit II grant 2474 to the MMI² project and partly by CEC Esprit III grant 6542 to the MIPS project. Organizations involved in the MMI² project are BIM (Belgium), ISS (Spain), ADR/CRISS (France), INRIA (France), EMSE (France), SERC RAL (UK), University of Leeds (UK). Organizations involved in the MIPS project are Longman Cartermill (UK), SERC RAL (UK), STI (Spain), SEMA Group Benelux (Belgium), Herriot-Watt University (UK), Trinity College Dublin (Eire), DTI (Denmark).

REFERENCES

Austin, J. (1962). *How to Do Things with Words*, Urmson, J. G. (ed.). Oxford University Press.

Behrendt, W., Hutchinson, E., Jeffrey, K. G., Kalmus, J., Macnee, C. A. and Wilson, M. D. (1993). Using an intelligent agent to mediate multibase information access. In Deen, S. M. (ed.) *Proceedings of the Workshop on Cooperating Knowledge Based Systems*, DAKE Centre, Keele, UK, September, pp. 27–43.

Bernsen, N. O. (1993). Modality theory: supporting multi-modal interface design. In Carbonell, N. (ed.) *Proceedings of the ERCIM Workshop on Multimodal Human-Computer Interaction*, Nancy, France, 2–4 November 1993, pp. 48–55. INRIA, Nancy.

Binot, J-L., Falzon, P., Perez, R., Peroche, B., Sheehy, N., Rouault, J. and Wilson, M. D. (1990). Architecture of a multimodal dialogue interface for knowledge-based systems. In *Proceedings of the Esprit '90 Conference*, pp. 412–433. Kluwer Academic Publishers, Dordrecht. (Also published on CD-ROM by CEC, Brussels).

Bolt, R. A. (1980). "Put-that-there": voice and gesture at the graphics interface. *Computer Graphics*, **14**(3), 262–270.

Burrill, V., Kirste, T. and Weiss, J. (1994). Time-varying sensitive regions in dynamic multimedia objects: A pragmatic approach to content-based retrieval from video. *Information and Software Technology*. (special issue on Multimedia), **36** (4), 213–224.

Bush, V. (1945). As we may think. *Atlantic Monthly*, July, 101–108.

Card, S. K., Robertson, C. G. and Mackinlay, J. D. (1991). The information visualiser: an information workspace. In Robertson, S. P., Olson, G. M. and Olsen, J.S. (eds) *Proceedings of ACM CHI '91: Human Factors in Computing*, pp. 181–188. ACM Press, New York.

Chapanis, A., Parrish, R. N., Ochsman, R. B. and Weeks, G. D. (1977). Studies in interactive communication: II. The effects of four communication modes on the linguistic performance of teams during cooperative problem solving. *Human Factors*, **19**(2), 101–125.

Chappel, H. and Wilson, M. D. (1993). Knowledge-based design of graphical responses. In Gray, W. D., Hefley, W. E. and Murray, D. (eds) *Proceedings of the ACM International Workshop on Intelligent User Interfaces*, pp. 29–36. ACM Press, New York.

Chappel, H., Wilson, M. and Cahour, B. (1992). Engineering user models to enhance multi-modal dialogue. In Larson, J. A. and Unger, C. A. (eds) *Engineering For Human-Computer Interaction*, pp. 297–315. Elsevier Science Publishers B.V. (North-Holland), Amsterdam.

Clarke, A. C. (1968). *2001: A Space Odyssey*: a novel. Hutchinson, London.

Cohen, P. R. (1984). The pragmatics of referring and the modality of communication. *Computational Linguistics*, **10**(2), 97–146.

Cohen, P. R. (1992). The role of natural language in a multimodal interface. In the *Proceedings of the Fifth Annual Symposium on User Interface Software and Technology*, pp. 143–149. ACM, New York.

Cohen, P. R., Morgan, J. and Pollack, M. E. (1990). *Intentions in Communication*. MIT Press, Cambridge, MA.

Cotton, R. and Oliver, R. (1993). *Understanding HyperMedia*. Phaidon Press, London.

Coutaz, J., Nigay, L. & Salber, D. (1993). Taxonomic issues for multimodal and multimedia interactive systems. In Carbonnell, N. (ed.) *Proceedings of the ERCIM Workshop on Multimodal Human-Computer Interaction*. INRIA, Nancy.

Crane, H. D. & Rtischev, D. (1993). Pen and Voice Unite. *Byte*, **18**(11), 99–102.

Dahlbäck, N., Jönsson, A., & Salber, D. (1993). Wizard of Oz studies – why and how? In Gray, W.D., Hefley, W.E., and Murray, D. (eds) *Proceedings of the 1993 ACM International Workshop on Intelligent User Interfaces*, pp. 193–200. ACM Press, New York.

Davis, H., Hall, W., Pickering, A. and Wilkins, R. (1993). Microcosm: an open hypermedia system. In Ashlund, S., Mullet, K., Henderson, A., Hollnagel, E. and White, T. (eds) *Proceedings of INTERCHI '93 Conference on Human Factors in Computing Systems*, p. 56. ACM, New York.

Feiner, S. and McKeown, K. (1991). Automating the generation of coordinated multimedia explanations. *IEEE Computer*, **24**(10), 33–41.

Fraser, N.M. (1993). Sublanguage, register and natural langauge interfaces. *Interacting with Computers*, **5**(4), 441–444.

Grice, H. P. (1975). Logic and conversation. In Role, P. and Morgan, J.L. (eds) *Syntax and Semantics*, Vol. 3, pp. 64–75. Academic Press, New York.

Guha, R. V. and Lenat, D. B. (1990). Cyc: a midterm report. *AI Magazine*. **11**(3), 32–59.

Hobbs, J. R. (1985). Ontological promiscuity. In *Proceedings of the 23rd Annual Meeting of the Association for Computational Linguistics*, Chicago, June 1985, pp. 61–69.

ISO (1992). *ISO/IEC JTC1/Sc18/WG8, Information Technology, Hypermedia/ Time-based Structuring Language (HyTime)*. ISO/IEC D18 10744.1.1.

Karlgren, J. (1993). Sublanguages and registers: a note on terminology. *Interacting with Computers*, **5**(3), 348–350.

Lenat, D. B. & Guha, R. V. (1991). Ideas for applying Cyc. Tech. Report. ACT-CYC-407-91. MCC, Austin, TX.

Mackinlay, J. (1986). Automating the design of graphical presentations of relational information. *ACM Transactions on Graphics*, **5**(2), 110–141.

Maybury, M. T. (1991). Planning multimedia explanations using communicative acts. In *Proceedings of the Ninth National Conference on Artificial Intelligence, AAAI-91*. Morgan Kaufman, Los Altos, CA.

Nelson, T. H. (1988). *Hyperdocuments and How to Create Them*. Prentice Hall, Englewood Cliffs, NJ.

Newcombe, S. R., Kipps, N. A. and Newcombe, V. T. (1991). The HyTime hypermedia/time based document structuring language. *Communications of the ACM*, **34**(11), 67–83.

Nickerson, R. S. (1977). On conversational interaction with computers. In *User-Oriented Design of Interactive Graphics Systems*, pp. 101–103. ACM, New York.

Oviatt, S. L. & Cohen, P. R. (1991). Discourse structure and performance efficiency in interactive and noninteractive spoken modalities. *Computer Speech and Language*, **5**(4), 297–326.

Pierce, J. R. (1980). *An Introduction to Information Theory: Symbols, Signals and Noise*. 2nd rev. edn. Constable, London.

Rubin, A. D. (1980). A theoretical taxonomy of the differences between oral and written language. In *Theorectical Issues in Reading Comprehension*, pp. 56–74. Lawrence Erlbaum, Hillsdale, NJ.

Stede, M. (1993). The search for robustnes in natural language understanding. *Artificial Intelligence Review*, **6**(4), 383–414.

Templeton, A. (1993). Strategies for business. In *European Multimedia Yearbook 93*, pp. 39–41. Interactive Media Publications, London.

Veronis, J. (1991). Error in natural language dialogue between man and machine. *International Journal of Man-Machine Studies*, **35**, 187–217.

Wrigley, A. (1993). In defence of sublinguistics. *Interacting with Computers*, **5**(4), 439–440.

About the Author

Michael Wilson is a Chartered Psychologist holding BSc and PhD degrees in experimental psychology. Since 1983 he has undertaken research into human–computer interaction at the MRC Applied Psychology Unit, Cambridge and Knowledge Engineering at the SERC Rutherford Appleton Laboratory where he is currently head of the Intelligent User Systems Section. At present he is the RAL team leader in the Esprit projects MMI^2 and MIPS, and acts as a monitor of research for the SERC. He has published over 50 book chapters and journal articles on task analysis, modelling human–computer interaction, knowledge acquisition, and multimodal and multimedia user interface design.

3 The design of the PROMISE multimedia system and its use in a chemical plant

J. L. Alty, J. Bergan and A. Schepens

3.1. INTRODUCTION

In the Spring of 1988, a number of interested parties met to consider problems which were perceived to be developing in the industrial process control area. Some of the parties at the meeting would shortly complete a major European ESPRIT-I project applying knowledge-based systems to interface design in power stations and communications networks (Alty and Johannsen, 1989). Others were from large industrial organizations whose main commercial activity involved complex operator-controlled processes. Additional attendees were from research organizations interested in interface design. There was general concern about the nature of the added cognitive demands which were being placed upon the operators of such systems and the consequential requirement for much higher levels of decision making. Operators' increasing difficulties were perceived to be related to a lack of "knowledgeable interfaces" and the use of rudimentary information presentation techniques.

Whilst some progress had been made in applying knowledge-based technologies (Johannsen and Alty, 1991; Monta *et al.*, 1992), the application of new presentation technologies (which might be broadly described under the generic term "multimedia") had not really been attempted in the process control area. It was therefore resolved to form a consortium to investigate whether such technologies might provide a solution. The resulting project was the PROMISE project (PRocess Operators Multimedia Intelligent Support Environment) supported by the European Commission under the ESPRIT-II program.

3.2. WHAT IS THE INTERFACE PROBLEM?

The successful operation of large plants, such as those found in the nuclear power or chemical industries, depends upon a balanced interaction between low level supervisory and control systems (which automatically control low and medium level operations of the plant) and strategic operator intervention. In the past, operators have been dissatisfied with process interfaces (Alty *et al.*, 1985), and although such interfaces have been greatly improved, the operators are now expected to do so much more and at higher levels of abstraction. Whilst improved training might better prepare the operator for these tasks, the inherent complexity of modern systems dictates that the designer of the plant must assist the operator through the provision of more intelligent advice and higher quality presentation. These two aspects must be considered together since more knowledgeable advice generally requires a more carefully organized presentation approach. Furthermore, operator competence comes from the internal cohesion of different images of the system (De Keyser, 1986), and improved knowledge and presentation ought to reinforce appropriate images.

One key feature of the human communication system which has not been fully exploited in operator interfaces is the extensive use, by the human processing system, of multiple media (Marmollin, 1992) to evaluate and assess the world (the term "multimedia" being used here to refer to communication media, not to storage media). Communication media commonly used by human beings include speech, graphics, pictures, moving pictures, animation, sound, text, diagrams and unmediated objects. Human beings are very effective in utilizing these many different media, in parallel, to understand and communicate information. Thus the presentation of information to operators might be considerably improved through the introduction of multimedia interface facilities.

The problem is not primarily a technical one. Multimedia systems can now be installed relatively cheaply on many personal computers such as the Apple MacIntosh or IBM PC, and are also available on other workstations such as the Sun. Even in 1989, although there were still some technical problems associated with synchronization, with the handling of large moving pictures and with real-time performance, most of these problems were expected to be solved within two or three years. The real difficulties associated with using multimedia presentation systems were perceived to stem from a total lack of a methodology for multimedia interface design. The real question was not *how* could different media be provided but *when* and to *what* effect. (A useful summary of PROMISE thinking in the first year of the project was presented at the Edinburgh HCI'91 Conference; Alty, 1991.) Furthermore, there appears to be a lack of research results on which types of media are appropriate in particular user circumstances.

The mission statement for the PROMISE project was thus formulated as:

the creation of a set of tools and a design method which will enable the designers of process control interfaces to exploit the potential offered by the multimedia approach and, as a result, improve the efficiency and reliability of operator performance in both normal and abnormal situations.

This will be achieved through the design, construction and evaluation of a multimedia toolset and a design method for:
a) creating interfaces which exploit multimedia capabilities
b) advising designers on the most appropriate media to use in given situations
c) providing software tools to assist designers in the multimedia interface design process

Although in 1990 some multimedia facilities were already beginning to appear in the market place, the project decided to build its own multimedia platform so that it would have complete flexibility in deciding which media to support, how to implement media consistency issues, and how to connect to remote plant. It was also agreed that a considerable amount of experimentation would need to be carried out in a behaviour laboratory and in real plant in order to understand how aspects of multimedia communication might solve current operator problems.

A live real-time environment was available in the form of a medium scale chemical plant owned by the DOW (Benelux) company at Terneuzen (Netherlands). DOW were keen supporters of the project throughout its life, and although it was inevitable that there would be severe constraints imposed by the commercial confidentiality resulting from the use of a real plant, the benefits were considered to far outweigh the drawbacks. Real environments put serious constraints on the evaluation environment. The clock cannot be stopped, unanticipated events can occur, the operators have a real job to do and the process constraints are real. Evaluations in such a real plant would therefore be truly "real". The project was also fortunate in having access, via Scottish Power (Glasgow), to a simulated environment where the nature of the upsets to the environment could be controlled, and operator performance could be monitored more effectively. Because of space limitations we will only report some of the real plant results here.

The project built a multimedia toolset with some novel features, carried out laboratory and real-world experiments to determine the possible advantages of using multiple media in the process control environment, and developed a methodology for multimedia interface design. We will first discuss the design features of the toolset and then report on some results from its use in the plant.

3.3.   THE DESIGN PHILOSOPHY OF THE PROMISE MULTIMEDIA TOOLSET

The PROMISE toolset was designed with a number of important factors in mind . These included the following.

1. A wide range of media should be available to the interface designer. These media should include graphics, text, audio, speech, animation and video.
2. A need for multimedia scheduling. The real-time complex nature of process control applications needs to be fully catered for. The presentation vehicle must be able to handle large fluctuations in the reception of process information particularly in exceptional circumstances. Such fluctuations will cause large variations in the quantity of information that must be communicated to the operator and hence will influence the type of media used. Since designers will not be able to anticipate when and how their interface renderings will be combined at run-time; the actual representation chosen

for displaying information may vary in different competing circumstances. For example, output destined for a speech synthesizer, will have to first check if the device is already in use. If so, an alternative representation will need to be found.

3. The toolset must provide support for integrating external applications into the environment in a uniform way.

4. Different applications may be required to run on separate host machines. The system must therefore provide support for communication between applications across a network of machines.

5. Data consistency: since data will be passed between several applications and renderings, the system must ensure that this data is consistent between all applications and all current renderings. Similarly, and most importantly, the information presented to the operator must be consistent with the data from the process and other applications.

6. Portability: as far as possible, the tools developed should be implemented with software which runs on different hardware platforms.

7. Performance: in process control environments the variables representing the underlying process may change very rapidly. It is essential that these changes are reflected to the operators and external software in real time.

8. Compilation-free interface creation: this would allow for rapid prototyping when designing the interface and implies the use of interpretative tools. This is far easier in NeWs-based approaches, and in early versions, tools based upon NeWs were used (later, the system moved closer to X-based approaches).

9. Interface creation through direct manipulation: this was expected to increase the speed of prototyping and would offer the additional advantage that the interface designer would not need to know a programming language.

An overall view of the resulting architecture is shown in Figure 3.1. To the far left is the Supervisory and Control System which is controlling "the process". The PROMISE components are in the shaded area consisting of two main components – the interaction data model (IDM) and the presentation system. Note that "process direct" input bypasses the systems completely. Thus the operators can control the process without passing through layers of PROMISE code. Similarly (not shown), all the usual mimic board output is available to the operator independently of PROMISE.

The IDM is an object-oriented database with active values, and is the central module of communication in the PROMISE system. It supports uniform communication with client programs written in a number of different programming languages, thus all applications, including the main process and the presentation system, communicate through it. It is responsible for ensuring that data is consistent between applications.

With such a system architecture it is very easy to integrate a variety of applications into the toolset. For example, client programs can run on different host machines. Such applications might be advisory and diagnostic expert systems or a natural language application.

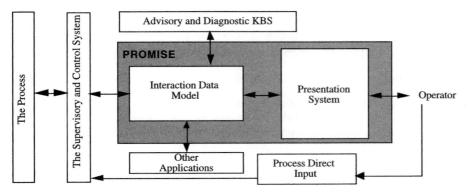

Figure 3.1.   The PROMISE overall architecture.

The presentation system is responsible for managing the user interface. It provides a uniform interface to the set of multimedia objects in the system, supporting dynamic allocation of media resources (explained later) to the different parts of the interface and enabling automatic updating of front end presentation objects.

The interface designer provides code for the IDM which describes the interface behaviour (and any other modelling of the application required). At the same time descriptions of the interface objects and their layout are provided interactively to the presentation system (see Figure 3.2).

Design and implementation of the application programs are completely independent from the construction of the user interface. Thus, the construction of a program consists of two main steps:

1. building the application itself with its application functionality;
2. building the user interface functionality, that is to say object creation, setting and getting presentation object instance variables, invoking presentation object methods etc.

We will now examine the IDM and the presentation system components in more detail.

3.4.   INTERACTION DATA MODEL (IDM)

The (IDM) is the component of the PROMISE system which provides:

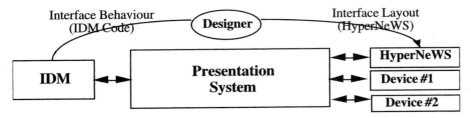

Figure 3.2.   The design process

1. a process and interface modelling capability;
2. connections between applications (and process variables) and their representations at the user interface;
3. consistency of data in the exchange between application entities and their presentation equivalents on various user interfaces.

The IDM module works as a centralized database, servicing requests from applications and from interface processes and other processes as well as maintaining data consistency between the different environments. A language (the IDM language, with syntax and semantics similar to "C") is provided to enable the designer to model appropriate parts of the process or plant. It is an interpreted language and so reduces prototyping and testing time. The language provides object declaration, deletion and modification; whole array operations; for/while/assignment statement execution; macro definition and execution; event definition and external C function calls.

In this language the designer defines a qualitative model of the application domain. For example, if we define an IDM model of boiler steam pressure, we can define another macro (an alarm macro) that infers the rule "steam pressure is too high"; this can generate an event about which, say, an expert system may have an interest. The expert system will then start to reason in order to understand the cause of the alarm. When the application does not need a complicate level of reasoning, the IDM's powerful modelling and reasoning facilities may be enough on their own.

Applications which communicate with the IDM can be written in C++, C or Lisp. An *IDM server process* monitors access to a database of objects and events and provides typical services such as fetch and store object values, event notification, etc. *IDM clients* interact with this server asking for specific services. The communication between the IDM server and its clients is based on the RPC (remote procedure call) network package and the TCP transport layer. Exchanged data between clients and the server are expressed in a standard transmission format supported by the XDR (eXternal Data Representation) library. Exchanged data between the IDM server and its clients may be heavily structured, for example variable size arrays, lists, structs, and so on.

3.5.   PRESENTATION SYSTEM

The presentation system is a high-level object-oriented tool kit for creating and controlling multimedia user interfaces. It supports a variety of presentation objects including many graphical objects, as well as audio, speech and video objects. To provide the designer with a uniform interface to both the underlying application and the user interface, and also to facilitate communication between the application and interface, these presentation objects are accessed and controlled from the IDM.

The HyperNeWS tool kit (Van Hoff, 1990) was used to build the front-end graphical objects. As HyperNeWS runs within the NeWs windowing system, its use was seriously debated within the consortium. Firstly,

NeWs is an interpreted environment which means that it is slower than compiled environments such as X tool kit client programs. Secondly, NeWs was effectively limited to Sun hardware, and even in 1990 it was thought likely that X-based systems would become the *de facto* standard (we now know that NeWs will not be supported by Sun's future operating systems). However, HyperNeWS was easily the best interactive tool kit for interface prototyping available at the start of the project, and even at the time of writing, few X tool kits exist which provide such powerful and easy to use environments.

A compromise was reached whereby the main part of the presentation system was coded in C++ and the parts of the interface design which are most naturally performed in an interactive manner, namely creating, laying out and modifying the visual interfaces, were carried out in HyperNeWS. This provided portable code as well as very good performance. Although this approach reduced the usefulness of the HyperNeWS interactive paradigm, it allowed the project to plan to move to a more standard front end, such as an X tool kit, by only reimplementing a small part of the system.

Since a designer can never be sure of the possible allowable combinations of output renderings which might be needed at any one time, all objects which are "presented" on the interface must be designed to have a number of possible media renderings. In times of high activity, screen "real-estate" may not be available, and output sound channels are usually limited to one source. A designer must therefore always provide alternative renderings for an object. This is achieved through the construction of a presentation object hierarchy for every object which needs to be rendered.

The two main types of classes in the hierarchy are nodes and leaves (see Figure 3.3). They differ in two respects. Firstly, nodes can have children whereas leaves cannot. They are abstract objects used to group parts of an interface in a subtree. Secondly, all leaves control a physical instantiation

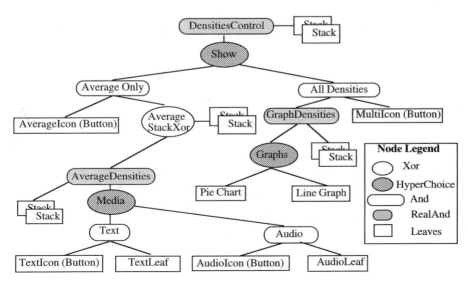

Figure 3.3.   A presentation hierarchy.

of themselves whereas node objects have no physical instantiation. The leaf instantiations are realized in the physical devices such as HyperNeWS (visual device) or the speech synthesizer (spoken audio device).

There are three basic types of nodes – AND, REALAND and XOR. AND nodes are used to specify presentation sub-hierarchies which should exist in conjunction, REALAND nodes are a specialization of AND (they are AND nodes with a realizable interface object such as a window), and XOR – used to specify alternative presentation sub-hierarchies.

For the object in Figure 3.3, the user can decide to show an Average Density (for a set of incoming readings) or a distinct Set of Densities. For Average Density presentation, the output can be text or sound. For the Set of Densities there are the alternative graphical presentations of a pie chart or a line graph. In this case the user decides which presentation to use, but the choice could equally well be made by the resource manager.

The architecture for the PROMISE presentation system has four main components (see Figure 3.4):

1. The presentation server;
2. Device managers;
3. The presentation database;
4. The resource manager.

3.5.1.   The presentation server

The presentation server is responsible for creating and maintaining the user interface. Instructions to create, update and modify presentation objects are received from the interface model in the IDM. The presentation server builds and stores the interface as a C++ object hierarchy.

Another function of the presentation server is to drive the interface automatically once it has been created. The IDM contains an interface model consisting of view objects and controller objects. These are connected to application data slots internally in the IDM. The presentation

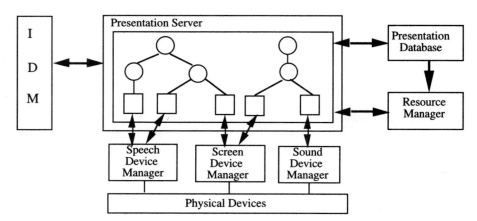

Figure 3.4.   Presentation system architecture.

server manages synchronous data connections between the view objects and the physical objects that the user interacts with. Whenever an IDM view object is updated, the presentation server is automatically notified of this through the IDM update mechanism. The presentation server then passes this update onto the appropriate leaf object which is responsible for updating its physical instantiation. Similarly, to drive the application from the interface, a connection is set up between an input attribute of a presentation object, such as the current selection on a pull down menu, and an IDM controller object. Again, the presentation server synchronously updates the controller object whenever the input attribute is modified by the user.

3.5.2. The device drivers

The device managers are responsible for interfacing the presentation leaf objects with the actual physical devices such as the screen and the speech synthesizer. Their main function is to translate high level presentation messages into low level device calls which can be understood by the hardware resource. The presentation system currently supports five physical devices, HyperNeWS (screen), MultiVoice and PcStem speech synthesizers, Sun audio sampler player and Parallax X video in a window.

It is worth noting that the animation and unmediated objects handle updates from the IDM in a different way from the other HyperNeWS objects. Since both of these objects receive a great deal of updates at a frequent rate, passing the updates through the presentation server would inevitably slow it down. To maintain a good level of performance it was decided that a bypass mechanism would be used to handle updates for these objects. However, messages from the IDM would still be handled in the normal way by routing them through the presentation server.

There are two speech synthesizer device managers, one for the English speech device and one for the Flemish speech device. These are both single access devices and can therefore only be accessed by one presentation leaf object at a time. A generic speech leaf has been implemented which allows the interface designer to select, at run-time, which language should be used for the speech output.

The audio device manager, also a single access device, is used to access the Sun workstation sampler player. The interface designer accesses the audio device through an associated presentation leaf object. A simple interface to the Parallax X video device has been implemented. This allows the interface designer play a video source in a window. Again this device is single access.

3.5.3. Presentation database

The presentation database is a general purpose database used to store facts. It can hold information such as device and media availability at a particular site. The database is also used to store contextual information which is used by leaf objects to evaluate their fitness in the overall interface.

3.5.4.   Resource manager

The resource manager is responsible for allocating the available device resources to the different parts of the user interface. The resource manager has two main functions. At times of competition for interface resources it prevents conflict in device usage. Alternatively, when there is no conflict to resolve, it selects the most appropriate interface from the alternatives specified by the interface designer.

The resource manager selects the best path through the presentation object hierarchy based on values calculated at the leaves in the tree. Each leaf object in the presentation system has an associated formula which calculates its fitness for the current presentation. This formula is a combination of four weighted components, multimedia usability rules, designer envelope, user preferences and local constraints. The weights for these components are stored in the presentation database and can be modified by the application designer.

Multimedia usability rules are general guide-lines about which media should be chosen in different contexts. Although many of these rules are yet to be formalized, an example could be that audio presentations should be used for alarms which are of high severity. The mechanism for specifying multimedia usability rules and local constraints is at present rather rudimentary. It involves storing relevant facts in the presentation database which can be retrieved by leaf objects when evaluating their fitness.

The designer envelope encompasses general or specific preferences about media usage defined by the designer. If, for example, a designer prefers visual to audio presentation this will result in lower weights for audio leaves. Operators can also express and modify their preferences about media usage (an operator may normally prefer audio presentations to visual presentations). The local constraints are facts which are specific to a particular site, such as whether a speech synthesizer is available for use. In a real application the facts will be more specific and complex than this.

The formula currently defined for every leaf in the presentation system is actually a default formula. However, application designers can write their own formulae, taking into consideration the context in which the object will be used. This is in accord with an early design criterion for the presentation system which was to make the mechanism as general and as adaptable as possible.

The process of resource allocation involves combining the fitness values for all the leaves that are part of a single path through the presentation tree into a value for the overall path. This value is then compared with the alternative paths and the most appropriate one is allocated. An important feature of the system is that the allocation and reallocation of resources takes place at run time. whenever information is updated in the presentation database the resource manager dynamically reallocates to achieve the optimal presentation.

3.6.   USE OF THE TOOLSET IN A MEDIUM SCALE CHEMICAL PRODUCTION PLANT

The PROMISE toolset has been used extensively in the Laboratory (Alty *et al* , 1993), in the simulator at Hunterston Nuclear Power Station (Scotland), and in the DOW plant at Terneuzen (The Netherlands). Some progress has also been made in the development of a methodology (Alty, 1993). In this section we report on use of the PROMISE toolset to develop a prototype process information exemplar, fully functioning in a real process plant environment.

A variety of prime chemical products (which are used as raw materials in other chemical industries) are produced in the Terneuzen plant in different proportions relating to external demand. During the process, a number of undesirable substances are produced as a result of side reactions, and these have to be separated out at different places in the process. An overview of the plant is shown in Figure 3.5.

The raw materials ethylene dichloride (EDC) and ammonia (NH_3) react, and a number of prime products of differing composition are formed, and some byproducts in lesser amounts. All the EDC is consumed in this reaction, but some ammonia remains which is recovered later. The mixture then goes to the neutralization section. Caustic soda is added to the mixture, giving primary products and salt. The remaining ammonia is evaporated. It is important to separate the salt as effectively as possible, and the separation process is simpler if the salt crystals are large and firm.

The size of the crystals is of great importance for the total removal of the salt: the larger the crystals are, the easier they are separated. If the concentration of the salt is too small, the salt is totally dissolved in the liquid. In order to reach the best size, the growth of the crystals needs to be promoted against the formation of new crystals. Therefore supersaturation needs to be kept low.

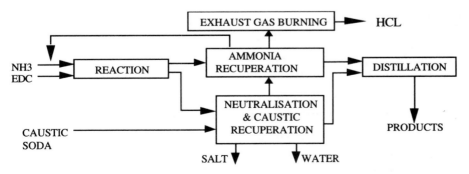

Figure 3.5.   Overview of the plant.

The input for the distillation section comes from the neutralization section. It is in this section that the prime products are extracted and made ready for shipment.

The neutralization section was chosen as a major applicable area for PROMISE. It was not the process itself that led to its choice, but rather the nature of the automation process and the way it is operated. It contains a mix of manual and automated (computer controlled) actions, and there was already an identified need for knowledge-based decision support.

Excellent salt quality is essential for successful neutralization. Since the caustic soda is recycled, an insufficient separation of salt leads to a recycling of salt which, in turn, further reduces the salt quality formed in the neutralizer. Low salt quality also has a negative effect in the amount of primary product incorporated in the salt crystals.

Surprisingly, the salt quality cannot be measured directly. The operator uses a lot of related information to determine the salt quality but a number of misconceptions can occur. The operators also have to cope with the fact that the neutralization section is heavily based on recycling. If a problem with certain effects occurs, it is possible that even after solving the problem itself, effects of the upset may still affect normal operation of the neutralization section after some time. If such problems do occur, the operators may be able to adjust the operation of the plant in such a way that the recycling effects are reduced to a minimum.

The operators therefore require better tools to operate the plant and it was hoped that a PROMISE multimedia system would provide better overview of the process, and assist in the control of a process based on such a fuzzy concept as salt quality.

The goal of the installed PROMISE system at DOW was therefore stated as follows:

The PROMISE system should help the operator in controlling the neutralization section. Essential for proper control is proper information at the right time. This can be achieved by enhancing the information flow to the operator. Beside a clear, structured and context-dependent overview of information and data, it is also hoped that more intelligent alarming, pre-alarming and diagnosis capabilities will be provided.

3.6.1.   PROMISE-supported applications

Knowledge based systems were developed to provide two main assistance functions for the operators controlling the neutralization section:

1. monitoring of salt quality;
2. handling of events coming from the automation system.

It was hoped that these systems together with good multimedia output facilities would solve a number of control problems.

1. immense data flows when problems occur;
2. unstructured information;
3. much improved help and glossary information;
4. overall consistency of approach.

The first exemplar installed had four applications – an alarm handler, a dynamic analyser, a glossary browser and a flowsheet browser. The second exemplar had seven applications (new were on-line manual, trending and an unmediated object).

Alarm handler. This allows operators to view current alarms and their status, and observe any new incoming alarms. New incoming alarms can be displayed using several media – text (a text line on the bottom of the screen where the latest alarm is always visible), voice (where the glossary of the incoming alarm is spoken after conversion to natural language), sound (to alert the operator if there is a new alarm) and animation (depending on the severity and the amount of alarms coming in, an exclamation mark will fall from along the left side of the screen).

Besides accessing the on-line manual it is possible to start the dynamic logic analyser from within the alarm display application to analyse a pending alarm. (Media used: text, colour, voice, sound, and animation.)

Dynamic logic and step analyser. This is a confidential application and cannot be described here. The results of analysis can be displayed by invoking the browser. It interfaces with an equipment mismatch expert system. (Media used: text, colour, graphics, speech and mouse selection.)

Glossary browser. This allows access to a set of "glossary cards". Each process variable has an on-line description relating it to a piece of equipment. In the current version four types of search actions are possible. The glossary browser is at the basis of a new approach of process control by operators. Rather than communicating to the process on the basis of a control language syntax/format, it will be possible to interact with the process on the basis of natural language. (Media used: colour coding and text.)

Flowsheet browser. This application allows the operators to browse through graphical representations of plant equipment and parts of the plant. These flowsheets can vary in level of detail from a high level representation of the whole plant to a detailed picture of a piece of equipment. In the current version flowsheets depicting the plant, sections and units are available. Operators can modify existing flowsheets and build new ones.

Flowsheets are linked in a hyper-hierarchy. Top-down browsing is achieved via plant and section overview flowsheets (double clicking on graphical representations loads the appropriate flowsheet). Horizontal browsing is possible at the section and unit level. The flowsheets are displayed in a scrolling canvas object. This object provides zooming and panning facilities.

The interface allows for other applications to be linked to flowsheet objects (i.e. after selecting a process variable by clicking a pop-up menu can be activated). Applications that can be accessed are the dynamic logic analyser, trending and the glossary. To access or create a trend the operator can select several objects on the flowsheet. (Media used: colour, graphics, voice and text.)

On-line hypermedia manual: This application allows one to access the on-line manual related to the PROMISE project. In this manual, general information about the PROMISE project and (rather detailed) help information about the different applications is available. At the same time a paper copy of the manual is available to the operators. Access is provided via two modes, browsing and updating. (Media used: text, graphics, images, graphical overlays, and recorded sounds.)

Trending information. This application allows operators to view, configure and create trends. Trends are based upon the history information of a group of variables for a certain time span and displayed with a certain accuracy.

Trends are displayed in a scrolling canvas object. This object allows panning and zooming. Several time spans can be displayed (30min to 8 days). For a given time span a trend can be viewed with different time steps varying from 1 s to 30 min. New trends can be created interactively via the set-up window or via collecting a number of variables in another PROMISE application (glossary browser or flowsheet). The notion of temporary trends exists within the trending application to indicate trends that "live" only once. (Media used: colour, graphics, text.)

An unmediated object was added to the display as a result of some research and literature studies by the project. In conventional control rooms experienced operators are able, at glance, to have an overview of the process, because they recognized certain patterns on the mimic boards. In the current control room, this is seldom the case. The mimic boards only contain status information so the operator has to use the PI-system, to look at analogue information.

The solution to this problem was thought to be an object that generates patterns from a set of variables. The pattern would have a regular shape for normal operation. Deviating variables would immediately disturb this pattern. This would help the operator in detecting abnormalities but could also give a guide as to which disturbances have occurred. This predictive feature will only be valid after a lengthy learning process. Since the unmediated object is unable to convey precise information, a link is offered to the trending package, in which the history of the variables can be seen or followed. (Media used: graphics.)

Table 3.1 displays a summary of the media used in the different applications.

Table 3.1. Media used in different applications.

	Text	Colour	Graphics	Speech	Animation	Sound
Alarm handler	x	x		x	x	x
Dynamic logic Inalyser	x	x	x	x		
Flowsheet browser	x	x	x	x		
Dynamic step analyser	x	x	x	x		
Trending facility	x	x	x			
Unmediated object			x			
Glossary	x	x				
Manual	x	x	x			x

3.7.   EXPERIMENTAL STUDIES WITH OPERATORS

We decided to carry out a series of longitudinal studies of operators interacting with the PROMISE system, relying mainly upon operator interviews for an assessment of its usability, backing this work with output
from logged operator activity. Qualitative information was gathered in
two ways: feedback comments from operators about the system were collected during system development, and the operators who used the system were interviewed when the complete prototype was finally installed.
Collecting feedback from operators during system development was very
important; however, it was unstructured and not very comprehensive. The
interviews therefore aimed to question about all aspects of the system and
the different types of tasks being performed, focusing particularly on the
success or otherwise of the use of the media in the presentations. A continuous log of events, both at the interface level and at the application
level, was recorded during the period from 30/9/1992 to 12/1/1993.

Interviews were carried out in Flemish/Dutch and translated into
English for analysis. They reflect operators' experience of using the
PROMISE prototype in the plant over a two month period. Nine plant
personnel were interviewed; seven of these were panel operators (sampled
from four crews), one was a shift supervisor, and one was a control engineer. All the panel operators were highly experienced, with between
three and 20 years spent working in the plant. Neither the shift supervisor nor the engineer had day-to-day experience of using the PROMISE
prototype in the plant.

In carrying out a study of this duration it is important to have a number of measures which indicate the amount and manner in which the various applications are used. We therefore collected data such as – the total
duration of use over the trial period, the number of times each application
was used, the average lengths of the sessions for each application, and the
amount of user interaction that took place with each application. Any of
these measures can be misleading when considered in isolation.

3.8.   OVERALL USAGE STATISTICS OF THE APPLICATIONS

In any longitudinal study it is important to ensure that applications are
adequately used so that the feedback is meaningful.

Table 3.2 shows the overall usage of each of the applications in terms
of the three measures mentioned above (total duration of use, frequency
of use and level of user interaction) as well as the duration divided by the
number of times used which gives an indication how long a typical
"session" with a particular application lasted.

All applications have been used for many hours. Some applications
were used considerably less than others. But for a new system introduced
with a minimum of training this is only to be expected. The initial
impression – that the PROMISE system at DOW is capable of providing
benefit to the users – is supported by these figures.

Table 3.2.   Overall usage of all applications.

Application	Total time used (hours)	Number of times used	Avg. duration of use (hours)	Avg. actions per hour
Unmediated	16.1	23	0.7	2.36
Glossary	28.8	18	1.6	1.53
Manual	69.2	40	1.7	0.14
Trend	199.8	79	2.5	2.07
DLA	212.4	114	1.9	0.08
DSA/flowsheet	355.0	70	5.1	0.84
Alarm	1756.9	87	20.2	23.61

The application that was used most was clearly the alarm display application. The 1757 h of use represent about 70% of the total duration of the trial period under consideration. Of the other applications it is notable that the trending, flowsheet and DLA applications were also used for relatively long periods.

The second column of Table 3.2 shows that the alarm application was used frequently. However, it is interesting to note that the DLA application was used most frequently of all applications. This application along with trending and flowsheet appears to have been used for shorter spells at more frequent intervals than, for example, the alarm handler. The third column in the figure confirms this impression. It is clear that an average session with the alarm application (20.2 h) typically lasted four times as long as with the flowsheet application (5.1 h). Sessions with the flowsheet application again lasted twice as long as with the trending application (2.5 h).

Further light can be shed on the duration of "typical" sessions by breaking down the total number of sessions by the length each session lasted. Table 3.3 shows the number of sessions of different durations with each application. The general impression that sessions with the alarm application lasted longer than the others is confirmed. On 38 occasions this application ran for more than 10 h and more than half the sessions with the alarm application lasted more than 5 h. However, it is also clear from the "Alarm" row that this application was used for shorter spells as well.

For the flowsheet, more than half the sessions lasted for less than 10 min indicating that the average of 5.1 h per session may not be very typical. However, there are still a large number of sessions lasting many hours with this application. It may be that this indicates that the flow-

Table 3.3.   Number of sessions of different duration for all applications.

Application	< 20 s	< 10 min	< 1 h	< 5 h	< 10 h	> 10 h
Unmediated	8	10	2	2	0	1
Glossary	5	8	3	0	1	1
Manual	20	16	0	1	1	2
Trending	12	40	8	10	2	7
DLA	35	55	6	4	6	8
DSA/flowsheet	3	35	5	10	4	13
Alarm	12	10	3	15	9	38

sheet application was used in a variety of ways for a variety of purposes. There are only three sessions of less than 20 s because it takes almost half of that time to load in the application and a complex process diagram. Clearly operators did not tend to use this application for "look-up" sessions lasting only a few seconds.

Moving on to the DLA and the trending applications it is clear that the vast majority of the sessions here lasted less than 10 min and were used very frequently for less than 20 s. We assume that this is because these applications were accessible through links from the other applications such as the alarm and the flowsheets. The DLA and the trending applications were used to look up particular logic statements or variable trends. When the required data had been found the operator would immediately close down the application and resume dealing with the problem at hand. The fewer sessions lasting several hours and beyond have contributed to average durations of sessions of around 2 h for these applications (Table 3.2) whereas Table 3.3 seems to indicate that a more typical session lasted for a much shorter period of time. However, we cannot discard the longer sessions as "freak occurrences" as both the trending and DLA applications had more than 20 sessions lasting longer than 1 h. It therefore seems that these applications were used in fundamentally different ways, perhaps by different operators. In addition to being used for short look-ups some operators may have used these applications to permanently display their "favourite" logic expression or variable set. These displays may have been primary sources for monitoring the process or secondary displays used to provide a "richer" view of the process.

In the case of the less-used applications, most lasted less than 10 min. It is therefore tempting to regard the very few sessions that lasted several hours with some suspicion as not being representative of the way the applications were used. For example, it was anticipated that operators would require long periods of familiarization with the Unmediated Display before the real benefits from it would be realized, but few very long sessions took place. Perhaps operators did not understand this display and did not expend any great effort in learning to use it. However, from the interviews it is clear that one operator, in particular, found the unmediated display very interesting and felt the concept could be exploited further. It is likely that much of the registered use can be attributed to this operator.

When asked about their usage of the PROMISE prototype, panel operators reported that they used it mainly for alarms – acknowledging alarms and analysing alarms. According to one operator, this was because the alarm-handling application was easy to use. This reported usage agreed well with the usage statistics based on the data logs, where the alarm-handler was the application most used by far.

From a consideration of the interviews as a whole, it seems that operators had different patterns of usage of the various applications available in the PROMISE prototype. By and large, all operators had extensive experience of the alarm-handler and the DLA, and to a considerable extent also of the trending and flowsheet applications. However, experience with the other applications was highly variable. Again this agrees well with the data logs.

It can be seen that the PROMISE system was very extensively evaluated and that the subsequent operator comments do relate to a serious attempt to use the system in a real environment.

3.9.   OPERATOR EVALUATION

3.9.1.   Relationship to the Existing System

To evaluate the PROMISE prototype in the context of the existing process information (PI) system, two things need to be considered. Firstly, with the present PI system, much information is presented as simple text and in fixed format screens. Thus much information is, of necessity, displayed textually which may be much more effectively communicated by, for instance, a graphic medium. The PROMISE prototype presented opportunities to redress such deficiencies. The prototype, therefore, represented a major shift from a mono-media fixed screen system to a multi-media flexible windowing system. This was not without its difficulties, as well as its benefits, for operators. The important issue arising here, of course, was education and training in the use of the new system.

Secondly, the PROMISE prototype did not replace the existing PI system in the plant. The intention with the prototype was to augment the current system and to be used in conjunction with it. Having said this, however, it is interesting to point out that there were two occasions when the existing PI system computers failed, but operators were able to keep the plant operational using the PROMISE prototype alone. On both these occasions, a total plant shut-down was avoided, saving the company from a number of days production loss. On the last occasion, the PROMISE prototype allowed for a major repair of the existing PI system to take place in circumstances where shut-down would ordinarily have been necessary.

Panel operators were asked whether the PROMISE prototype helped to solve plant problems more quickly, and whether they were less likely to make errors and mistakes. Operators responded that handling of alarms was easier and quicker, and it was easier to monitor a controller or a plant section with the flowsheet and trending facilities. Operators also reported that the PROMISE prototype had helped them avoid mistakes related to the analysis of alarms. With the existing system, it was easy for operators to get lost in their browsing of complex control statements when trying to find the reasons for true or false conditions. There could be a wrong analysis of alarms, and a long search time to find the proper reasons. With the PROMISE prototype, "analysis of alarms is automatic, no mistakes".

When asked whether the new system features had made a difference to the PI system, operators felt that the impact was not as great as it could have been. There was agreement that the PROMISE prototype offered more and better functionality, but as one operator reported: "I suspect if I had to use it more often, that some things I now perceive as being difficult would have made life easier for me." The comment of another operator expanded this point: "since we weren't forced to use the system, in critical situations we often used the old system. We must say that there are probably a lot of features we don't know about, but the demo/training sessions were just not enough to explain everything."

Clearly the operators felt that they were not able to do full justice to the PROMISE prototype with such brief experience of using it, and there was an expressed need for more training in the use of the system. This emphasizes the need for really extensive longitudinal studies with in-depth training.

3.9.2.   Perceived strengths and weaknesses of the PROMISE prototype

The strengths and weaknesses of the PROMISE prototype were assessed by all operators. The speed with which the system allowed critical information to be accessed and processed was highlighted favourably by all. This is very important for operators where the system buys time for the operator when dealing with critical events. Also favoured were the integrated and interconnected nature of the system applications, and the facility within an application for calling other applications in a context sensitive manner. More specifically, most operators appreciated the ease of alarm handling and the ability to link directly to the logic analyser (DLA) for immediate analysis of alarm events. The flowsheets, with their direct link to trending and the DLA, were also favoured. Operators had their personal preferences; one focused on the dynamic step analyser, another on the unmediated object with its opportunities for pattern recognition, and another mentioned configurability.

All operators found the new system complex and difficult to use. However, different operators took different attitudes to this complexity. One found it fun to experiment with new opportunities. Another found the new system too tedious to work with, and used the (still available) old familiar system. Another prominent dislike was that the mouse was difficult to manipulate (especially for left-handed people). The main reason for this was the particular mouse pad (which was necessary for good operation and had to be in a correct position to work properly) and a cable which was too short. Also the cursor was often hard to find. A number of operators drew attention to the poor quality of the voice output. The use of sound was disliked as there were too many sounds in the plant. Operators also had individual dislikes; one felt that unrestricted configurability was a weakness, another disliked the overlapping of windows. The operator view of the PROMISE strengths and weaknesses are summarized in Table 3.4.

To view features like the complexity and unrestricted configurability of the PROMISE prototype as "weaknesses" is, perhaps, to view things somewhat like the novice user. Operators appreciated this themselves as was reported above. Operators had difficulties in learning the new system, and more training in the use of the system would have been advantageous. One may speculate that the very successful participative approach adopted to system development, of involving operators from the

Table 3.4.   Strengths and weaknesses as perceived by the operators

	Strengths/likes	Weaknesses/dislikes
Overall system features	Speed Integration	Complexity Instability
Specific system features	Alarm handling Explanation of control logic Flowsheet/trending	Speech and sound Sun mouse
Individual preferences	Step analyser Unmediated object configurability	Overlapping windows Unrestricted configurability

earliest stages and integrating their feedback comments into system design, may have contributed to an oversight for the need for a thorough training programme. The gradual introduction of new presentation ideas to operators over an extended time period may, perhaps, have led to a slippage in the perceived importance of training when the full system was finally to be put in place. For whatever reason, to the extent that the PROMISE prototype seems to represent something of a paradigm shift for operators on a number of fronts, the need for more training was clearly evident.

It is interesting also that configurability and unrestricted configurability were reported as strengths and weaknesses respectively. Equally interesting is the fact that it was the same panel operator who made both these reports. This again underlies the issue of training and its importance for being able to use comfortably the many new powerful functionalities in the PROMISE prototype.

3.9.3.   Comments on media usage

The default media for presenting alarms were text and animation. This was clearly the mode preferred by the operators, as it was used 89% of the time the application was open. Although animation and text were used considerably more in total than any of the other combinations it is notable that the media-rich combination of animation, text and speech, which was used on 11 occasions, lasted on average nearly 15 h each time. The same media with the addition of sound were used nine times for a total of 10 h. A curious case is the combination of text and sound which was only used once in a "session" lasting 25 h.

A number of other combinations of the four media animation, text, sound and speech were tried out by the operators. But these "sessions" did not amount to any real usage. It is notable that the auditory media of sound and speech, were criticized by most operators regarding the quality or relevance of the output, were in fact used for so many hours. It is true that the synthesized speech was of modest quality, but it was possible to understand it. It is also true that audio notification of alarms was redundant since most alarms are accompanied by another audio pre-alarm from the automation system. The fact that the auditory media were used for relatively long periods despite this indicates that useful information could still be assimilated from these sources.

Animation was present in all media combinations that were used for any reasonable period of time. However, animation on its own was only used for a total of 1 min over the trial period. This is hardly surprising as animation was only intended as a gentle way of alerting the operators of incoming alarms and also to provide some visual feedback about the number of pending alarms. Most operators did not perceive the animation as a benefit. It may have fulfilled its purpose of drawing operators attention to alarms but operators did not acknowledge it. As the animated icon was most often accompanied by the scrolling text display, it may be that operators were drawn to incoming alarms by a combination of the dropping icon and incoming lines in the text field. These are both movements in the visual field which could be noticed.

Operators commented more favourably on the text display is because it is filled with detailed information about the alarms which the operators require. The line of text representing each alarm was colour coded according to state and severity of the alarm. This display also provided direct links to other applications (such as the trending, DLA and unmediated). It is therefore not surprising that the text display was also present for the majority of the time the alarm application was in use.

3.10.   CONCLUSIONS

There has been little previous experimental evidence to support the view that a multimedia interface will necessarily provide a "better" interface than a monomedia one. By "better" we presumably mean that it enables the user to perform a task more efficiently in terms of time to complete, or in terms of making fewer errors, or both. Additionally it may also make the job more enjoyable or acceptable. The experiments we have carried out with the PROMISE tool kit in the DOW plant have been extensive. A brief glance at the usage statistics will confirm that the system was heavily used and carried out real tasks. This was no simulator or mock-up plant. The plant was a real one producing important and costly chemical components. In such a complex environment it is neither possible nor desirable to carry out controlled experiments. Thus our results cannot be interpreted in a precise way. What they do show, however, is that the system, as installed, generally did improve the way in which operators carried out their tasks, and they further perceived this to be so.

One difficult question to answer is whether the operators' improved performance and favourable disposition towards the system was due to the knowledge in the expert systems or to the quality of the multimedia interface. This question cannot be answered directly, and we suspect the answer is "both". Either on their own could fail. We need knowledgeable interfaces *and* good presentation.

All the evidence collected has not been reported in this paper because of space limitations. We hope to report later on a more detailed analysis.

ACKNOWLEDGEMENTS

The PROMISE project gratefully acknowledges receipt of a grant P2395 in the ESPRIT-II work programme of the European Commission. In a project of this size, many people have contributed to the reported results. We would like to thank the management team – Prof. J. L. Alty (University of Loughborough), Prof. M. Rijkaert (University of Leuven), Dr A. Schepens (DOW), Dr C. Dolphin (Work Research Centre, Dublin), Mr R. McKee (Scottish Power) and Dr Stephanie Pieroni (EXIS) for their significant contribution to all phases of the project work. Special thanks are also due to Dr B. Massop and Dr M. Verboven (DOW) for data collection and analysis of the operator data in the DOW plant.

REFERENCES

Alty, J. L. (1991). Multimedia: what is it and how do we exploit it?, Keynote address to HCI'91, Diaper, D. and Winder, R. (eds), pp. 31–44. Cambridge University Press.

Alty, J. L. (1993). Using multimedia techniques in process control: operator perceptions and design issues. In *IEEE International Conference on Systems, Man and Cybernetics*, Le Touquet, France, pp. 361–366.

Alty, J. L. and Johannsen, G. (1989). Knowledge based dialogue for dynamic systems. *Automatica*, **25**(6), 829–840.

Alty, J. L., Elzer, P., Holst, O., Johannsen G. and Savory, S. (1985). Literature and user survey of issues related to man–machine interfaces for supervision and control systems. ESPRIT P600 Pilot Phase Report (available from CRI Copenhagen).

Alty, J. L., Bergan, M., Craufurd P and Dolphin, C. (1993). Experiments using multimedia interfaces in process control: some initial results. *Computers and Graphics*, **17**(3), pp. 205–218.

De Keyser, V. (1986). Technical assistance to the operator in case of incident: some lines of thought. In Hollnagel, E., Mancini, G. and Woods, D.D. (eds) *Intelligent Decision Support in Process Environments*, pp. 229–253. Springer-Verlag, Berlin.

Johannsen, G. and Alty, J. L. (1991). Knowledge engineering for industrial expert systems. Automatica, **27**(1), 97–114.

Marmollin, H. (1992). Multimedia from the perspectives of psychology. In Kjelldahl, L. (ed.) *Multimedia: Systems, Interactions and Applications*, pp. 39–52, Springer-Verlag, Berlin.

Monta, K., Hayakawa, H. and Naito, N. (1992). Human reliability in process control during malfunctioning. A survey of the nuclear industry with a case study of man–machine systems development. In *Proceedings 5th IFIP/IFAC/IFORS/IEA Confence on Man–Machine Systems*, The Hague.

Van Hoff, A. (1990). The HyperNeWs interface. Available from the Turing Institute, Glasgow.

About the author

James L Alty was appointed to the Chair of Computer Science at Loughborough University in 1990 where his main research is Human–Computer Interaction, concentrating upon providing better interfaces for process control applications using multimedia techniques. He is also Head of the Computer Studies Department.

Professor Alty has held a large number of research grants, and has published a large number of research papers and four books. He lectures extensively in Europe, Asia and the U.S.A.

Julie Bergan was employed on a RACE project MITS whose aim was to investigate and develop novel metaphors for multimedia interfaces to telecommunications systems of the future. Currently she is working as a Research Engineer at Det Norske Veritas Research, Norway, on an ESPRIT III project, MARITIME. The project is aimed at improving the sharing and exchange of product data within the Eurpean maritime industries by concerted application of modern information and interface technologies throughout the life cycle of maritime products, in particular ships.

Andre Schepens joined Dow in 1981 as a process control engineer. He has done and led plant automation projects both as engineer and project leader. He has had active involvement in plant start-ups. This led to the interest in the field of man–machine interfacing for computer operated plants and he was the project leader of DOW for an ESPRIT funded project (PROMISE) on the use of multimedia and expert systems in control rooms. His current interest and activity is in the use of state-of-the-art software for the generation and maintenance of plant automation systems.

PART 1

Systems: Techniques

4   The essential elements of hypermedia

Michael A. Harrison

4.1.   INTRODUCTION

The last few years have seen an explosion of interest in multimedia, hypertext, and hypermedia systems and software. Mass-market magazines such as *Business Week* and *Time* have prominently featured articles on multimedia, while journals, conferences, books, and seminars have proliferated. The first major conference on hypertext took place at the University of North Carolina in 1987. Over 200 interested people attended and a fine time was had by all. While there was a sense of excitement, it was clear that there were important principles yet to be formulated. There has been a large amount of literature created since that time and a variety of commercial systems are now becoming available. It is now time to speculate about what is needed to develop the promise of hypertext and hypermedia systems.

The purpose of this chapter is to offer yet another definition of hypermedia systems. Working definitions, by their very nature, must be concise. We believe that this area is fundamentally important and that there are important principles to be found, systems to be built, and significant industrial applications to be created. Hypermedia has the potential to revolutionize the development and delivery of applications as well as the sophistication and usability of those applications. Therefore, this chapter enumerates the fundamental properties that a system must have to deserve the name "hypermedia system".

Industrial users of such systems should demand hypermedia systems that meet this set of requirements. Designers of such systems should meet these criteria and extend them. Only in this way will the technology advance and will everyone benefit.

4.2.   HISTORY

Almost 50 years ago, Vannevar Bush wrote an article (Bush, 1945) in which he described a system called Memex which could be said to have multimedia capabilities (typed items, photographs, and hand-written annotations on microfilm). The system also had associative memory and links representing "trails" between its objects. It is fair to credit Bush with being the parent of these concepts, even though the technology did not exist to implement them at the time.

Another major event was the appearance of the Augment System of Douglas Englebart in the 1960s (Englebart, 1984; Englebart and English, 1968). This system employed a mouse and an optional one-handed chord keyset, and offered genuine hypertext capability. It appears to be much harder to identify the first system that genuinely employed multiple media because the list of candidate systems is unclear. Ted Nelson's role as a visionary should also be mentioned: he first saw that these principles could be extended to a hypertext network of all of society's documents (Nelson, 1981). Moreover, he expressed his visions in colourful language ("If computers are the wave of the future, displays are the surfboards" (van Dam, 1988)).

In 1987, the HyperCard program (Goodman, 1990) was supplied to all purchasers of Macintosh computers. While HyperCard may be regarded as a primitive hypermedia system, its widespread availability stimulated interest in this area, and thousands of HyperCard stacks were created. For a general discussion of such systems, see Halasz (1988) and Haan et al. (1992),

NoteCards (Halasz et al., 1987; Halasz, 1988) was developed at Xerox from a different conceptual basis. It was intended as a supporting system for collecting and organizing ideas, each repesented by a card and organized by links.

Intermedia (Haan et al., 1992; Yankelovich et al., 1988) was a major multi-user hypertext system intended to focus on scholarly and educational applications. With its annotation service, link browser and linguistic tools, it intended to be both an authoring and reading tool. Certain implementation decisions have prevented Intermedia from being adopted more universally. These are documented in Haan et al. (1992).

The extensive multimedia work done in Project Athena at MIT (Hodges and Sasnett, 1990) was contemporaneous with the development of Intermedia.

The decade of the 1990s is bringing larger systems which work on multiple platforms, serve scores of users, and are becoming commercially significant. Companies like MacroMedia and Gain Technology (Chen, 1991) have comprehensive sets of products and are moving in different directions. The recent heavy emphasis on video is also opening up new applications.

There are also important applications of these technologies in software engineering. An early application was Neptune (Delisle and Schwartz, 1987). A current example is Ensemble (Graham et al., 1992), an enviroment for the uniform analysis and synthesis of software and multimedia documents. It is a framework for the integrated support of interactive development of complex natural language and formal language documents. The system has direct manipulation capabilities as well as services for formal description of syntax, semantics, and transformations of structured objects and representations. Users can edit and view compound documents of many types of components represented in a variety of media. Views can display the logical structure of a document as in a tree-structured representation or a view might display the output of a transformational process such as a printed view of a program.

4.3. DEFINITIONS

The computer systems we discuss all operate by visiting a sequence of "pages", sometimes called cards or scenes. A "simple page" might be a page containing text, graphics, animations and other objects. A "page" would be made up of some number of simple pages. (In a system that works with programs, e.g. Ensemble (Graham *et al.*, 1992), a "page" might represent a "module" in the programming language.) A *hypertext* system is a system as described above for which a user may also

1. create or delete pages;
2. insert or delete one or more links between two previously defined pages;
3. edit pages;
4. visit a page by following a link.

Thus it is fair to talk about traversing a graph of pages in a hypertext document.

A *multimedia* system is a system as above where the pages may be of different individual media types or compound pages which may include many media types. We discuss in Rule 1 below the different types of media that minimally should be included here. It is important to note that the list of types should be open-ended since the computer field advances dramatically whenever new media types are introduced (think of I/O devices such as the laser printer which drove the development of desktop publishing).

A *hypermedia* system is defined as a comprehensive multimedia system that also has hyperlinks between its "pages".

There are many other definitions of hypermedia. Halasz (1988) chooses a similar definition, but his view is very circumscribed. In NoteCards, each idea maps onto a card which is (prematurely) organized into a somewhat static structure. On the other hand, Nelson's vision (Nelson, 1981) could include all existing documents, hence his term "docuverse". We are thinking of powerful systems, network connections, large displays etc., which can be brought to bear on mission-critical applications which might involve collaborative development and use. Links are an important feature of such systems, but they are not paramount.

That is, a hypermedia system is a hypertext system that incorporates a significant number of distinct media types. We prefer the term hypermedia because the term "multimedia" does not connote hypertext functionally.

There are two important aspects of hypermedia systems: building applications (or authoring), and making those applications available to their intended users (reading or browsing). The process of building or creating these applications is frequently called "authoring". Programming refers to creating applications in programming languages by experienced and highly trained programmers. Authoring, however, encompasses a wider range of techniques than programming and a much larger group of less experienced developers. The authors are accomplished people in their disciplines but generally not software experts. The word authoring has its roots in the publishing world, since building a hypermedia application is much more similar to creating a document than it is to writing pages of programming code. One could argue for the movie production paradigm of MacroMedia Director.

There are many types of multimedia or hypermedia systems available, ranging from the type which is essentially a controller of media devices (e.g. Drapeau, 1993). At the other extreme is GainMomentum (Chen, 1991) from Gain Technology which attempts to provide a comprehensive set of media editors and services.

In what follows, we offer a dozen criteria by which to compare and evaluate hypermedia systems. At the end we shall categorize the criteria.

4.3.1.   The multimedia rule

1. A hypermedia system should support both user-driven and time-driven input and output of the full range of sensory-rich multimedia types, including not only those items that are stored internally in the system but also those stored externally in other data sources.

Most popular application-development systems today support only the traditional data types common to commercial data processing: text, numbers, and dates. All of these are displayed to the application user in character form, either as dot-matrix characters on traditional CRT displays or in various fonts and sizes on high-resolution workstation display screens.

The full range of sensory-rich multimedia types includes not only these familiar business data types but also several more that can leverage the tremendous power and sophistication of human eyes and ears as peripheral devices to the brain:

static 2D (two-dimensional) colour graphics
static 3D (three-dimensional) colour graphics
animated 2D colour graphics
animated 3D colour graphics
audio
static images
full-motion video
text and fonts
widgets

Graphics are computer-rendered representations of real-world or imaginary entities. For example, they might be drawings of every-day objects such as telephones or automobiles, drawings of cartoon characters, models of phenomena or concepts such as a graph of an organization's financial performance over time, or a map of the highway and railroad systems in an area of the country. Well-designed colour graphics can convey a tremendous amount of information in a very compact, memorable, and visually appealing form.

Many graphics are static and unchanging after they have been displayed on a screen. Animation is the process of bringing these static graphical objects to life. Animated objects can appear or disappear through various special effects such as slow fades, change colour or shape before your eyes, or move across the screen over a variety of paths. Animation can be used to add realism to artificial objects or surrealism to images of real objects. Well-designed animation adds interest to applications and increases the memorability and retention of the multimedia information they display. Animation editors for multimedia systems provide path and destination animations and perhaps frame animation.

Audio refers to recorded voices, music, or other sounds that are later played back. Well-chosen audio not only increases information retention but also provides ways to communicate with application users when their eyes are not fixed on their display screen. Audio is also increasingly being used as an input medium, completing the use of typewriter-style keyboards and pointing devices such as mice. Audio animation can be effective in moderation.

Images are static pictures of real-world objects or scenes that have been captured and recorded on photographic film, video tape, optical disc, or other physical media. Full-motion video refers to pictures of an event captured and recorded over a period of time at a rate that on playback can exactly duplicate the captured event. Today's video technologies record and play back at 30 frames (or pictures) per second. This rate is adequate for most applications. It is above the minimum frequency (fusion frequency) at whch the human visual system interprets sequences of static images and believes it is watching real-world motion. In addition, full-motion video on playback can be slowed down, speeded up, paused, and even played backwards in time.

A hypermedia system must not only manipulate multimedia objects as described above but also store and retrieve these objects on computers. For improved system performance, these objects might be stored within the software system itself. However, bidirectional (i.e., read and write) access to objects outside the system is also a requirement. Multimedia objects, especially live-video clips, consume immense quantities of storage space. In addition, organizations will receive and manage multimedia objects in a variety of physical media such as CD-ROM and laser discs. For them, the conversion and redundant storage of multimedia would be additional overhead that is both inconvenient and expensive. Video boards are now available for most systems which provide reasonable quality. Current software-only solutions are less satisfactory. An incredible amount of time and money is being spent on research and development for systems to provide video on demand over existing phone and cable lines.

Early applications of multimedia have been to education, including computer-based training, as well as to marketing separate tracks of audio, image, and video into a presentation that is played by the user in the author's predetermined sequence from beginning to end. Significant business applications that employ multimedia, by contrast, must be user driven and not time driven. The user of the application, rather than its author, must be able to control the pacing and sequencing of application elements. The user needs to respond to environmental or application-sensitive events and continually decide what actions he wants to take next at the time he is running the application.

Multimedia promises to improve significantly the processing and retention of information by application users. However, a multimedia object in isolation is not particularly interesting or beneficial. The real power of multiple multimedia objects appears when they can be used together. For example, consider a hypothetical hypermedia architectural application. The user interacts with a two-dimensional graphic of a building. With his pointing device such as a mouse, he clicks on a floor of the building. The two-dimensional building graphic is then joined by a three-dimensional representation of the floor layout. The user then clicks on a menu item that opens a window on the screen and plays a synthetic three-dimensional graphical walk-through of that floor, with the user controlling the speed and direction of the walk-through. Another mouse click invokes a video clip of a person actually walking around the floor – from the eye level and point of view of that person. Accompanying the video clip the user hears an audio recording of the person recounting his impressions of the colour schemes and spaces that he encounters on this walk.

4.3.2.   The object rule

2.   A hypermedia system should employ object metaphors for system interaction, system storage, and application creation.

The terms "object" and "object oriented" have become so overloaded that a few words of history may be helpful. Object-oriented software began at Xerox PARC (Palo Alto Research Centre) in the 1970s. It may be thought of as the encapsulation of data plus the "methods" or functions that operate upon that data. Objects can communicate by sending messages to one another as in the Smalltalk-80 language (Goldberg, 1984). For example, a laser printer and its font library might be represented as an object. Another object may "send" a message to that object with a request to print a particular file in a particular font on the printer. The object metaphor is a powerful one in modern programming and is especially useful in creating software such as direct-manipulation systems.

"Inheritance" is a mechanism that allows new classes of objects to be defined as extensions to previously defined classes. It is the key notion that provides the leverage to construct new objects from previously defined ones instead of starting from scratch. The importance to the user of being able to customize a system through simple modification of existing system objects is difficult to overstate. For example, the elegant MediaView multimedia-document publishing system (Phillips, 1991) is relatively easy to implement by subclassing objects in the Application

Kit based on Objective C and supplied by a workstation vendor. Then new behaviour is added to the subclassed objects or their existing defaults are overridden.

Another use of the word "object" concerns object-oriented database management systems (OODBMS). One needs to store heterogeneous multimedia objects such as text files, images, and video clips in a persistent store where they outlive the applications that created them. There can be many such multimedia objects in a sophisticated hypermedia application. Their granularity or size can vary widely and they can be related or "linked" in various ways for subsequent fast retrieval from large object collections. Hierarchical flat-file systems, such as those of the UNIX or VMS operating systems, lack important object-storage management capabilities, such as version control, check-in and check-out, and fine-grain security and access control over small objects below the file level.

An object-oriented development and storage environment offers a high degree of control and flexibility in developing applications. Application authors receive precise control over basic system objects such as tools, pages, graphics, widgets, and user-defined objects. They can share and reuse these objects to develop modular applications much faster than with other programming methods.

After all this discussion, Rule 2 is still ambiguous. First, we meant it to apply to the objects in the application. Moreover, we are advocating the use of an object-oriented data base. Both recommendations are arguable.

Experience with users suggests that the use of objects is intuitive, and easily learned by non-technical people. Actors are sometimes proposed as an alternative so as to preserve message passing and reusability but to do away with the containment hierarchy. There are classless systems (Ungar *et al.*, 1992; Harward *et al.*, 1992) which do away with any hierarchy of object types.

The object-oriented data base industry has failed to live up to its early promise (so far). One must choose between generality and performance. In a well-designed system, the user may not notice the difference except through performance and scalability. Some commercial systems have fixed size limits. From the point of view of building systems, it is conceptually easier and more elegant with an object-oriented data base.

4.3.3. The scripting rule

3. A hypermedia system should provide a rich, user-accessible scripting language for extending and modifying the behaviour of the system and its application elements.

Authoring in a hypermedia system is not and must not become ordinary programming in an imperative language. A scripting language should be as non-technical as possible. For example, a scripting language such as HyperTalk (Goodman, 1990) is much easier for a novice to use than, say, LISP or Scheme.

A scripting language is used to compose scripts – very short programs based upon the user's native language. Scripts can imitate user actions or respond to external events such as the clicking of a mouse button. A well-crafted hypermedia system will help its user by providing templates of code fragments for standard events. For example, the code fragment

```
on buttonPressed
    <statements>
end buttonPressed
```

can be selected from a menu of templates and then the template <statements> can be replaced by actual instructions written by the user.

How are scripts deployed? The hypermedia world is made up of objects such as documents, pages, text boxes, buttons, etc. A script can be attached to any object to specify its behaviour under various conditions.

Significant hypermedia applications require a functionally and semantically rich scripting language, the details of which are beyond the scope of this chapter. However, a complete scripting language should provide the ability to perform at least the following functions:

send messages to objects (for example, "turn green and blink");
receive messages (for example, "the mouse button has been clicked on you");
manipulate objects and modify their behaviour (for example, add a script to a buttom so that the button changes colour when it is clicked with the mouse);
perform some data processing functions (for example, sort a list of names into alphabetical order);
interface with arbitrary programs (for example, send a SQL query to a relational database system and receive back data to be presented).

There is a debate about how rich a scripting language should be, especially in the area of data types and data structure. However, an interesting functionality test for a hypermedia system is whether a user can construct with it an interface builder – a set of objects and behaviour that can be easily subclassed and modified to construct quickly custom user interfaces for his applications.

A good scripting language shares some important attributes with the 4GLs (four-generation languages) that are increasingly used today to build standard data-processing applications. A scripting language is non-sequential and much more suited for the asynchronous, non-linear control-flow environments of the object-oriented hypermedia world. A scripting language also allows environment-specific primitives to be integrated into the syntax of the language instead of appearing as externally callable routines. And a good scripting language allows an application author in a single integrated environment to move quickly back and forth between building a new routine and testing it in operation.

Finally, scripting and object inheritance must work well together. For example, a message may be sent to any object – a simple button or graphic, or a larger object such as a document page that contains the simple object. If an object receives a message and no response, i.e. message handler, is defined for that message, the system passes the message up the object inheritance hierarchy to that object's parent class. Only if no message handler in the object hierarchy can respond does the user receive an error response that the message was not understood.

The International Multimedia Association is seeking to standardize on a scripting language for the industry. The leading candidates are ScriptX from Kaleida Labs and GEL from Gain Technology.

4.3.4. The multi-user rule

4. A hypermedia system should support the collaborative building of applications by multiple concurrent authors on networks of heterogeneous computers and the execution of those applications by multiple concurrent users.

We are now enjoying (some would say enduring) the fourth generation of computing – networks of heterogenous desktop and deskside computers. Network computing fosters cooperative work within groups of users by allowing group members to collaborate electronically on shared projects and to exchange data and other relevant information quickly and easily. Complex applications can now be built by teams instead of individuals, and be deployed on networks of computers from multiple manufacturers with multiple operating systems and network protocols.

Hypermedia systems must support these collaborative client-server environments. Those who build hypermedia applications must be able to work together electronically through their software. An object (for example, a control panel with radio buttons) created by one application builder must be both accessible to and shareable by the others. If multiple users attempt to access and modify the same object concurrently, the system must resolve the conflict, either by allowing only one of the users to "check out" the object or by giving each user access to his own copy of the checked-out object while keeping track of and managing the copies in their different versions.

When the developed application is placed into production, its users must also operate without interfering with or invalidating the work of others. For example, users of an order-entry application must be able to enter concurrent orders for identical inventory items without selling more items than physically exist in the inventory. The system must resolve such concurrency conflicts while maintaining the integrity of the data and the application.

It is not only application building and application processing that must be distributable among groups of users. The storage and management of application data and application objects needs to be distributed as well. The system must mask the presence of the network, the size of the collaborating group, and the distribution of data and multimedia objects while creating the illusion that the network is a single computer with a single object store and a single user. And the system must sustain this illusion of network transparency as group size changes or as objects are redistributed so that applications need not also be changed. This is not easy with video over a network and special protocols must be introduced to control jitter (Ferrari *et al.*, 1992).

4.3.5.   The scalability rule

5. Applications developed with a hypermedia system should continue to work well and with predictable performance characteristics when deployed in production environments that contain much more data and many more concurrent users than existed in the prototype or pilot version of the application.

The folklore of commercial application development abounds with tales of prototypes that demonstrated well but failed miserably when deployed in their target environments. Such failures are often errors of scalability, where the success of the application depends on the scale of the problem or other factors to which it is applied.

The size or complexity of application problems can rarely be predicted. Therefore, a hypermedia system must be scalable. Scalability allows an author of hypermedia applications to build prototypes for test environments with the confidence that their performance and usability in the target production environments will not depend on the number of concurrent users, on the number, size, or distribution of objects employed, or on the number of mix of media types employed. For example, if the number of application users doubles, users' response times must not double as well.

Without such scalability, a developed application would have to be extensively tested and debugged in the target environment itself, often at great financial or organizational expense. With scalable software, applications can be delivered more quickly and enjoy longer lives if their environments undergo change.

Unfortunately, scalability is difficult or impossible to prove formally in advance.

One must build scalability tests into prototypes and must speak with other users of the software to determine if their scalability expectations have been met. I remember a case in which a programmer developed an algorithm which was judged satisfactory on the basis of small test cases. In practice, it performed poorly. When the algorithm and the code were examined, it was possible to change one line of code which reduced an $O(n^2)$ algorithm to an $O(\log n)$ algorithm. In multimedia systems, n does get very large!

4.3.6.   The interoperability rule

6. Hypermedia applications should be able to exchange both data and control not only among themselves but also with external applications and data stores such as SQL relational data bases.

Open systems and interoperability are requirements for survival and prosperity in today's computing world. In the workstation arena, this is accomplished with a common operating system while in the PC area, hardware compatibility has been the norm.

Interoperable applications allow you to leverage the work of other application authors instead of doing all the work yourself. An interoperable application can cooperate and communicate with other applications so that you can solve new classes of more complex problems faster.

The most common example of interoperability is that of preparing a text document using a word-processing program and embedding a portion of a financial spreadsheet within that document. Of course, a static textual copy of the spreadsheet cells could be created with the spreadsheet program and then inserted into the document. (There are "dirty tricks" that can be played with PICT files of spreadsheets but the spreadsheet functionality is still lost.) However, if the spreadsheet were later changed, someone would have to notice the change and explicitly insert the updated data into the document. Interoperability between the word processor and spreadsheet programs would eliminate the need for this manual intervention. A "live" link between the document and the spreadsheet would allow the document always to see and present current data from the spreadsheet whenever the document is viewed on a screen or printed on a printer.

Application interoperability requires three important capabilities. The first is that interoperable applications can communicate and exchange data with one another. The communication may occur in various ways, such as through intermediate temporary or persistent data files, through message store-and-forward systems, or via inter-process communication facilities such as "pipes" or "sockets". Inter-application data communication often must also be bidirectional, with either application being the source or destination (or both) of the communication.

The second capability is bidirectional control flow. This means that interoperable applications must be able to initiate and, where permitted, terminate one another. For example, an order-entry application may need to launch a packing-slip application to print packing slips for the shipping department and be informed when the packing slips are done.

The third capability is interoperability with foreign, external applications. For example, a hypermedia order-entry application that displays images of ordered items may need to invoke an electronic-mail application to communicate order status automatically to field salespeople and an SQL database server to retrieve and update customer credit information.

Interoperability is fostered and nurtured by standards (see Rule 12) such as OLE (Microsoft, 1992–93) (object linking and embedding) and ORB (object request broker). Standards for bidirectional data flow and control flow between applications mean that a software vendor need implement interoperability only once according to those standards, and thereby achieve interoperability with all other software whose vendors have done the same. Without such standards, interoperability among products requires all their vendors to do substantial work. If there are n vendors who want to interoperate, for example, the amount of their work increases from n to $(n-1)/2$.

4.3.7.   The hyperlink/hyperview rule

7. A hypermedia system should allow users to establish navigable relationships among objects of different media types, to browse and navigate those relationships in an ad-hoc non-linear manner, to determine readily one's location among them at any time, and to return easily to any prior location on a navigated path.

When multimedia objects are used together, they must be linked to one another through some appropriate navigable internal mechanism. For example, a multimedia object representing an employee's personnel file might be linked to an image object containing a photograph of that employee. That same photograph might participate in a second link from an object representing the company's baseball team for which the employee plays third base. A company executive viewing an employee's personnel file will want to see the employee's picture appear as part of that file. The baseball coach, however, will want the picture to appear as part of the baseball-team object whenever he views it. In both cases, it is the same image that appears in two different locations. A separate copy of the image object could have been created instead, but that would have required redundant storage space for each identical copy. Linking to the image object from several other objects conserves storage space and ensures that any changes to the image object (for example, a new photograph is taken because the employee grows a beard) are immediately visible from all linked objects. These kinds of read-only, single-level, automatic links are called *view links* and are an essential capability of hypermedia systems.

Now let us continue with our example. The same executive viewing the same personnel-file object notices that the employee works in the engineering department. The executive decides to visit the engineering department's project file (which may reside on another computer on the network) and creates a link to that object. Upon "arrival" in the project-file object, the executive notices several other engineers, creates and follows a link to the picture of the first of those engineers, then creates and follows a link from that engineer's picture to his employee file. These kinds of multi-level links are called *hyperlinks* and the process of traversing them in an *ad-hoc* non-linear manner is called *browsing*. Both hyperlinks and browsing are also essential capabilities of hypermedia systems.

In a large hypermedia application or electronic hypermedia document, the link structure can become complex. To return to our example, the executive has now forgotten exactly where in the link structure he is and how he got there. He is "lost in hyperspace", or more accurately, lost in a network of fundamental objects such as pages. He needs to be able to "step back" and view a roadmap of his current location and determine how he can return to where he began, either by retracing all of the steps he navigated or following a single link back. In some systems, the network of linked objects itself is displayed on a page where it can be edited to add and delete object nodes as needed (Halasz *et al.*, 1987). This ability to take a bird's-eye view of the environment at any time and from any altitude is called hyperviewing and is an essential capability of hypermedia systems.

In large hypermedia systems such Intermedia (Yankelovich *et al.*, 1988; Meyrowitz, 1986), the link structure can become complex. Conklin (1987) discusses this phenomenon and provides a vivid example of the phrase "lost in hyperspace". We need to find scalable hyperviewing mechanisms.

It should be possible to perform general computation in a hypermedia system as discussed in Rule 3. But since the hyperlinked network of objects itself is describable as a hypermedia document, it should also be possible, at least in principle, to search that entire network and compute some function on each object node (for example, the number of times an author uses the word "really" as a synonym for "very") or to generate links automatically based upon content rules.

A hypermedia system's browser and hyperviewer should support a graphical interface. That is, one's location in a complex link structure should be both diagrammable in and manipulable through a roadmap-like graph. This graph-layout problem is not easy. Designing a visually attractive, scalable, and efficient solution is a challenge. Techniques such as elision, holophrasting, and fly-overs have been used in various viewing systems and need to be adopted and adapted here for hypermedia systems.

4.3.8.   The technology independence rule

8. A hypermedia system should provide independence from any particular vendor's technologies and guarantee that the hypermedia applications will continue to work without change as the underlying technologies evolve.

Applications occupy a precarious perch in the computing world. They sit atop a constantly shifting layered pyramid of hardware platforms, operating systems, network protocols, data formats, graphical user interfaces, and other technologies. Yet applications are often used to perform mission-critical functions for groups or entire organizations, so they must be fault tolerant, operate error free, and survive without modification over long periods of time.

Underlying technologies change frequently and quickly. For example, processors increase in speed. Memory chips become denser, faster, and less costly per bit. Colour display screens become larger with higher pixel densities. New colour display standards are adopted. And new technologies such as HDTV and laser discs constantly appear. How can one simultaneously achieve the seemingly incompatible goals of application stability and taking advantage of new or better technologies?

You can and should demand that your hypermedia system gives you technology independence today and assures you of technology independence tomorrow. The hypermedia system must run in a variety of popular technology environments in various combinations. How the vendor achieves this portability is not your concern (though we do offer vendors a methodology in Rule 12). But the benefit for you is that you will not have to play the role of a riverboat gambler and make irrevocable bets that your choice of underlying technologies will win.

Numerous technology choices are available. Here are just a few examples in several categories.

Operating systems: MS-DOS, Windows NT, UNIX (various flavours), OS2.
Processors: Intel, Sparc, Mips, Motorola, VAX, Alpha.
Network protocols: TCP/IP, DECnet, IPX/SPX, XNS, ISO protocols, etc.
Multimedia hardware: TV, HDTV, CD-ROM, Laser Disc, DAT, DVI, etc.
Graphical user interfaces: MS Windows, Macintosh, OpenLook, Motif, DECwindows, Presentation Manager, Win32 etc.

Having a superior technology is neither a necessary nor sufficient condition for widespread market acceptance. (One example suffices: Windows versus the MAC graphical user interface.) Market dominance for a particular technology or product is a function of so many other unpredictable factors. If you choose a hypermedia system that is inextricably bound to a particular operating system, graphical user interface, or network, your applications will also become bound to those technologies.

4.3.9.   The extensibility rule

9. A hypermedia system should be easily extensible and contractible in functionality and user interface in order to solve wide classes of application problems and to accommodate users of all types.

It is impossible for those who build and sell software tools to anticipate all of the kinds of problems to which users will apply them. For example, an application-building system might be designed for creating standard data-processing applications such as order entry, yet be unsuitable for computer-based training applications without the addition of new functions such as cross-matching, multiple-choice question types.

An extensible hypermedia system allows application builders to implement new system functions through a scripting language or an interactive dialogue instead of through modification of the source code of the system itself, and to integrate these functions seamlessly into the system as if they had been there all along. Extensibility includes the abilities to add or delete items from standard system menus, to create custom menus, to hide or diable portions of or entire system menus, and to integrate new error messages and other communications into standard system-user advisories or dialogues.

The designers of the successful personal-computer spreadsheet programs recognized the importance of extensibility, and provided facilities such as macros for the customization of menus, user interactions, and program functionality. This enabled spreadsheet programs to be applied to unanticipated classes of problems outside the sphere of standard financial modelling. Designers of hypermedia systems must provide similar extensibility in their products.

4.3.10.   The multilingual rule

10. A hypermedia system should support user interaction, user communication, and data storage and retrieval in languages other than American English.

Some 60% of the users of the world's computer systems are not native English speakers. This percentage is continually growing as computer applications become more accessible to non-technically trained users. What is more, global networks, high-resolution graphical displays, and laser printers with large font libraries are continually driving this expansion.

English as a written language is remarkable for its simplicity in that there are no diacritical marks, no context sensitivity, a small character set, few ligatures, and a phonetic representation. The Roman characters of the English language are also used in other common languages such as French, German, Polish, Spanish, Norwegian, etc., but with significant differences among them in ligatures and diacritical marks.

The variety of alphabets and syllabaries involved in non-English use of computers is astounding. These include Russian and Ukrainian with their Cyrillic alphabets, Greek, Devanagari, Hebrew, Arabic, Thai, and Korean. Chinese and Japanese are also important but stand apart because of their complexity. Phonetically, Japanese is one of the simplest languages, while Chinese is very complex with up to eight tones per character.

Japanese language processing involves the use of Hiragana which is a syllabary capable of representing all the sounds of the language. Katakana, like Hiragana, is derived from Chinese, but is used for represeing foreign words and for emphasis. Kanji consists of about 10,000 Chinese ideograms, of which an educated adult may need to know about 2500. The standard computer representation for Japanese (JIS-X-0208) uses a 16-bit code. Thuse software for this character representation requires two bytes per character and may necessitate changes to a computer's operating system.

A consideration of the multilingual problem in computing (Becker, 1984) has led to the Unicode (for "unique code") standard which also uses 16-bit encoding. Unicode defines alphabets for Arabic, Hebrew, Roman, Cyrillic, Greek, Japanese, Chinese, Korean, Symbols, and Han (including Hanzi, Kanji, and Hanja).

Users of hypermedia systems must be allowed to create, store, and manipulate text objects in multiple languages. In addition, user menus and other system-user communications such as error messages and documentation must be easily customizable and switch-selectable into these languages. For example, users should be able to communicate with their hypermedia software entirely in Kanji, Hiragana, and Katakana.

Multilingual hypermedia software reduces training time, accommodates larger user populations, and increases acceptance of the software by its users. Hypermedia systems that hope to be useful globally must either support a Unicode mode or offer special provisions for simulaneous use of several languages.

4.3.11.   The performance support rule

11. A hypermedia system must accommodate both novices and power users, allowing them to author visually and to debug user-friendly applications that can become self-contained electronic performance-support systems for their users. A hypermedia system must also be its own electronic performance-support system.

Complex, highly functional software systems can become quite inscrutable and inaccessible by all except highly trained users. If hypermedia systems are to achieve their promise, they must overcome these usability barriers. And there are several important requirements they must fulfil in doing so.

A hypermedia system must carry minimal prerequisites for its use. Users with only a basic knowledge of how to use a graphical user interface such as a Macintosh must be able to begin using the system and become productive in it without further formal training. This requirement entails some other requirements which are discussed below.

A hypermedia system must accommodate both expert users and novices. This usually means that the system must interact with its user through a graphical interface. But the system must also allow the user to perform a wide range of application-building tasks via visual authoring – the direct manipulation of multimedia application objects and their behaviour through pull-down menus, dialogue boxes, and other object manipulation such as rearranging screen layout with drag-and-drop or other techniques. And while being easy to use, the system should not restrict the expert's access to all the system functions he needs. For example, creating a link between two objects (see Rule 7) should be no more complicated than pointing at the two objects and then selecting a menu item to perform the link. Yet an expert user should be able to change one of an object's links by directly editing the link information on the object's property sheet instead of by the possibly more time-consuming though simpler process of visually deleting the link and then recreating it.

A hypermedia system should also employ multiple media in communicating with its user and not restrict use of multiple media to the applications developed by the user. For example, system error messages might include audio played back through a workstation loudspeaker in addition to error text appearing on the screen. (Such a system might be acceptable in a private office but would be inappropriate in a software factory setting.) Some system messages might even be communicated through audio alone. For example, a "resource busy" advisory message might be communicated with a telephone-style "busy" signal on the loudspeaker.

If the user requires assistance with a system feature or procedure, a simple click of a key or the mouse should invoke that assistance on-line. The system should respond with the help that is exactly appropriate for the user's context and not force the user to locate the relevant material beginning with a top-level table of contents. Yet if the user desires to browse or search through the on-line reference material, the system should support a variety of search techniques and even allow the user to leave bookmarks and to annotate what he finds with electronic yellow "post-it" notes. Both the on-line help and on-line reference materials must be multimedia themselves. For example, a request for help in coping with a "printer is out of paper" message might invoke a video clip slowing how to refill the printer's paper tray instead of the less-helpful message "put more paper in the printer".

A hypermedia system must also allow the user to create and maintain multiple contexts within the system. For example, the user must be able to invoke the on-line help facility in a scrollable window on the screen while concurrently working in another window with that part of the system for which the help was sought.

A helpful hypermedia system not only accommodates users of different experience levels but also acts its own self-contained electronic performance system, obviating the necessity to consult reference material in hard-copy manuals or to obtain direct assistance from other humans.

The name of this rule was debated among my colleagues. Those who work more closely with new users favoured using the phrase "user friendly". Those who associate with advanced users favour the name selected. "Performance support" was chosen because of the importance of electronic performance support systems (Gery, 1991) and because this name covers several classes of users.

4.3.12. The standards rule

12. A hypermedia system should support and comply with all relevant formal and market standards.

A computing-industry pundit once opined that the nice thing about standards is that there are so many of them to choose from. Yet the computing world would be truly chaotic without them. Standards reduce the number of choices to a tractable number. In so doing, they allow product vendors to innovate and add truly useful features to their products instead of devoting time to proprietary implementations of common functionality. And standards-adherence by vendors gives the consumers of their products the confidence that the products will be compatible with other products in those areas.

There are two kinds of standards. *Formal* standards are debated and agreed upon by formal standards organizations or industry consortia. For example, the International Standards Organization (ISO) over the years has published standards in a variety of areas. For example, ISO has defined 8-bit encodings for Roman character sets, the architecture and functionality of network protocol stacks, and the syntax and semantics of the SQL database-access language. Formal standards are published in standards documents and widely disseminated in the hope that the relevant vendors will incorporate them in their products.

Market standards undergo a different process. They become standards by virtue of being purchased and used in significant quantities. For example, the X Window System has become a market standard because all the important hardware manufacturers offer implementations of it and all the major software vendors now write their user interfaces to conform with it. Instead of being voted upon with a show of hands by a standards committee, market standards are determined by the vote of dollars in the marketplace.

Hypermedia systems must comply with and support all relevant formal and market standards. This will not help different standards-compliant software products to interoperate but will also helps ensure their integration into your standards-compliant operating environments. Standards also simplify a vendor's problem of making their systems portable to a variety of platforms and environments.

Unfortunately, multimedia and hypermedia are still such a young set of technologies that the standards process for them has not yet run its course.

However, a few standards such as JPEG, MPEG, Unicode, MIDI, HyTime, and MHEG have emerged (Markey, 1991; Kretz and Colaitis, 1992). Such standards must be supported in hypermedia systems and not replaced by equivalent proprietary methods.

4.4.   CONCLUSIONS

Industrial-strength applications are built today with tools such as 4GLs and forms packages. We believe that hypermedia systems as described as described herein can dramatically alter the process and speed of building such applications as well as the sophistication and usability of those applications.

We have offered twelve criteria by which to judge putative hypermedia systems, and these rules are summarized in Table 4.1.

Not all of these criteria have equal weight. Rules 1, 3, and 7 are essential and unchallenged. Rule 2 is largely agreed upon but other approaches may yet prove viable (Unger *et al.*, 1992).

It is interesting to compare our rules with the work of Halasz *et al.*, (1987) on NoteCards in which he lists seven fundamental issues for hypermedia. Our two approaches are very different since our underlying assumptions differ radically. NoteCards is a system to help people organize

Table 4.1.   The 12 criteria for hypermedia systems.

1.	The multimedia rule
2.	The object rule
3.	The scripting rule
4.	The multi-user rule
5.	The scalability rule
6.	The interoperability rule
7.	The hyperlink/hyperview rule
8.	The technology independence rule
9.	The extensibility rule
10.	The multilingual rule
11.	The performance support rule
12.	The standards rule

their ideas. The users of NoteCards are assumed to be authors, designers, and researchers. On the other hand, we envision hypermedia systems as tools for building large industrial-strength performance-enhancing systems. All but one of the Halasz criteria are explicit or implicitly covered in our own rules. An apparent exception is his rule on "Virtual structures".

Virtual structures are an attempt to overcome the static nature of the basic NoteCards model. A user of NoteCards must map his or her ideas into individual units which are stored one to a card. Each card gets a title and is placed into a "filebox". This means that the user must predefine a static structure and Halasz (1988) calls this the "problem of premature organization". A virtual structure is only a view in the sense of Date (1990) or a multiple representation in the sense of Chen and Harrison (1987). But, since we demand access to relational databases in Rule 6, we have freedom in how data is stored as well as powerful retrieval methods. Thus the virtual structures suggested in Halasz (1988) are implied by the database access criterion of Rule 6.

The only system we know with access to industrial-strength databases is GainMomentum 2.0. Data is retrieved (by simple search or a query language, e.g. SQL) which may be presented using the full hypermedia functionality. As data in the database changes during the application, so does the display.

Halasz (1988) has other desiderata in his reflections about visual structures which could be classified as artificial intelligence (AI) oriented. Recent work on vision and new paradigms for reasoning suggest going even further by adding a reasoning tool to such systems. For example, such a tool could aid in the design and representation of a object based on weakly understood uncertain casual processes. To be more concrete, an intelligent assistant for a landscape architect might utilize geographical data, wind patterns, botanical data etc. in devising a design for a garden and its irrigation system. More mission-critical examples would include crisis management, intelligent vehicle and highway systems, etc.

ACKNOWLEDGEMENTS

This work was sponsored by the Defense Advanced Research Projects Agency (DARPA), under Contract N00039-88-C-0292, monitored by Space and Naval Warfare Systems Command and under Grant MDA972-92-J-1028.

It is a great pleasure to acknowledge the significant contributions of Eugene Shklar. Special thanks to Denise Kiser for asking the right question at the right time.

REFERENCES

Becker, J. D. (1984). Multilingual word processing. *Scientific American*, **251**(1), 96–107.

Bush, V. (1945). As we may think. *Atlantic Monthly*, **176**, 101–108.

Chen, P. (1991). An object oriented framework for developing hypermedia applications. Technical report, Gain Technology Inc., Palo Alto, CA.

Chen, P. and Harrison, M. A. (1987). Multiple representation document development. *IEEE Computer*, **21**(1), 15–31.

Conklin, E. J. (1987). Hypertext: an introduction and survey. *IEEE Computer*, **20**(9), 17–41. (A more detailed version is available as Technical Report STP-356-86, Dec. 1986. Microelectronics and Computer Technology Corporation, Austin, TX.)

Date, C. J. (1990). *An Introduction to Database Systems*, 5th edn. Addison-Wesley Publishing Company, Reading, MA.

Delisle, N. M. and Schwartz, M. D. (1987). Neptune: a hypertext system for software development environments. *Database Engineering*, **10**(1), 54–59.

Drapeau, G. D. (1993). Synchronization in the Maestro multimedia authoring environment. In ACM (ed.), *ACM Multimedia 93 Proceedings*, New York, June, pp. 331–339.

Engelbart, D. C. (1984). Authorship provisions in Augment. In *Proceedings of the 1984 COMPCON Conference*, San Francisco, CA, 27 Feb.–1 Mar. pp. 465–472.

Engelbart, D. and English, W. (1968). A research center for augmenting human intellect. In *Proceedings of FJCC*, Montvale, NJ, Vol. 33, No. 1. pp. 395–410. American Federation of Information Processing Societies, AFIPS Press.

Ferrari, D., Banerjea, A. and Zhang, H. (1992) Network support for multimedia – a discussion of the tenet approach. Technical Report TR-92-072, October, International Computer Science Institute, Berkeley CA.

Gery, G. J. (1991). *Electronic Performance Support Systems*. Weingarten Publications, Boston, MA.

Goldberg, A. (1984). *Smalltalk-80: The Interactive Programming Environment*. Addison-Wesley Publishing Company, Reading, MA.

Goodman, D. (1990). *The Complete HyperCard 2.0 Handbook*, 3rd edn. Bantam Books, New York.

Graham, S. L., Harrison, M. A. and Munson, E. V. (1992). The Proteus presentation system. In Weber, H. (ed.), *Software Engineering Notes*, pp. 130–138. ACM Press.

Haan, B. J., Kahn, P., Riley, V. A., Coombs, J. H. and Meyrowitz, N. K. (1992). Iris hypermedia services. *Communications of the ACM*, **35**(1), 36–51.

Halasz, F. G. (1988). Reflections on note cards: Seven issues for the next generation of hypermedia systems. *Communications of the ACM*, **31**(7), 836–852.

Halasz, F. G., Moran, T. P. and Trigg, R. H. (1987). NoteCards in a nutshell. In *Proceedings of ACM SIGCHI+GI'87 Conference*, Toronto, Canada, April, pp. 45–52.

Harward, V. J., Schlusselberg, E. and Tedrow, J. (1992). Athenamuse eventscript: user manual. Technical report, MIT Center for Educational Computing Initivitives, Cambridge, MA.

Hodges, E. and Sasnett, R. M. (1990). *Multimedia Computing*. Addison-Wesley Publishing Company, Reading, MA.

Kretz, F. and Colaitis, F. (1992). Standardizing hypermedia information objects. *IEEE Communications Magazine*, **30**(5), 60–70.

Markey, B. D. (1991). Emerging hypermedia standards. In *Proceedings of the Summer '91 USENIX Meeting*, pp. 59–74.

Meyrowitz, N. (1986). Intermedia: the architecture and construction of an object-oriented hypermedia system and applications framework. In *Proceedings of 1st ACM Conference on Object-Oriented Programming Systems, Languages, and Applications*, Portland, Oregan, September, 1986. Published as *ACM SIGPLAN Notices*, **21**(11), 186–201.

Microsoft. (1992–93). *Object Linking and Embedding*. Creating Programmable Application. Microsoft Corporation, Redmond, WA, pre-release edition.

Nelson, T. (1981). *Literary Machines*. Self published, Swarthmore, PA.

Phillips, R. L. (1991). Mediaview: An editable multimedia publishing system developed with an object-oriented toolkit. In *Proceedings of the Summer '91 USENIX Meeting*, pp. 125–136.

Ungar, D., Smith, R. B., Chambers, C. and Hölze, U. (1992). Object, message and performance – how they coexist in self. *Computer*, **25**(10), 53–64.

van Dam, A. (1988). Hypertext '87 keynote address. *Communications of the ACM*, **31**(7), 887–895.

Yankelovich, N., Haan, B. J., Meyrowitz, N. K. and Drucker, S. M. (1988). Intermediate: the concept and the construction of a seamless information environment. *IEEE Computer*, **21**(1), 81–96.

About the author

Michael A. Harrison is a Professor of Computer Science at the University of California at Berkeley. He received his Ph.D. from the University of Michigan in Ann Arbor and immediately joined the University of California at Berkeley. Harrison's research areas have included switching theory, automata theory, formal language theory, fast parsing techniques, protection in operating systems, electronic document environments, and software development environments. Harrison has been a Guggenheim Fellow and is a Fellow of the American Association for the Advancement of Science and the IEEE. He has been Vice President of ACM and a Director and Trustee of a number of organizations. Harrison has written five books and well over 100 technical publications. He is a founder of Gain Technology Incorporated. His current research interest is in hypermedia systems.

5 Hypermedia tools for multimedia information management

Wendy Hall

5.1. INTRODUCTION

This chapter explores the issues and concepts involved in multimedia information management. It presents the argument that hypermedia tools are a crucial part of any multimedia information system and shows how an open hypermedia system, can be used to provide a links service that permits hypermedia link following from any application to a set of multimedia resources. The chapter starts by looking at the evolution of hypertext and hypermedia systems, and continues by considering what we mean by a multimedia information system. Open hypermedia systems are discussed and the Microcosm system is presented in detail. Finally, some examples of current Microcosm applications are used to illustrate the argument made in the paper.

5.2. HYPERTEXT AND HYPERMEDIA

The terms hypertext and hypermedia are often used quite interchangeably. Hypertext in the strict sense only applies to text-based systems; hypermedia is simply the extension of hypertext to include multimedia data. The invention of both terms is credited to Ted Nelson in 1965. His vision of a universal hypermedia system, Xanadu, is most fully explored in his book *Literary Machines* (Nelson, 1981) but is more easily accessible in papers published in conference proceedings (Nelson 1980, 1988). Nelson defines hypertext as non-sequential writing, but the ideas the term encapsulates are wider than that and include cross-referencing and associative indexing. He states that

There are no intellectual subjects. For someone used to learning, to grabbing vocabulary and ideas, the elements of a new subject can come quickly. The more diagrams you have seen, the more words you know, the more theories you have heard, the more easily you can grasp the next one and assimilate it to the snow-ball of ideas already rolling around in your head. (Nelson, 1981).

Here Nelson is presenting a vision of the type of knowledge management environment that hypertext can help to support.

The inspiration for Nelson's ideas came from the writings of Vannevar Bush and the pioneering work of Douglas Engelbart. Bush proposed a theoretical design for a system that we would now call a hypertext system (Bush, 1945). He foresaw the explosion of scientific information and predicted the need for a machine to help scientists follow developments in their discipline. Bush called his system Memex (memory extender) which he described as "a sort of mechanised private file and library". The system was never implemented, but the ideas formed the basis of much of the later work on hypertext systems. Engelbart started work on his Augment project at Stanford University in 1962 (Engelbart, 1963). He foresaw a world of instant text access on screens, interconnections that can be made and shared, a new style of shared work amongst colleagues, and the use of computers to augment the human intellect. One part of the Augment project was NLS (for oN-Line System), which had several hypertext features, even though it was not developed as a hypertext system, and was first publicly demonstrated in 1968.

These then were the visionaries. It should be clear already, that the sort of hypermedia environments generally available to us on our personal computers today could not provide support for the large scale information management outlined above. Halasz describes Augment and other hypertext research projects that were originally mainframe based, such as Fress, as first generation hypermedia systems (Halasz, 1988). Work on second generation hypermedia systems began in the early 1980s with the emergence of various workstation-based systems including NoteCards (Halasz *et al.*, 1987), KMS (Akscyn *et al.*, 1988), Neptune (Delisle and Schwartz, 1986) and Intermedia (Yankelovitch *et al.*, 1985). For more information on these systems and basic definitions of hypertext and hypermedia concepts the reader is referred to the classic survey by Conklin (1987) and the more recent book by Nielsen (1990).

The first hypertext products released commercially for PC-based systems were Hyperties (Shneiderman, 1987) and Guide (Brown, 1987). When it was first released, Hyperties worked on the plain text screens of IBM PCs and PS/2s, although a Microsoft Windows version has recently become available. Hyperties was initially developed for two reasons: firstly, as a practical and easy-to-learn tool for browsing in instructional databases, and secondly, as an experimental platform for studies on the design of hypertext interfaces. As a practical tool it has been used extensively in applications such as museum information systems, and many of the design choices in Hyperties follow from this original emphasis. Guide was developed by Professor Peter Brown at the University of Kent in the UK as part of a research project that started in 1982. It was released as a commercial product initially for the Macintosh platform by Office Workstations Ltd in 1986. An IBM PC version soon followed and for some time Guide was the only hypertext system available for both platforms. In its original conception, Guide was designed to support text processing and large-scale information management. It is based on scrolling text windows and a hierarchical structure. Link anchors are associated with text strings and move as the user scrolls or edits the text. The commercial version supports four different hypertext link types – expansion (replacement), note (pop-up), reference (jump) and command (executes external commands). The different kinds of hypertext links in Guide are revealed to the user by the changing shape of the cursor as it moves over the text. The link anchors are usually referred to as buttons, but it is up to the author whether they are highlighted in any way.

Apple's release of HyperCard in 1987 did more to popularize hypertext than any other event. Timing was everything. Apple needed a product to make its computers attractive to new markets. In 1987, the majority of computer users were unwilling to pay the higher prices for Apple machines in order to take advantage of Apple's advanced graphical user interface (GUI), mainly because the many advantages that GUIs bring to the computing environment were not then widely understood. HyperCard was not designed as a hypertext product from the beginning. Its designer, Bill Atkinson, readily admits that he originally built it as a graphic programming environment and many of the features built into HyperCard actually have nothing to do with hypertext (Neilsen, 1990).

Nielsen (1990) discusses the reasons behind HyperCard's popularity. The most pragmatic one is that Apple took the decision to bundle it free with every Macintosh sold. This together with the fact that it is very easy to prototype applications in HyperCard because of the powerful programming language HyperTalk that is built into it, made HyperCard an instant success. Its release effectively sounded the death knell for Guide on the Macintosh, although it was not until 1992 that OWL announced they were no longer supporting the product. HyperCard's availability meant large numbers of people who might never have otherwise heard of hypertext were introduced to the concept and found themselves creating HyperCard stacks.

HyperCard introduced the concepts of hypertext to the computer-using community at large. It ceased to be solely a topic for research and became a widely accepted technique for application development, particularly in education. By the early 1990s, many new products on the market claimed some sort of hypertext/hypermedia functionality, even though most of the time all they were providing were buttons and elementary hard-wired links. This is particularly true of multimedia presentation and authoring systems. Techniques such as clicking on an object to initiate some action have become a standard feature of computer interfaces today, but it must be remembered that these are just interface techniques that give the system a hypertext-like feel, they do not make the application a hypertext system.

The dominance of the HyperCard approach to hypermedia application design and the resulting limitations on the development of such applications is still very much in evidence today (Hall, 1994). It has spawned many derivatives such as SuperCard, now produced by Aldus, Asymmetrix Toolbook and IBM's Linkway, to name but a few. HyperCard, SuperCard and Toolbook are now used extensively on both sides of the Atlantic to develop educational applications. Whilst some excellent applications have been developed using these systems, they tend to exaggerate some of the popular myths and misconceptions about hypertext such as the problem of being lost in hyperspace and the idea that every link (static or dynamic) must have a button at its start point.

They are also blind alleys as far as hypertext development is concerned. The end-products are often one-off products, they are difficult to tailor, maintain and up-date, and cannot be integrated into other desktop tools. They impose limits on the size of files etc. that they can handle, and data once imported into the application cannot be reused externally because it has been converted into a format that is proprietary to the authoring system. Using such limited systems, it would be impossible to build the global hypertext environments envisaged by Bush, Nelson and Engelbart.

5.3.   MULTIMEDIA INFORMATION SYSTEMS

To computer users today, the term *multimedia*, if it means anything at all, means the presentation of different media types (text, graphics, animations, images, video, sound, scientific data etc.) in a unified computing environment. The term *multi*media is used rather than media, because it ensures that the concept of multiple, integrated, concurrent communications is understood. Today, most users manipulate multimedia data by using a commercial presentation production system such as MacroMind Director or MediaMaker, or using the multimedia toolkits provided with windows programming environments. Alternatively they use authoring systems, such as Authorware Professional or IconAuthor, to create interactive multimedia learning environments in the same genre as the more traditional computer-based learning applications with varying degrees of branching capability and some superficial hypermedia functionality. Commercial hypermedia authoring tools, such as HyperCard and Toolbook, also contain utilities for manipulating and displaying multimedia data. However, in all these systems, presentation is everything.

The ability to display digitized video on a computer screen alongside some explanatory piece of text or diagram while listening to a soundtrack that describes the event in the video is still a marvel of technology. In the future this will be taken for granted. Today it is still a novelty. Most multimedia applications are produced in a one-off manner. There is no concept of a registry to record what multimedia resources (images, video, sound files etc.) have been used in the application, there is no system-supported way to allow authors to find out if someone else in the organization has already digitized a particular photograph or produced a video sequence that could be reused in the new application, no way to allow an author to query an image database to find suitable images etc. As the novelty of multimedia presentation wears off the need for multimedia document management systems that allow the user to browse through and query large sets of multimedia resources will become increasingly apparent.

Much work has been done on extending traditional database architectures to incorporate multimedia data types (Grosky and Mehrota, 1989; Rhiner and Stucki, 1991). However, the term database implies a set of structured data. The integration of traditional database management systems (DBMS) with text retrieval systems is by no means trivial because the text documents may have no inherent structure and database systems are not designed to handle fields of free text. The situation is inherently more complex when such a system is extended to include any multimedia data type. This leads to the definition of a multimedia information system (MMIS) as a repository for all types of electronically representable data which can be manipulated and processed by users in whatever way is most appropriate to the type of data they wish to access and/or the type of query they wish to make (Goble *et al.*, 1991, Grosky, 1994).

Multimedia resources are expensive to produce, and highly specialized tools are required to manipulate them. Many different editors and processing tools will be required, as well as specialized query handling, storage and retrieval devices for the different media types. It will not be cost effective to implement all of these tools within a single closed system but rather as a set of loosely coupled communicating processes with access to a common multimedia resource base. Additionally, unlike traditional databases where it makes little sense to access the data from outside the structure of the DBMS, it makes every sense for people to want to access unstructured data types such as text, images, video and audio from whichever application package they happen to be working in.

Developments in operating systems and graphical user interfaces are making integration between applications easier to implement at least at the level of sharing common objects but generally this involves the embedding of the (virtual) object within an application. In this chapter we suggest that to take the greatest advantage of the availability of multimedia information within computer systems, we need the flexibility provided through the use of hypermedia tools as provided by the new generation of open hypermedia systems.

5.4.   OPEN HYPERMEDIA SYSTEMS

Whilst the world has been building relatively small-scale hypermedia applications in HyperCard and its derivatives, the hypertext research community has continued to explore the development of hypertext systems that handle information on a large scale. It is clear that authoring effort and the management of links are major issues in the development of large hypertext and hypermedia applications. This has led to the design of systems which separate the link data from the document data. (In this chapter, "document" means a piece of information that may be of any multimedia data type.) This enables information about links to be processed and maintained like any other data rather than being embedded in the documents themselves. Research effort has been concentrated on the development of open hypermedia systems that enable hypermedia functionality to be integrated into the general computing environment and allow linking from all tools on the desktop. The hypertext management system then becomes much more of a back-end process than a user interface technology.

The paper by Malcolm *et al.* (1991) is an excellent summary of user requirements for hypermedia that extend well beyond the scope of the current generation of commercial hypermedia systems. The paper in fact argues for the development of open hypermedia systems that fulfil the following criteria: an adaptable environment for the integration of data tools and services that do not confine users to a particular suite of editors and specialized software packages; a system that is platform independent and distributed across platforms; a system which makes it easy for users to find, update, annotate and exchange information; and a system in which all forms of data and media are treated in a conceptually similar manner.

It is clear that the current generation of hypermedia systems do not fit any of these criteria. This is because they are all to a greater or lesser extent closed systems. A closed hypermedia system provides a fix set of encapsulated applications which are normally tightly integrated with the hypermedia linking mechanisms. The hypermedia links are generally embedded in the data which is stored in a proprietary document format. It is therefore not possible to access the data or the links from outside of the hypermedia system. In contrast, an open hypermedia system provides a protocol that allows any application to participate in the hypermedia service. The applications are loosely integrated with the hypermedia linking mechanisms but the degree of openness can vary considerably according to the restrictions that the protocol imposes on the applications, ranging from complete control to none at all. A hypermedia link service and an associated protocol is therefore an essential part of any open hypermedia system.

In his book *Literary Machines* (Nelson, 1981), Nelson describes Xanadu as a "universal open hypermedia environment". Unfortunately Xanadu has never been fully implemented, but Nelson's ideas certainly laid the foundation for the development of such systems. The Intermedia project (Yankelovitch *et al.*, 1985) was also a pioneering project in this respect. Sun's Link Service (Pearl, 1989) was probably the first implementation of a hypertext system that could be truly described as an open system. Running on Sun workstations, in a distributed environment, it consists of a link database service that is integrated with registered applications through a library that implements a communication protocol. It therefore provides a link service to existing applications, and dedicated applications for editing and processing information are not required. However, an application has to be aware of the link service and be registered with it in order to make use of the service. It must be able to send information to the link service that identifies the element in the document from which a link is to be followed.

Following on from these early developments a number of research groups have developed various models of open hypermedia systems. These include Microcosm (Davis *et al.*, 1992), Multicard (Rizk and Sauter, 1992), Hyper-G (Kappe, 1992), and HyperBase (Schutt and Streitz, 1990). Such systems are largely still in the province of the research laboratory although commercial versions of some of them are envisaged. The openness of the system and the scope of the link service varies in each case. We shall present the Microcosm system in detail and explain how it can be applied to multimedia information management.

5.5.   THE MICROCOSM APPROACH

The Microcosm system has been under development at the University of Southampton since 1989. The philosophy behind its development and on which we based the original design is shown in Figure 5.1. This three-layer model is similar to the three-level architecture of a traditional DBMS. Just as the conceptual level of a DBMS maps the user's view of the data onto the internal storage structure of the database, so the link service maps the data in the application to the multimedia information catalogued by the document management system.

Our principle criteria in the design of Microcosm were:

the separation of links from data;
the need to maintain a database of links;
no requirements for proprietary document formats;
the ability to apply links to other applications and to read-only material;
the use of the selection–action metaphor as the basic link interaction mechanism;
a declarative model for link specification;
an open system to encourage portability across different hardware platforms;
a highly modular system to allow for easy extensibility;
no ultimate distinction between author and user.

The consequences of these design principles were the need to develop a link management system and a method of allowing links to be applied to applications that are not under the control of the hypermedia system. We also wanted to keep the system as open as possible so that link following was just one type of action that could be applied to an object in a data file. Our aim was to produce a generalized multimedia information management environment based on the availability of an open hypermedia system.

Microcosm is currently implemented on MS-Windows 3.1. Versions of the software are also currently under development for the Apple Macintosh and Unix systems running an X-Windows front-end. The model was first described in Fountain et al. (1990), but has subsequently been fundamentally altered and extended in order to keep all aspects of the system open (Davis *et al.*, 1992). It is best understood as a set of autonomous communicating processes (agents) which supplement the facilities provided by the operating system.

In Microcosm the user interacts with a *viewer*. A viewer is any application in which data may be displayed. Messages to perform actions are sent from the viewer to Microcosm, which then dispatches the message through a chain of *filters*. Each of these filters is then given the opportunity to respond to the message by blocking it, passing it on or changing it before passing it on. Based on the message contents, some filters may add new messages to the chain. Eventually the message(s) will emerge from the filter chain and arrive at the Link Dispatcher. This will examine the messages to see if they contain any available actions (such as links to follow), and if so it will offer these actions to the user.

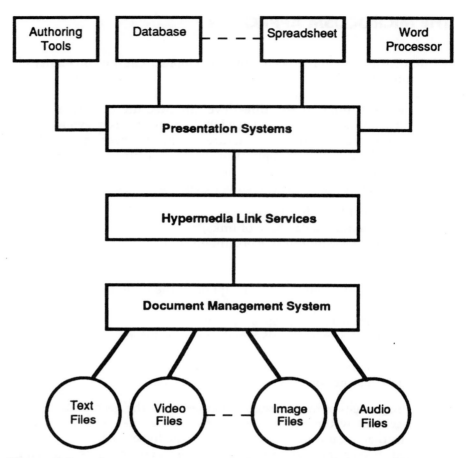

Figure 5.1. The Microcosm system architecture. (Copyright © Wendy Hall, University of Southampton.)

Filters in Microcosm are independent processes, and may be dynamically installed, removed or reordered (Hill *et al.*, 1993). Particularly important filters are the link databases, or linkbases as we call them, which contain all the information about link availability. When a message arrives at a linkbase requesting a link to follow, the process looks up the source anchor in a data file and, if found, returns details of the link destination, which are passed on to the link dispatcher. There can be any number of linkbases in the filter chain: the user can install and delete linkbases at run-time so it is easy to present different views of the data to different users. Other filters include processes to aid navigation (such as a history mechanism and local map device) and processes to compute dynamic links.

The Microcosm model for creating and following links is based on the process of *selection* and *action*. The user selects the information they are interested in, which may be for example a word or a phrase in a text document or an area in an image, and chooses an action from a menu to be performed on this selection, such as *follow link* or *make link*. This enables us to create a spectrum of link types. Specific links are defined on an object at a specific point in a particular source document. Local links are defined on an object at any point in a particular source document. Generic links are defined on an object at any point in any document. The local and generic links, which have dynamic source anchors, are the features that enable the Microcosm link service to be applied to other applications. This spectrum of links is naturally extensible to links created dynamically by any process that can be applied to the source selection. For example, we have implemented text-retrieval links which are created dynamically using a text-retrieval search based on the source selection.

We have implemented buttons in Microcosm, but they are merely a special case of a specific link, where the *follow link* action is tied to the specific source selection. When a document is viewed through Microcosm, the linkbases are automatically queried to search for buttons in that document, which are then highlighted on the screen. When the user clicks on a button the *follow link* query is automatically initiated without the user having to select the action. This side-effect of what is essentially a declarative model for hypertext linking causes a number of problems, and buttons can only be displayed in viewers which can receive messages from Microcosm.

We currently have three categories of viewers. Fully aware Microcosm viewers are generally ones we have written ourselves to display different multimedia datatypes including text, graphic images, video, animations and sound. They have the full range of Microcosm functionality. Partially aware viewers are applications from external sources, such as word processors, databases and other hypermedia systems, that have been adapted to be Microcosm aware, i.e. send messages to Microcosm. For example, in the Microsoft Windows environment almost any application that has a level of programmability and access to the DDE can be made Microcosm aware. Unaware viewers are applications that cannot sent message to Microcosm: in the Windows environment this usually translates into applications that have no DDE access. To enable Microcosm link services to be applied to such applications, we have introduced the idea of "clipboard links". Microcosm can be set-up to monitor the contents of the clipboard and to perform link processing actions on this data. In this way, the Microcosm link service can be applied to different desktop applications as well as used to support hypermedia authoring in the large.

In order to ensure that the system is kept as flexible as possible, we have adopted a tagged ASCII message format. Any viewer or filter may introduce any tag and data it likes into the message. Filters respond to the tags they know and ignore the rest. Microcosm for Windows makes use of the dynamic data exchange (DDE) facility to pass the messages from process to process The Macintosh system uses Apple events, and the Unix version uses sockets for the message passing.

Writing a new filter is a simple task that could be undertaken by any Windows programmer without any special understanding of Microcosm internals. A procedure is written to analyse the incoming message for the required tag(s) and to take appropriate actions. This is then inserted into a standard shell which takes care of all the communication with the DDE channels, and the new filter is then compiled. This flexible modular approach makes it easy for a programmer to make major changes to the functionality of the system.

We have developed our own document management system (DMS) which registers the multimedia information available within particular applications. This has been implemented to provide users with a catalogue of available information and can be used directly to find and retrieve information. The list of data types that can be stored in the DMS is extensible and can contain virtually any media data type. Additionally links can lead to third-party application programs, these can also be declared as data types in the DMS.

5.6.   EXAMPLE APPLICATIONS

Microcosm has been used extensively to manage and create hypermedia versions of large multimedia archives. The first example of this was the personal archive of the Earl Mountbatten of Burma, which is held at the University of Southampton. It consists of approximately 250,000 text documents and 50,000 photographs plus a sizeable collection of cine-films, videotapes and sound recordings of speeches. The material spans Mountbatten's entire life and the remit of the University Library is to make this material available for use by authorized researchers. The multimedia nature of the archive makes this impossible by "traditional" methods. Our long-term aim is to create an electronic version of the entire archive and make this available over the Internet. Using Microcosm, the authoring effort is greatly reduced because of the generic link facility and it is possible to create different "views" of the data for different users by creating different linkbases. It is also possible for users to create their own "views" of the data in the archive. Integration with database and information retrieval systems provides a powerful environment for browsing and exploring the archive.

A similar approach is being taken by the Department of History in the creation of a multimedia archive for use in teaching. This is based on material concerning the Yugoslavian Civil War of 1941–45 (Colson and Hall, 1992). A Microcosm version of this archive has been successfully used as the basis of a third year undergraduate course by the historians. The students have access to the material on workstations based in the University Library and create "multimedia dissertations" using Microsoft Word for Windows, drawing on material in the archive for evidence. This is a very easy and natural thing to do using an open hypermedia system such as Microcosm. The student hands-in their dissertation as a Word file plus a Microcosm linkbase. The tutor can examine both the "interactive" dissertation and the linkbase for evidence of the student's ability to extract information to support an argument from a set of archive material. A screen shot from this application is shown in Plate 3 (colour section).

Another application that has been successfully used in teaching is the Cell Biology application shown in Plate 4. This shows abstracts of video sequences (micons) which are used to help the user browse the available video sequences. This application has been used several times as part of the first year biology course at the University of Southampton

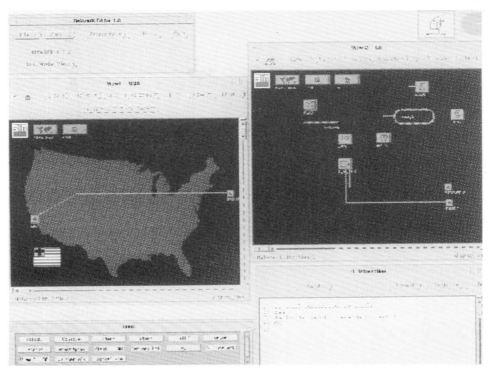

Plate 1 An example screen image from the second MMI² demonstrator for monitoring computer network performance showing different interaction modes: a map overlaid with the physical structure of the network; natural language input mode, the logical structure of the computer network.

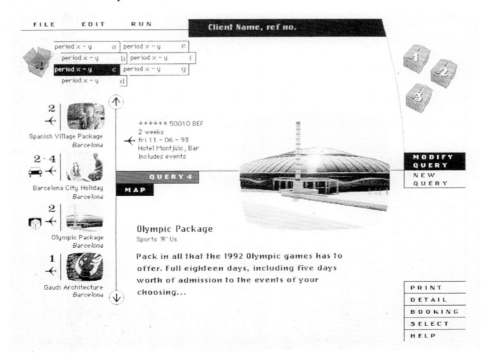

Plate 2 Screen design for a hypermedia tourism application for the Barcelona 1992 Olympics using the MIPS presentation system. The main image is a short video of the site.

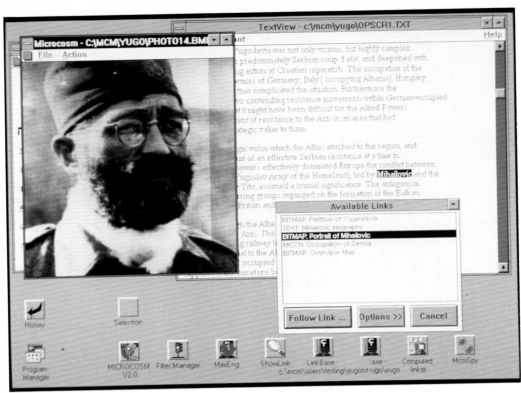

Plate 3 A screen shot from the Yugoslavian Civil War application. (Copyright © Wendy Hall and Frank Colson, University of Southampton.)

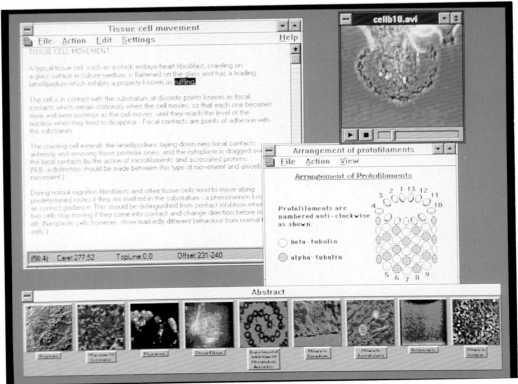

Plate 4 A screen shot from the cell biology application. (Copyright © Wendy Hall and Gerard Hutchings, University of Southampton.)

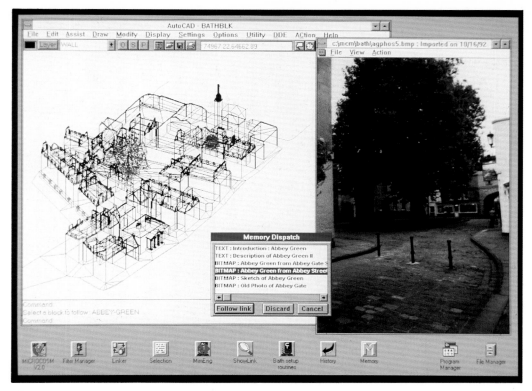

Plate 5 A screen shot from the City of Bath application. (Copyright © Wendy Hall and Hugh Davis, University of Southampton.)

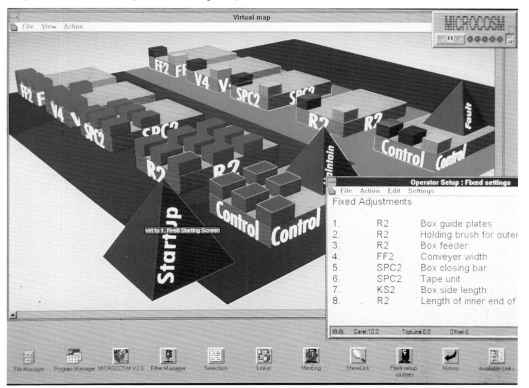

Plate 6 A screen shot from the advanced manufacturing technology application. (Copyright © Wendy Hall and Richard Crowder, University of Southampton.)

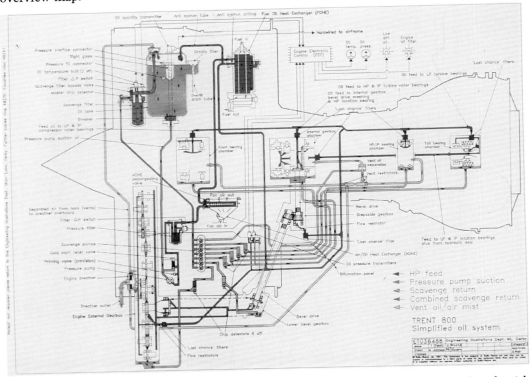

Plate 7 Simplified oil system diagram (original size 44.2 × 26.8 cm). (Reproduced with permission from Rolls Royce plc.)

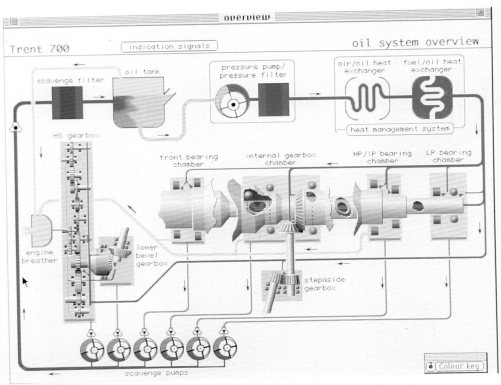

Plate 8 Overview map of the oil system cinegram (original size 22.6 × 16.9 cm).

Plates 9 & 10 Pressure pump and filter component view. "Replace filter element" sequence.

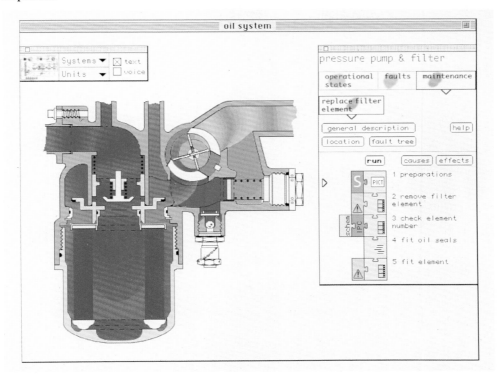

Plate 9 Preparations.

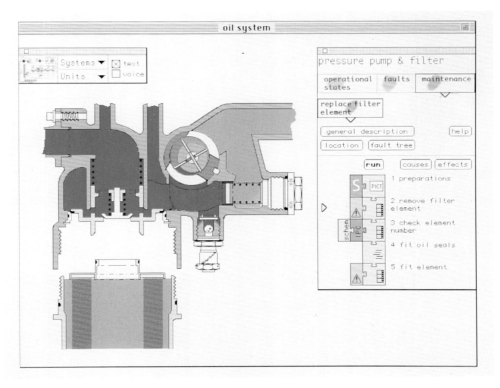

Plate 10 Remove filter element.

Plates 11 – 14 Scavenge filter component view. Filter blockage sequence.

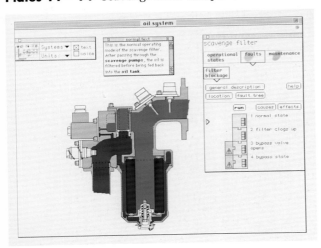

Plate 11 Normal state.

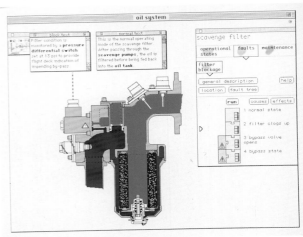

Plate 12 Filter clogs up.

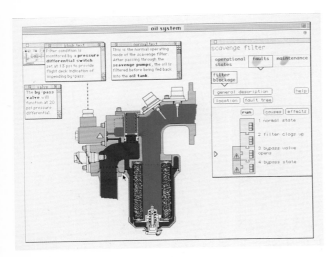

Plate 13 Bypass valve opens.

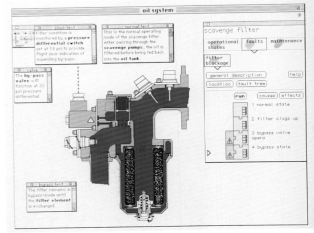

Plate 14 Bypass state.

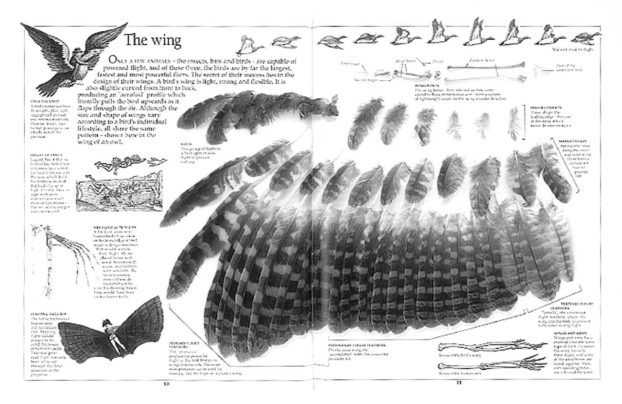

Plate 15 *Eyewitness Guide:* Bird. Copyright © Dorling Kindersley.

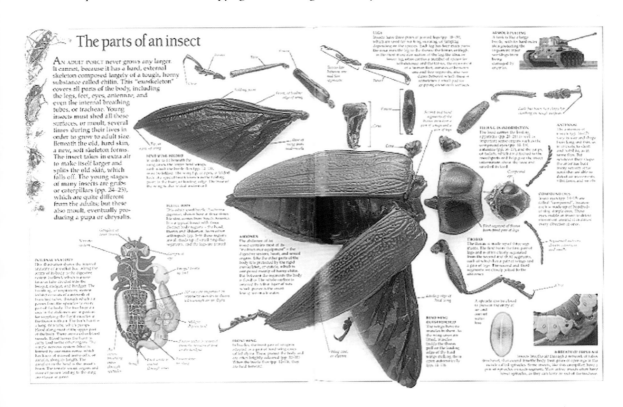

Plate 16 *Eyewitness Guide:* Insect. Copyright © Dorling Kindersley.

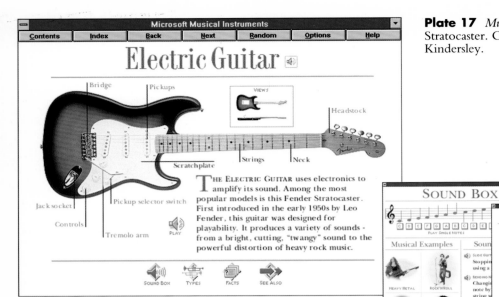

Plate 17 *Musical Instruments:* Fender Stratocaster. Copyright © Dorling Kindersley.

Plate 18 *Musical Instruments:* Drum Kit. Copyright © Dorling Kindersley.

and has formed the basis of a number of evaluations (Hutchings *et al.*, 1993).

Another interesting development is the integration of Microcosm with 3D-modelling packages such as Autocad. Every object in an Autocad drawing is given a unique name. This name can be used as the anchor for a Microcosm link. When the user selects an object in Autocad and chooses the Microcosm *follow link* action from the menu bar, a message is sent to Microcosm and the corresponding link entries retrieved from the database. The object name is independent of the spatial position of the object on the screen, as a result the user can access multimedia information about objects in the drawing from whatever perspective they are viewed. We have used this functionality to link a set of hypermedia documents to a 3D model of the City of Bath as illustrated in Plate 5. This work has been undertaken with the Centre for Advanced Studies of Architecture at the University of Bath and has been designed to support the teaching of urban planning. A number of animations have been built demonstrating "fly-overs" and "walk rounds" of various areas in the model using packages such as 3D-Studio. The same set of hypermedia links can be applied to the animations as to the main 3D model.

This technique has been extended for use in maintenance, training and fault diagnosis applications in industry. In particular, we are working with Pirelli Cables, UK, to explore the potential of an open model for hypermedia as an operational interface in the advanced manufacturing environment, and the formulation and application of large scale multimedia resource bases to support this activity. We are using a particular system in the packaging line at Pirelli's factory in Aberdare as a case study. This is illustrated in Plate 6. The same technique can be used to link multimedia information to a geographical information system: in this case it is the co-ordinates of the map that become the anchor of the link.

5.7. CONCLUSIONS

These are just some of the ways in which we are experimenting with using Microcosm to integrate different applications and application packages to large sets of multimedia resources. Microcosm is the basis of the University of Southampton's institutional Teaching and Learning Technology Project (TLTP). Using Microcosm, authors can customize and reuse multimedia and hypermedia material to best suit their particular teaching requirements. It enables tutors to take material developed at other sites and link it to their own multimedia teaching resources (slides, videos, lecture notes etc.). We have used authoring environments such as Authorware and Toolbook as front-ends to multimedia resource bases held in Microcosm, so that all the facilities of such environments are available to authors whilst not restricting them to always working in a closed system.

The flexibility of the Microcosm model makes the possibilities endless. We are currently experimenting with the development of many different types of filters to generate links automatically to reduce authoring effort, and to create links dynamically according to different algorithms. For example, we are using rule-based algorithms to create an intelligent agent device. The integration with visualization systems such as Autocad is allowing us to experiment with different metaphors for the development of user interfaces to a large sets of multimedia data.

An open hypermedia system like Microcosm has an intrinsically different feel from closed hypermedia systems. The onus is on the user to interrogate the system in order to ask for more information rather than expecting the system to announce to the user that there is more information about a particular subject. The infinitely more flexible model allows us to customize the hypertext environment to the user's needs. On an even wider scale, filters can be built to generate links to wide area information servers such as WAIS, WWW and Gopher.

This chapter has shown how an open hypermedia system can be used to provide a very flexible model of multimedia information management and to provide access across a whole range of standard applications to large sets of multimedia resources. Since these resources are stored in standard formats and no mark-up is imposed on them, it is possible to use standard editing and processing tools to create and interact with them. The material is also in a form in which it can be easily converted to hypermedia interchange formats such as MHEG and HyTime as they become more widely used in the future.

ACKNOWLEDGEMENTS

The author would like to acknowledge and thank the entire Microcosm team without whom this paper would not have been possible, and all the authors and developers in the groups with whom we are producing applications. Funding for the Microcosm project has largely been provided by the SERC, the HEFC and the University of Southampton.

REFERENCES

Akscyn, R., McCracken, D.L. and Yoder, E. (1988). A distributed hypertext for sharing knowledge in organisations. *CACM*, **31** (7), 820–835.

Brown, P.J. (1987). Turning ideas into products: the guide system. In *Proceedings of the Hypertext'87 Workshop*, University of North Carolina at Chapel Hill, 13–15 November, pp. 33–40.

Bush, V. (1945). As we may think. *Atlantic Monthly*, **176**, 101–108.

Colson, F.C. and Hall, W. (1992). Pictorial information systems and the teaching imperative. In Thaller, M. (ed.) *Images and Manuscripts in Historical Computing*, pp. 73–86. Scripta Mercaturae Verlag.

Conklin, J. (1987). Hypertext: an introduction and survey. *IEEE Computer*, **20** (9), 17–41.

Davis, H.C., Hall, W., Heath, I., Hill, G.J. and Wilkins, R.J. (1992). Towards an integrated information environment with open hypermedia systems. In *Proceedings of ECHT'92*, pp. 181–190. ACM Press.

Delisle, N. and Schwartz, M. (1986). Neptune: a hypertext system for CAD applications. In *Proceedings of ACM SIGMOD'86*, Washington D.C. 28–30 May, pp. 132–142. ACM, New York.

Engelbart, D.C. (1963). A conceptual framework for the augmentation of man's intellect. In *Vistas of Information Handling*, Vol. 1. Spartan Books, London.

Fountain, A.M., Hall, W., Heath, I. and Davis, H.C. (1990). Microcosm: an open model for hypermedia with dynamic linking. In *Proceedings of ECHT'90*, pp. 298–311. Cambridge University Press.

Goble, C., O'Docherty, M., Crowther, P., Ireton, M., Daskalakis, C., Oakley, J., Kay, S. and Xydeas, C. (1991). The Manchester multimedia system. In Kjelldahl, L. (ed.), *Multimedia: Systems, Interaction and Applications*, pp. 244–268. Springer-Verlag.

Grosky, W. (1994). Multimedia information systems–a tutorial. *IEEE Multimedia*, pp. 12–24, Spring.

Grosky, W. and Mehrota, R. (eds.) (1989). *IEEE Computer*, Special issue on image database management, December.

Halasz, F.G. (1988). Reflections on NoteCards: seven issues for the next generation of hypermedia systems. *CACM* **31** (7), 836–852.

Halasz, F.G., Moran, T.P. and Trigg, R.H., (1987). NoteCards in a nutshell. In *Proceedings of the 1987 ACM Conference on Human Factors in Computer Systems* Toronto, 5–9 April, pp. 45–52.

Hall, W. (1994). Ending the tyranny of the button *IEEE Multimedia*, **1** (1), 60–68.

Hill, G.J., Wilkins, R.J. and Hall, W. (1993) Open and reconfigurable hypermedia systems: a filter based model. *Hypermedia* **5** (2), 103–118.

Hutchings, G.A., Hall, W. and Colbourn, C.J. (1993). Patterns of students' interactions with a hypermedia system. *Interacting with Computers*, **5**, (3), pp. 293–313.

Kappe, F., Maurer, H. & Sherbakov, N. (1992). Hyper-G – a universal hypermedia system, IICM Technical Report, Graz University of Technology, Austria.

Malcolm, K.C., Poltrock, S.E. and Schuler, D. (1991). Industrial strength hypermedia: requirements for a large engineering enterprise. In *Proceedings of Hypertext'91*, pp. 13–24. ACM Press.

Neilsen, J. (1990). *Hypertext and Hypermedia*. Academic Press.

Nelson, T. (1980). Replacing the printed word: a complete literary system. In Lavington, S.H. (ed.) *Proceedings of IFIP Congress 1980*, pp. 1013–1023. North Holland.

Nelson, T. (1981). *Literary Machines*. Published by the author.

Nelson, T. (1988). Unifying tomorrow's hypermedia. In *Proceedings of Online Information '88*, London, 6–8 December, pp. 1–7.

Pearl, A. (1989). Sun's Link Service: a protocol for open linking. In *Proceedings of Hypertext'89*, pp. 137–146. ACM Press.

Rhiner, M. and Stucki, P. (1991). Database requirements for multimedia applications. In Kjelldahl, L. (ed.) *Multimedia: Systems, Interaction and Applications*, pp. 269–282. Springer-Verlag.

Rizk, A. and Sauter (1992). Multicard: an open hypermedia system. In *Proceedings of 4th ACM Conference on Hypertext*, pp. 4–10. Milan, Italy.

Schutt, H.A. and Streitz, N.A. (1990). Hyperbase: a hypermedia engine based on a relational database management system. In *Proceedings of ECHT'90*, pp. 95–108. Cambridge University Press.

Shneiderman, B. (1987). User interface design for the hyperties electronic encyclopaedia. In *Proceedings of the ACM Hypertext'87 Workshop*, University of North Carolina at Chapel Hill, 13–15 November, pp. 189–194.

Yankelovich, N., Meyrowitz, N. and van Dam, A. (1985). Reading and writing the electronic book. *IEEE Computer*, **18** (10), 15–30.

About the author

Wendy Hall is a professor of computer science at the University of Southampton. Her research interests include multimedia information management systems and their application. She and her team started work on Microcosm in 1989, which has developed into a large research project and a commercial enterprise. She is also Co-Director of the Interactive Learning Centre at the University of Southampton.

6 Analysis and evaluation of multimedia systems

William M. Newman

6.1. INTRODUCTION

Multimedia systems are becoming the focus of increasing attention from the IT research community. Interest stems in part from recognition that multimedia technology, useful though it is on its own, can offer much greater benefits if it is incorporated into full-scale systems. At the same time it is clear that important new problems in system design are raised by the need to integrate multimedia and computer-systems technologies. The other chapters included in this volume provide evidence of the wide range of new problems that are arising and that are being addressed by research.

A central pair of questions need to be addressed by this research community, indeed by anyone in research: who are the recipients for the research, and how will they benefit? These questions are especially important these days, when researchers are often short of funds and under pressure to demonstrate the value of their work. We may regard ourselves, working in this rapidly expanding area, as fortunate in the sense that the need for research is obvious. However, this does not imply that the identity of our recipients and the fashion in which they can benefit are obvious too. Perhaps we are not as fortunate as we think.

This chapter identifies *designers of multimedia systems* as important recipients of research results, and suggests that they will benefit most from *improved tools and methods*. Some explanation is needed for taking this particular view, and is provided in Section 6.2. Section 6.3 is a discussion of analysis and evaluation, looking at how it supports design, and Section 6.4 looks at how research can generate better methods. The point is made that these methods rely on the availability of analytical models of solutions, which take time to emerge from research. As a result, the choice of method may depend on whether the solution adopted is novel or mature, i.e., on the stage of the solution in its life-cycle of development from a novel idea to an established technology.

Section 6.5 surveys some recently published accounts of analysis and evaluation of multimedia systems at various stages in their life-cycles. It

ISBN 0-12-227740-6

draws some conclusions about usage and development of analysis and evaluation methods.

6.2.   IDENTIFYING THE RECIPIENTS AND THE BENEFITS

Why should multimedia systems research focus on product designers as its customers, and on analytical models and tools as its outputs? The next two sections attempt to provide answers to these questions.

6.2.1.   The product designer as recipient

The design of multimedia systems is, or should be, an engineering discipline. In other words, multimedia systems should be designed and built according to scientific principles, not just by craft and intuition. Unless there is a strong scientific basis to system design, the results are bound to be unpredictable and possibly catastrophic. If we need any evidence of how catastrophic a system design failure can be, we need only study the accidents that occurred in the use of the Therac-25 X-ray system, in one of which a patient (who later died) was out of contact with the operator due to a malfunctioning audio link (Leveson and Turner, 1993). Incidents like this underline the urgent need for an engineering discipline of multimedia systems design.

Engineering disciplines arise through the application of science to all stages of design, construction and use, but particularly to design because this depends so much on the ability to predict the outcome. We can see this emphasis on assisting design when we look at research outputs from any established field of engineering. Here, published research offers improvements to analytical models, improvements to designers' tools, and improvements to the actual designs in use (Newman, 1994). These offerings provide direct benefits to product designers, and meanwhile add strength to the underlying science (Rogers, 1983).

This is the philosophical argument in favour of trying to help designers, but there is also the more direct argument that we need to do something about design failures. We see reports on these failures increasingly often. Since Therac-25, there has been the recent failure of the London Ambulance Service system, which also depended on multimedia equipment (London Ambulance Service, 1993). We can be sure that these published reports are only the tip of the iceberg.

6.2.2.   Better analytical methods as the benefit

As we have already seen, analytical methods provide two kinds of benefits to designers. In a direct sense, they help the designer to make accurate predictions about the outcome of design, by virtue of their underlying scientific theory. More indirectly, research into analytical methods helps to strengthen scientific theory and thus has an important role in strength-ening the overall practice of engineering design.

In spite of these obvious benefits, little research tends to get done into developing better methods of analysing and evaluating interactive systems. In a fast-moving technological area such as Multimedia, research usually focuses on inventing new artefacts and paradigms, or on studying the properties of new inventions (Newman, 1994). This is where the pay-off from interactive systems research is often held to lie.

On the other hand, almost anyone can invent a new artefact, whereas hardly anyone except a researcher can develop a new method of analysis or evaluation. Only a researcher is likely to have the necessary training, resources, time and motivation to carry out the research. If researchers are diverted into inventing new products, less effort will go into developing new analytical methods.

Of course, analytical methods are not the designer's only means of evaluation: another approach is to build and test a prototype. Prototypes have a vital role to play in engineering design, but they play this role alongside analytical methods, not in place of them. Used in place of analysis, prototyping is expensive and time-consuming, and often produces results too late to affect the design. It can also be somewhat unreliable in the kinds of collaborative settings where multimedia systems are used and where "real" conditions are hard to guarantee during testing. The designer needs methods for evaluating design options on paper, without resorting to prototyping every time. Analytical methods serve this essential purpose.

6.3.   ANALYSIS AND EVALUATION IN SYSTEM DESIGN

Analysis and evaluation have each acquired their own meaning in the context of system design. The term *analysis* is usually applied to activities performed on data, such as the "systems analysis" performed on data collected in user interviews and surveys. *Evaluation* is usually considered to apply to actual designs, primarily with a view to verifying that they comply with specifications or that they meet users' needs. Unlike analysis, evaluation is often carried out by building and testing a prototype.

There is, however, a degree of overlap between analysis and evaluation. Both pre-design analyses and post-design evaluations involve collecting data and analysing them. Furthermore, it is debatable whether we should distinguish sharply between pre- and post-design data collection and analysis, because their real value emerges when they are used in conjunction. By comparing the results of the pre- and post-analyses the designer determines whether things have changed in the ways intended.

6.3.1.   The methods available to product designers

Multimedia systems are aimed almost exclusively at supporting users' activities interactively. As a result, analysis and evaluation is largely a matter of assessing how well the systems provide this support to users' activity. The measure of a good design is whether the activity can be performed faster, with fewer errors, by fewer people, with shorter learning times, with fewer breakdowns, etc. Most of these measures come under the heading of usability, and so the designer relies heavily on *usability assessment methods*.

Methods for usability testing and analysis cover a wide spectrum. With few exceptions, the methods have been developed for general use, i.e., for assessing any kind of interactive system. Some useful studies have been conducted to compare the effectiveness of different methods (Jeffries *et al.*, 1991; Desurvire *et al.*, 1992). However, most of the findings concern the usability properties each method offers, rather than the type of system to which they are suited. The principal methods include:

Usability testing (Whiteside *et al.*, 1988). This method involves live testing of a working system under controlled conditions. It permits the identification of problems in the design, and the measurement of various usability factors such as speed of task performance and occurrence of errors. It is generally held to be the most thorough and versatile method of evaluating the usability of a product, or of prototypes of a product, but is expensive to conduct and is inappropriate for early evaluation when the design is not yet ready to be prototyped.

Heuristic evaluation (Nielsen and Molich, 1989). In this method, a panel of evaluators draws up a list of problems that they have identified in the design, using a list of heuristics or design principles for guidance, e.g., "Simple and natural language", or "Be consistent". The technique has been tested extensively, showing that four evaluators form the most cost-effective team (Nielsen and Landauer, 1993). In several studies of alternative methods of evaluation, heuristic evaluation was found to be the most efficient, especially in predicting problems that might prevent the user from completing the task.

Cognitive walkthrough (Lewis and Polson, 1990). This method is analogous to the code walkthrough technique, focusing on identifying problems by stepping through the performance of a task and identifying problems on a basis of cognitively-based simulation of the user's interaction. It has been applied particularly effectively to walk-up-and-use systems such as automated tellers. It has also been found effective in identifying errors likely to occur during system use.

In summary, the designer's two main options are to build a prototype and conduct a full-scale usability test, or to use a more economical method that identifies problems in the user interface analytically. Neither of these will help the designer, during the early stages of design, to make quantitative predictions. In particular, neither of them can help at this stage in predicting the speed of operation of the interface, often a vital factor in assessing whether the system will save money.

6.3.2.   Extending the range of methods

Why is the range of methods for measuring usability so limited? What can we do to extend the range? The answer lies in understanding the

dependence of the methods on scientifically valid *models* of the interaction whose usability is being assessed. Thus the cognitive walkthrough
method relies on a model of exploratory learning that predicts how the
user will choose between alternative steps in the dialogue (Polson and
Lewis, 1990). Heuristic evaluation is less dependent on a single model: it
draws more on the individual models invoked by the evaluators in
response to the heuristics. Usability testing can employ a variety of different models, depending on the insights of the analyst and the nature of
the data gathered.

The development of new models for assessing usability is a major focus
of HCI research. There have been some important breakthroughs over the
last decade, not all of which have contributed to evaluation of products in
general. For example, the GOMS model of Card *et al.* (1983) provides a basis
for predicting the speed of operation of interfaces used by trained operators to perform routine tasks. It relies on measurements of the times to
perform keystroke-level operators, and on a model of how these operators
affect the speed of performance. The limited scope of application of GOMS
has meant that it still does not figure prominently in the evaluator's repertoire, but it has been highly influential in suggesting how research should
be conducted towards improving our methods of analysis and evaluation.

Although the focus of modelling research in HCI has been on general-
purpose methods, real advances may be easier to achieve in modelling
specific types of solution supporting particular kinds of task. The development of a model that successfully predicts the performance of any type
of interactive solution may be too hard a problem to solve. In a sense, we
can see evidence of this in existing models such as the exploratory learning model, which applies well to walk-up-and-use systems, and in GOMS
which applies to systems that support repetitive task performance.
Ultimately, accurate modelling and prediction of performance involves
fitting the model to the form of the solution.

6.4.   HOW MULTIMEDIA SYSTEMS RESEARCH CAN HELP

These problems in developing better models cannot reasonably be laid at
the door of product developers: they belong with the interactive systems
research community. Of course this community has other responsibilities to other product domains besides multimedia systems. It also has a
variety of personal motivations, such as gaining Ph.D. degrees and
achieving academic tenure, that sometimes distract it from the goal of
assisting designers. As a result the overall thrust of systems research
tends not to focus directly on problems in analysis and evaluation.
Instead it spreads across a number of activities:

inventing radically new artefacts and paradigms;
conducting studies of new inventions, and gaining experience of their
use, leading to the development of design guidelines and bodies of experience;
incremental advances in models, tools and technologies.

A fast-moving field of technology like multimedia systems needs to keep pace with the inventions that are driving the technology forward. This is where the real challenge lies, and it is generally tackled by focusing on invention as a research activity. In other words, researchers devote themselves to *tackling radically new problems or inventing radically new artefacts*. The value of this research lies in the new opportunities it offers, to product developers, supporting industries, and to other researchers in need of interesting problems to tackle.

New inventions do not make analysis easier for the designer; they may even make it more difficult. They may give rise to new applications and solutions that nobody knows how to compare with existing ones. It takes time, usually measured in years, before these applications settle down. In the meantime, progress is made by conducting studies of a more exploratory form. Initially, the invention is tested in the laboratory; then it may be tried out in relatively artificial "user testing"; it may go through a year or more of experimental use, leading to observations about its behaviour and to formulation of experiments to establish *design guidelines* (of which an example might be "Cooperative hypermedia authoring systems should include version support"; see Haake and Haake, 1993). These guidelines may eventually form a basis for the development of analytical models.

Incremental advances are likely to emerge in the more stable situations where the technology has "settled down" into an accepted form, and where applications and usage patterns have become well-established. If we are interested solely in developing better methods of analysis, we may well direct our attention here. We will then try to identify applications to which we could apply analytical modelling techniques; we will develop enhanced models where necessary, in the manner of GOMS, and will build them into design tools; we will make incremental improvements to the technology and measure the effects. In other words, we will conduct our research in the way most engineering disciplines conduct theirs.

6.5.   THE LIFE-CYCLE OF MULTIMEDIA SYSTEMS ANALYSIS

As the preceding section points out, multimedia systems research can be tackled on a broad front, ranging from radical invention through exploratory studies to incremental advances in models, tools and solutions. In effect, research practice reflects the *life-cycle* of development that any truly novel invention must go through before it can become a part of accepted design practice. At present, however, most of the activity in multimedia systems research is going on at the earlier stages of the life-cycle. It is being applied largely to inventing and assessing novel solutions.

The life-cycle of innovation is important because it involves the progressive refinement, not only of the invention itself, but also of the accompanying models and techniques for analysing and evaluating designs. The methods we apply to multimedia system designs must reflect the stage of refinement of the technology. This section therefore looks briefly at the techniques used in analysis and evaluation of systems at each point in the life-cycle. It exposes some of the challenges in developing better techniques for analysis and evaluation, which are summarized in the final discussion.

6.5.1.   Preliminary studies prior to system design

Designing a new system must involve gaining some familiarity with the environment that will receive it. After all, design is concerned with bringing about change (Simon, 1979; Jones, 1980), and this change is impossible to predict without an understanding of the receiving environment. When new application domains are considered for multimedia systems, it is vital to conduct pre-design studies. A variety of techniques have been proposed for preliminary studies, including task analysis (Diaper, 1989), systems analysis (Weinberg, 1988; Bingham and Davies, 1992) and field study (Lofland, 1971; Klein, 1976).

The value of preliminary studies in multimedia system design can be seen most clearly in those that generate unexpected findings. For example, a study was undertaken by Heath and others of a dealer room with a view to designing a system to capture records of deals through voice recognition. The study showed quite conclusively that such a system would fail (Heath *et al.*, 1993). Studies by Goodwin of airport control rooms likewise showed that a conventional distributed system might fail, because so much of the collaboration between controllers relied on overhearing each others' work. Likewise Harper *et al.* (1991) learned through their studies of air traffic control that new technology must present the state of the airspace to the entire control-room team, not just to the controller. The value of these studies lies in their ability to focus designers on those problems that have a realistic chance of solution.

Pre-design studies have always been an accepted component of the systems analyst's methodology. However, recent research suggests that there is plenty of room for new methods, particularly those with a sociological or ethnomethodological basis. The standard analyst's approach of eliciting descriptions of work from half-hour interviews with prospective users has come under serious question from several quarters (Suchman, 1987; Eldridge *et al.*, 1994).

6.5.2.   Exploring new paradigms through simulation and envisionment

Radically new designs and paradigms must go through a certain amount of analysis and evaluation before they can justify the effort of building working prototypes. The challenge in conducting the analysis lies in the shortage of analytical tools that can be applied to designs when they exist only in paper form.

The use of *envisionments*, i.e., of mock-ups and simulations that emphasize key design features, is an increasingly popular approach to analysing designs in the pre-prototype phase. In the domain of multimedia systems, this is often done with the aid of video: a well-known example is the "Knowledge Navigator" video envisionment produced by Apple Computer (Apple, 1986). On a more modest scale, video has been used by Wellner to envision a set of techniques for interacting with paper documents on a "DigitalDesk" (Wellner, 1991).

These examples illustrate the power of envisionment to involve users in the design process and elicit their reactions. This in turn assists the designer in learning about the technology's potential to solve users' problems. In the case of the DigitalDesk, for example, users' evaluations pointed towards focusing on a particular form of interaction illustrated in the envisionment, shown in Figure 6.1. The Knowledge Navigator envisionment was distributed widely, and led to a number of analyses covering, for example, the question of whether video links should be symmetrical or should favour one of the participants at the expense of the other.

6.5.3.   Building and experiencing new paradigms

The task of building a prototype of a new multimedia concept is a major undertaking. It is not uncommon for resources to run dry before

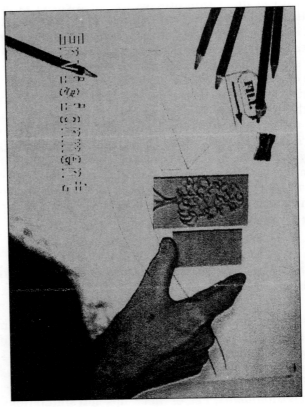

Figure 6.1. DigitalDesk application; this particular application was selected for prototyping after envisionment of a number of applications (Wellner, 1991).

implementation is complete. Even if this does not happen, there may be little effort available to evaluate the final result.

We see many instances of prototypes of new ideas in which relatively little effort is devoted to evaluation. In another DigitalDesk project, for example, a simple experiment was conducted to demonstrate the usefulness of providing access to an on-line dictionary through direct interaction with paper documents in foreign languages (Newman and Wellner, 1992). The experiment indicated the general effect of the technology on the reading task, and enabled the researchers to learn about the immediate reactions of users. Borning and Travers (1991) described two designs of a radical nature, involving the use of low-resolution images to promote awareness between collaborators. They were able to make some preliminary observations about symmetry and user control, but their primary analysis was in terms of recommendations for future work.

The ultimate value of many new inventions may lie not so much in the insights gained by the designers from evaluations, as in the inspiration the inventions provide for future work, possibly elsewhere. In this respect, the advantage of encouraging researchers to invent is the relative frequency with which their inventions are made public, and thus are able to inspire follow-on work by others. Inventions that occur in commercial development are less likely to see the light of day.

6.5.4.   Compiling experience from longitudinal studies

In most cases, the build-up of understanding of new multimedia system designs begins only when the design is subjected to full-scale, longitudinal testing under relatively "real" conditions. This is especially true of designs for the support of communication and collaboration, which cannot usually be tested in the laboratory.

The study by Nardi *et al.* (1993) of video usage in neurosurgery illustrates the kinds of knowledge gained from allowing new applications of multimedia technology to be tested more thoroughly and realistically. The researchers were able, for example, to identify important uses of video lying outside the usually-cited use for person-to-person communication. In the operating theatre, video was used to access information and thus permit surgeons to operate more independently, and was employed as a means of sharing information between members of the operating team. A long-term study of the use of an audio/video "mediaspace" by Gaver *et al.* (1992) resulted in a number of findings concerning shared work support, privacy, awareness and blurring of boundaries.

The difference between immediate and longer-term evaluation can be seen in the studies of video-supported awareness by Dourish and Bly (1992) that followed on from the initial designs of Borning and Travers. In the second project, observations over a period of several months showed that users valued the passive awareness they gained through the display of low-resolution, regularly updated video images of their colleagues (see Figure 6.2). Although the images occupied a large area of the screen, users found them sufficiently valuable to justify this use of screen space. In this follow-on study, therefore, specific findings were starting to emerge.

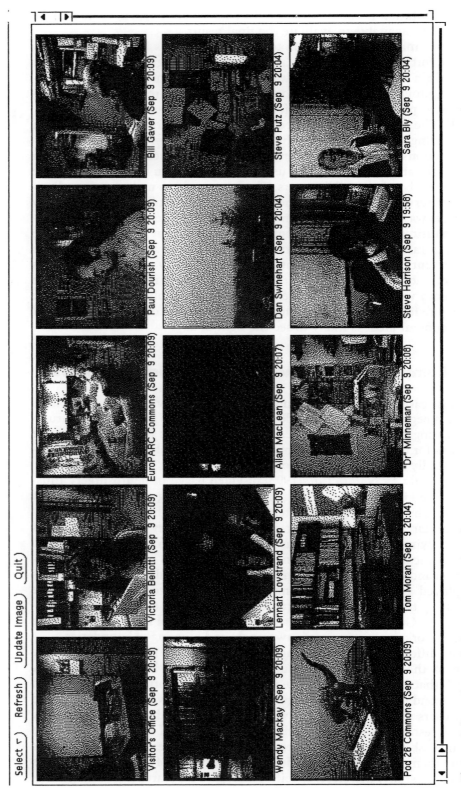

Figure 6.2.   The Portholes system, used in follow-on studies of the long-term support of passive awareness (Dourish and Bly, 1992).

6.5.5.   Extracting design guidelines from experience of more mature designs

To the product designer, studies of novel designs may be of limited in value because they do not generally provide answers to specific questions. After conducting in-depth studies, however, the researcher may begin to see ways to offer these answers. Patterns of use may start to emerge, and these may lead to the formation of hypotheses that can be tested in experiments designed specifically for this purpose. The result is to extract *design guidelines* that can be applied more generally to designs of a similar kind.

Some multimedia systems research has been conducted into design guidelines. However, this research is relatively sparse for the obvious reason that not many multimedia designs have attained the necessary maturity. One exception is the analysis by Dourish *et al.* (1994) of long-term use of video connections, which established the somewhat unexpected design guideline of allowing a wider view than the usual "head-and-shoulders" to enable larger groups of people to interact across the video link. Other examples of guideline research are found in the work of Mynatt *et al.* (1992) on the relative usability of hypertext and books and of Haake and Haake on the need for version support in hypermedia systems (Haake and Haake, 1993).

Guideline-oriented research is time-consuming and often inconclusive. It may not prove or disprove anything of value. An example of the guideline researcher's difficulties is found in the study by Sellen (1992) of speech patterns in video-based communication. Her initial hypothesis was that use of video would produce a number of differences in conversational patterns; tests showed, however, that the differences were much less than expected; instead, unanticipated effects were found in users' ability to attend to particular audio or video streams. Another project with an unexpected outcome is the study by Olson *et al.* (1992) of the use of a shared editor to support design, which showed a reduction in exploration by the design team instead of the expected increase.

6.5.6.   Modelling and incremental enhancement of an established technology

Examples of true engineering science flowing from multimedia systems research are few and far between. As the earlier comments suggested, these kinds of results tend to emerge only when both the technology and the application achieve considerable maturity.

One celebrated instance of successful modelling and incremental design, lying on the fringes of multimedia systems, is found in "Project Ernestine", a study of the design of telephone operator workstations (Gray *et al.*, 1992). These workstations involve multimedia to the extent that they employ recorded speech messages and involve the operator in concurrent interaction with one or more subscribers and with a variety of computer systems. In the work of Gray *et al.*, a model of the operator's task was developed, building on previous GOMS research, and was used to analyse both an existing design and a proposed improvement. The analysis showed that, contrary to expectations, the new design would be slower in use than the existing design, and would therefore cost several millions of dollars in extra operating costs to the phone company concerned. This research provided the workstation designers with an analytical model capable of predicting the performance of new workstation designs and thus preventing repeated embarrassments.

6.6.   DISCUSSION

The main thrust of this brief survey is to show that there is no single answer to the question, "How should we evaluate multimedia systems?" Rather, there is a need to perform different kinds of analyses and evaluations throughout the life-cycle of system solutions, as they progress from novel ideas to initial prototypes and from there into fully-tested solutions, initial products and well-established solutions. These include:

preliminary studies of users' needs;
user-participatory analyses of mock-ups and envisionments;
documenting initial impressions of novel designs for the benefit of future research;
conducting longer-term studies of new designs in order to make useful observations about their use;
conducting more sharply-focused research in order to establish design guidelines;
constructing analytical models of mature designs and applications in order to support predictive analyses of designs.

This sequence of analyses and evaluations is played out *during the life-cycle of the solution*, not just the development of the product. The distinction is an important one, for it implies that we cannot apply any method to any solution; we must choose our method according to the solution's maturity. Thus a novel design will need to be evaluated by means of preliminary studies, envisionments and initial impressions, whereas a mature design will justify the development of guidelines and the use of analytical modelling. This point may go some way towards explaining why comparisons of evaluation techniques have given conflicting results (Desurvire *et al.*, 1992): they have been applied to solutions of differing maturity.

6.6.1.   Studying existing solutions

The sequence of methods is also important in suggesting what to expect from multimedia systems research. As we have seen, most of this research takes place in the context of novel designs and proposed new paradigms. Most of the success in developing useful evaluation methods, however, occurs when mature solutions start to emerge. As a result of this, multimedia product designers should not expect to receive much in the way of useful tools for analysing or evaluating their designs. They must expect to rely heavily on "late evaluation" techniques such as product beta-testing.

This provides a clue to how progress might be made towards a more analytical basis for multimedia product design. It would involve shifting the emphasis of research towards existing solutions and away from new designs. An emphasis on preliminary studies of existing work settings would undoubtedly result in fewer misdirected inventions; an emphasis on long-term studies of existing systems in real work settings would provide data of a much more reliable nature, from which guidelines and models could be developed.

One important message, therefore, is that researchers need access to real work settings, including settings where established multimedia products are in everyday use. They need this access in order to gather data on which to base new models and new design tools. Researchers also need opportunities to validate these models and tools. This validation involves gaining access to design information in order to understand how existing products work and how they might be enhanced, because enhancement and testing are essential steps in model validation. At present, none of these forms of access is easy for a researcher to gain.

6.7.   CONCLUSIONS

This chapter has made a case for paying attention to the analysis and evaluation of multimedia systems, and has explored some of the implications of doing so. The case rests on the need of product designers for adequate models and tools for use in analysing their designs. The main implication, given the relative novelty of multimedia system designs and applications, is that this need is far from being met. If events play out their normal course, the development of engineering-strength design methods will involve waiting until solutions have achieved a much greater degree of maturity.

Whether or not progress can be made in methods of analysis and evaluation, advances will undoubtedly be made in technologies supporting new applications of multimedia systems. There are important questions regarding the impact of these new and relatively untested technologies on society. Technological progress is always accompanied by failures; we need to do all we can to limit their impact on society, and this involves making sure that critical developments have a sound basis of engineering science.

REFERENCES

Apple Computer (1986). *The Knowledge Navigator*. Videotape.
Bingham, J. and Davies, G. (1992). *Systems Analysis*. Macmillan.

Borning, A. and Travers, M. (1991). Two approaches to casual interaction over computer and video networks. In *Human Factors in Computing Systems, CHI '91 Conference Proceedings*, pp. 13–19.

Card, S. K., Moran, T. P. and Newell, A. (1983). *The Psychology of Human Computer Interaction*. Lawrence Erlbaum Associates, Hillsdale, NJ.

Desurvire, H. W., Kondziela, J. M. and Atwood, M. E. (1992). What is gained and lost when using evaluation methods other than empirical testing. In Monk, A. et al. (eds) *People and Computers VII*. Cambridge University Press.

Diaper, D. (1989). Task observation for human–computer interaction. In Diaper, D. (ed.) *Task Analysis for Human-Computer Interaction*. Ellis Horwood.

Dourish, P. and Bly, S. (1992). Portholes: supporting awareness in a distributed work group. In *Proceedings CHI '92 Conference*. ACM SIGCHI.

Dourish, P., Adler, A., Bellotti, V. and Henderson, A. (1994). Your place or mine? Learning from long-term use of video communication. Submitted to CSCW '94 Conference Rank Xerox Research Centre, 61 Regent Street, Cambridge CB2 1AB, UK.

Eldridge, M. A., Barnard, P. and Bekerian, D. (1994). Autobiographical memory and daily schemas at work. *Memory*, **2**(1), 51–74.

Gaver, W., Moran, T. P., MacLean, A., Lovstrand, L., Dourish, P., Carter, K. and Buxton, W. (1992) Realizing a video environment: EuroPARC's RAVE system. In *Proceedings CHI '92 Conference*. ACM SIGCHI.

Gray, W. D., John, B. E. and Atwood, M. E. (1992). The précis of project Ernestine or, an overview of a validation of GOMS. In *Proceedings CHI '92 Conference*, ACM SIGCHI.

Haake, A. and Haake, J. (1993). Take CoVer: exploiting version support in cooperative systems. In *Proceedings InterCHI '93 Conference*.

Harper, R. H. R., Hughes, J. A. and Shapiro, D. Z. (1991). Harmonious working and CSCW: computer technology and air traffic control. In *Proceedings ECSCW '91 Conference*. North Holland.

Heath, C., Jirotka, M., Luff, P. and Hindmarsh, J. (1993). Unpacking collaboration: the interactional organisation of trading in a city dealing room. In *Proceedings. E-CSCW '93*.

Jeffries, R. J., Miller, J. R., Wharton, C. and Uyeda, K. M. (1991). User interface evaluation in the real world: a comparison of four techniques. In *Proceedings CHI '91 Conference*.

Jones, J. C. (1980). *Design Methods: Seeds of Human Futures*. John Wiley.

Klein, L. (1976). *A Social Scientist in Industry*. Gower.

Lewis, C. H. and Polson, P. G. (1990) Testing a walkthrough methodology for theory-based design of walk-up-and-use interfaces. In *Proceedings CHI '90 Conference*.

Leveson, N. G. and Turner, C. S. (1993) An investigation of the Therac-25 accidents. *IEEE Computer*, Vol. 26, 7, July 1993.

Lofland, J. (1971). *Analyzing Social Settings: A Guide to Qualitative Observation and Analysis*. Wadsworth.

London Ambulance Service (1993). *Report on the Inquiry into the London Ambulance Service*. (Available from: Communications Directorate, South West Thames Regional Health Authority, 40 Eastbourne Terrace, London W2 3QR.)

Mynatt, B. T., Leventhal, L. M., Instone, K., Farhat, J. and Robinson, D. S. (1992). Hypertext or book: which is better for answering questions? In *Proceedings CHI '92 Conference*.

Nardi, B. A., Schwartz, H., Kuchinsky, A. and Leichner, R. (1993). Turning away from talking heads: the use of video-as-data in neurosurgery. In *Proceedings InterCHI '93 Conference*.

Newman, W. M. and Wellner, P. (1992). A desk supporting computer-based interaction with paper documents. In *Proceedings CHI '92 Conference*.

Newman, W. M. (1994). A preliminary analysis of the products of human–computer interaction research, using pro forma abstracts. In *Proceedings. CHI '94 Conference*.

Nielsen, J. and Landauer, T. (1993). A mathematical model of the finding of usability problems. In *Proceedings. InterCHI '93 Conference*.

Nielsen, J. and Molich, R. (1989). Teaching user interface design based on usability engineering. *ACM SIGCHI Bulletin*, **21**(1), 45–48.

Olson, J. S., Olson, G. M., Storroesten, M. and Carter, M. (1992). How a group-editor changes the character of a design meeting as well as its outcome. In *Proceedings CSCW '92*.

Polson, P. G. and Lewis, C. L. (1990). Theory-based design for easily-learned interfaces. *HCI*, **5**, 191–220.

Rogers, G. F. C. (1983). *The Nature of Engineering*. Macmillan.

Sellen, A. J. (1992). Speech patterns in video-mediated conversations. In *Proceedings CHI '92 Conference*.

Simon, H. A. (1979). *The Sciences of the Artificial*. MIT Press.

Suchman, L. (1987). *Plans and Situated Actions*. Cambridge.

Weinberg, G. (1988). *Rethinking Systems Analysis and Design*. Dorset House.

Wellner, P. (1991). The DigitalDesk calculator: tangible manipulation on a desk top display. In *Proceedings ACM UIST '91 Conference*. Hilton Head, NC, November.

Whiteside, J., Bennett, J. and Holtzblatt, K. (1988). Usability engineering: our experience and evolution. In Helander, M. (ed.) *Handbook of Human Computer Interaction*, pp. 791–817. Elsevier.

About the author

William Newman is a Principal Scientist at Rank Xerox Research Centre in Cambridge, England. He was previously a member of research staff at the Xerox Palo Alto Research Center from 1973 to 1979, and then worked for some years as an independent consultant in the UK. He joined Rank Xerox in 1988. He has published on a wide range of research topics including computer-aided design, computer graphics, user interface design and office systems design. While at Rank Xerox he has worked principally on applications of ubiquitous computing to the support of human memory, and on methodologies in support of interactive system design. He has been a Visiting Professor at the University of London, Queen Mary Westfield College, since 1980.

PART 2

Applications: Simulation

7 Multimedia in simulation and training

Stefan Nowak

7.1. INTRODUCTION

Simulations in training generally require the user to gain an understanding of the underlying mathematical model through real-time interaction. This is particularly important where the model itself represents a continuous process over which the user has a degree of control. In some simulations, e.g. a chemical reaction, the user simply wants to experience something that may not be easy, or safe, to do in real-life. In other situations, it may be necessary to simulate a process or environment, prior to exposing the user to the real thing. A complex system that needs specific control skills, such as an aircraft or power station, may not be suitable for "on-the-job" training, due to the possibility of unacceptable levels of risk or undue expense.

The underlying rules governing the systems behaviour, the simulated world model, are usually expressed as mathematical equations, although simple simulations can be reduced to a set of logical rules. The sophistication of the simulation is reflected, in part, by the complexity of this mathematical model. Many simulations, such as weather forecasting, require such complex mathematical models that even the most powerful computers cannot simulate the process in real-time. (What is real-time in relation to weather forecasting? Giving a result before the time being predicted – you want tomorrow's weather today!) Some simulations can usefully be done in less than real-time, e.g. scientific experiments, where the outcome may be more important than the process itself – all the interaction is essentially at the beginning, inputting data parameters, rather than during the process.

Flying an aeroplane is not only potentially dangerous to life but also expensive in fuel consumption and repairs if damaged through misuse. This type of application has therefore been a prime candidate for simulation for many years. Traditionally, it has always been an expensive form of simulation, due to the complex nature of an aircraft and its environment in flight. Applying flight simulation technology to other applications has not really been a viable economic proposition. However, multimedia technology is able to bring many of the key features of this type of simulator into the desktop computing environment. The two key

MULTIMEDIA SYSTEMS AND APPLICATIONS
ISBN 0-12-227740-6

components of a simulation are the underlying *processor power* for running the mathematical model, and the *visualization* of the user's interaction with the environment or the system that this represents.

7.1.1.   Processing power

Current desktop computers have CPUs capable of processing millions of instructions per second, and are able to handle the computation of complex mathematical models in real-time. What would have required a mini-computer or mainframe a few years ago can now be performed on a PC. The latest generation of CPUs, such as the Intel Pentium, Digital Alpha, and MIPS R4000 continue this trend, and are now being coupled with portable operating systems, such as Microsoft Windows NT, and associated software tools that allow easier access to this power for application developers. As well as being applicable to number crunching the mathematical model, this power can also be applied to the display side of the system.

7.1.2.   Visualization

Most simulations require the visualization of the environment being modelled. Although certain simulations, such as scientific experiments, may be visualized through simple graphics displays, others require a more realistic representation of the world. Modern flight simulators, for example, can display high-resolution, photo-realistic images of the view from the cockpit. This traditionally required custom-designed, proprietary graphics hardware in order to achieve any degree of realism with real-time interaction. Increasingly this territory is being invaded by workstation manufacturers, such as Silicon Graphics, who can provide off-the-shelf systems with increasingly powerful graphics capabilities. Although top-of-the-range systems, such as the Silicon Graphics Reality Engine, are still too expensive for many potential simulation applications, the price/performance ratio continues to improve, and within a very few years this capability will be available on the desktop for a few thousand pounds.

7.1.3.   Multimedia solutions

Desktop multimedia systems, whether based on PCs or entry-level workstations, now offer sufficient processing capability and graphics performance to provide a useful platform for visual simulations. This can also include digital video and audio, as well as interfacing to appropriate real-world controls, which can easily be accomplished using off-the-shelf hardware components. The traditional simulator market is not only being supplemented by multimedia systems, but also by the application of virtual reality techniques. There is an increasing overlap and convergence in these technologies, as the following case studies show. They describe recent work done in the field of simulation and training by Hodos Ltd, a multimedia development company.

7.2. CASE STUDIES: TRAIN DRIVING SIMULATION

These two case studies illustrate the application of multimedia technology to produce effective simulations. Although both applications simulate driving a train, they differ in the techniques used – the first is a part-task driver training simulator and uses digital video technology; the second is a visualization simulator for railway engineers and uses 3D graphics modelling implemented with a virtual reality toolkit.

7.2.1. British Rail

Training needs

British Rail's Driver Training Programme was studied between January and April 1990 to establish the potential use of simulation. Part of this programme requires the trainee to complete 40 periods of duty, or turns, in the driver's cab of service trains. This is to gain first-hand experience of the duties of a driver, and no training personnel are involved. On completion of this period the trainee undertakes a 21 week programme covering both procedural and practical aspects of train driving. The traction unit used for practical exercises is specifically assigned for training purposes, and special arrangements have to be made for it to travel on mainlines. The unit has a low priority and can, therefore, be subject to cancellation and delay. This programme is therefore time consuming and expensive to resource, yet its completion is essential for the training of safe and competent train drivers.

This needs analysis showed that there was great scope for the use of simulation for Route Learning and Basic Traction Handling. The aim was to allow practical exercises to be given on the simulator in the classroom prior to actual traction handling, thus achieving not only savings in time and resources, but more importantly raising the quality levels and safety standards.

BR had commissioned simulators before and traditional solutions had been expensive, costing hundreds of thousands of pounds, yet achieved mixed success. The proposal put forward by Hodos was to design a part-task simulator based clearly on the perceived training and safety requirements, rather than an engineering specification for a locomotive. Limiting the functionality in this way would reduce the cost of implementation, but the innovative approach proposed to the technological problem could enable a more cost-effective solution to be realized.

Multimedia solution

Hodos were able to attract funding for a prototype from the government's Training Agency with support from British Rail who recognized the potential benefits. Over the following three years, six part-task simulators were developed and installed in BR regional training centres in Glasgow, Newcastle, Leeds, Plymouth, Ilford and Croydon.

The key enabling technology was Intel's Digital Video Interactive (DVI), which consisted of additional hardware to allow a standard PC to decompress and display digital video from hard-disk or CD-ROM. DVI had all the elements in a single board to be able to simulate the audio-visual environment of driving a train. Essentially, the digital video can have its frame rate varied to simulate speed changes, and simultaneous sound effects can be generated using digitized audio samples. In addition, graphic overlays to show different signal aspects can be combined with the digital video. All of this was achieved using a single DVI card and a modest 386 PC. Actual train controls in a full-size mock-up desk were used to drive the digital video shown on a computer monitor. A second screen relayed the driver's performance to an instructor, who could also control the signal setting along the route.

The use of the simulator was evaluated by BR and the overall opinion was that it was certainly capable of meeting several training objectives during initial driver training. The following areas were highlighted:

General coordination, in particular hand, eye and hearing coordination when using the controls and responding to the automatic warning system (the AWS sounds a horn when the driver is approaching a warning or stop signal and must be cancelled by the driver otherwise the brakes are automatically applied – correct response to this is a key training requirement). The simulator will make it possible to gauge a trainee's coordination in the safety of a classroom prior to driving a real train.

Response to external conditions, i.e. signals and track conditions, predefined by the instructor to test particular scenarios.

Use of the brake and throttle, i.e. to achieve smooth and economic driving technique.

Overview of the AWS, i.e. how it works relative to the signals ahead and how to response correctly.

Orientation, i.e. location of major controls in the cab.

Overall "feel" of a train's characteristics, i.e. understanding the train's dynamic behaviour.

Interpretation of rules and regulations in a practical and visual situation.

Learning the road, i.e. route learning, currently a very time consuming activity much of it spent on the footplate.

This success in applying new technology to meet these training objectives was recognized by the British Interactive Multimedia Association in 1992 with an Award for Innovation.

7.2.2. Dutch Rail

User requirement

In 1992, the Dutch Rail (Nederlandse Spoorwegen) Engineering Department were investigating a new type of signalling system which they wanted to be able to visualize and simulate in use in order to test the validity of their proposal. It should be noted that this was not a training need but purely a visualization exercise for railway engineers. Being familiar with the British Rail simulator, they wondered if a similar approach, using digital video, could provide a solution to their problem.

Further discussions revealed the full scope of their requirement. The simulator should ideally have the ability to:

create track layouts representing typical configurations of track;
position signals and signs (both existing and new types) anywhere on this layout;
drive through the visualized layout at variable speeds, with synchronized sound effects, both manually and via other programs;
utilize existing CAD data, i.e. for track, signals, signs, etc.;
be usable by non-programmers.

Multimedia solution

These requirements conflicted with the known capabilities of a digital video solution, so a feasibility study was undertaken to explore the possibilities of a 3D computer graphics visual system. Prior experience with a product called WorldToolKit (WTK), a virtual reality development system, suggested that it might be suitable for real-time modelling of a 3D environment. Performance would be a key issue, particularly as it was essential to use existing PC-based hardware rather than a graphics workstation. WTK was originally developed by the Sense8 Corporation of California, with funding from Intel, to run on DVI technology. As DVI developers, this was the version with which Hodos had experience – in this application the DVI board was being used as a powerful graphics processor rather than for digital video. One of the unique features of the DVI implementation of WTK was its ability to render not only shaded polygons but also texture-mapped surfaces. The technique can produce a higher level of realism with fewer polygons – for example, in modelling a building, rather than drawing each individual brick in a wall, the whole surface is rendered with a photorealistic image of brickwork applied to the wall as a whole, which is now just a single polygon. DVI hardware is particularly efficient at warping a bit-mapped image on to any arbitrary polygon in this manner.

The feasibility study proved the capability of WTK and DVI technology to produce a 3D graphics environment. The prototype model was produced using existing CAD files of track, gantries, signals and signs which were imported into WTK via Autocad's DXF format. A short length of track was modelled with limited texture-mapping and gave adequate performance at a resolution of 512 x 480 pixels with a 16-bit colour depth. However, this was essentially a static model and the final design needed to address the requirement to be able to easily create arbitrary track layouts.

Train track layout can be created from a finite number of standard components, pretty much like a model train set, so it was proposed to implement this idea in 3D graphics. In WorldToolKit the 3D environment is composed of objects which are typically imported from CAD data, but rather than build a static model as in the prototype, it was decided to try a dynamic approach. The standard components (track, gantries, signals, etc.) are initially loaded as models, and then copies, or instances, of them are placed in view as and when required. In order to maximize the possible length of the layout, the track objects are only laid ahead of the viewpoint as far as the horizon, and once passed are deleted. This minimizes the amount of storage required and maximizes performance, as it is only necessary to render the track currently in view. When objects are deleted from the view they are not actually removed from memory, merely marked as free for reuse at a later point in the model. This approach makes efficient use of a small number of objects, which can get redisplayed many times in different locations, and also minimizes fragmentation of memory.

To facilitate the creation of layouts using this a technique, a command set was devised to allow the user to load object definitions and locate any number of copies of them, using absolute or relative 3D coordinates, as well as specify the position, orientation and movement of the viewpoint. These commands are simply ASCII text strings which the visual system, i.e. the WTK application, interprets at run-time, allowing both static and dynamic control of the 3D environment. This program, which runs in MS-DOS 32-bit protected mode, can receive input either from the keyboard, a text file, or via the serial port which allows control from a second computer. This latter feature was fully utilized in the final system, both to automate the creation of track layout from graphics drawings and to control the run-time environment, i.e. driving down the simulated track in real-time. The command structure would also allow alternative programs to be employed, either to generate track layouts or to control movement of the viewpoint.

One of the problems encountered during implementation was the complexity of the CAD models being imported. They typically contained several hundred polygons, and had an obvious impact on performance. Efforts were made to simplify these, both by redrawing from scratch and by using level of detail functions within WTK, which automatically reduced the number of polygons drawn according to viewing distance. However, the results were still unsatisfactory, both in terms of polygon count and visual realism, so a different approach was adopted.

Making use of WTK's capability of rendering textured polygons, with optional shading or transparency, all of the objects were redesigned to consist of a series of flat surfaces with bit-mapped images on them. Although the resulting objects were essentially flat, the 3D effect and detail was actually much better, and the speed of rendering increased significantly. This worked so well that it was even possible to replace a complex model of an overhead gantry with a single polygon containing a transparent texture. A similar technique was used to create scenery in the form of scanned images of trees placed on flat surfaces. The effect is rather similar to a theatre with scenery flats and works because the viewpoint and motion path is only in one direction. These objects are very easy to create, even manually, using WTK's neutral file format, an ASCII text file, to describe the geometry and surface textures and colours.

Although these design changes improved the performance of the DVI-based PC, it was decided to replace the graphics hardware by a faster device, the Spea Fire card which is based on Intel's i860 processor. This enabled a further increase in performance of five to ten times. The only changes required to the program were a recompilation of the source code, written in C, and conversion of the texture graphics files to TARGA format. This hardware also allowed a higher graphics resolution and more detailed texture maps, giving a further increase in image quality. WTK is in fact portable across a number of platforms, from a version running on a standard Windows PC up to a Silicon Graphics Reality Engine. Surprisingly, none of the workstations currently supported between these extremes can cope with real-time texture mapping as well as the i860/PC system despite the hardware being a fraction of the price.

The second system, providing the user interface, was based on a standard Multimedia PC configuration. Using a high level development tool, Asymetrix Multimedia ToolBook, it was possible quickly to produce a graphical user interface that could communicate with the visual system via standard serial ports. This system performed two functions – the first was to allow the creation of track layouts by drawing them on the screen; the second was to control the run-time aspects of the visual simulation.

The track layout drawing program used the concept of nodes and links, where a node represented the location of a signal, sign or track junction, and a link the track section connecting two nodes. From the diagram created the program generates set of commands that defines all of the objects and their positions in the visual system. This file only contains ASCII text, so can easily be edited manually if required, and can be uploaded via the serial link to the visual system for subsequent execution. The files can also be used to drive the visual simulation "off-line".

Once the model is loaded, the visual simulation can be "driven through" by sending commands from the second machine which essentially just move the viewpoint. The audio capabilities of the multimedia PC are used to play looped samples of sound to simulate train and track noises. The run-time system can not only control the speed of motion but can also trigger events at specific locations, for example to change signals or sound effects. The ability of the visual system to replace entire objects "on-the-fly" can be used for simple signal changes or animating a series of objects, for example simulating a level crossing barrier being raised.

The whole system can be completely reconfigured by the user by means of initialization files. These define everything from the object definitions (geometry and textures) through to the menu text without modifying any of the source code. It would, in fact, be perfectly feasible to change the entire visual environment from a train track layout to any other driving simulation.

7.3.   CONCLUSIONS

Although the systems described in these case studies may lack the sophistication of larger systems, being based on standard, off-the-shelf, multimedia PC hardware makes them significantly cheaper. This allows the effective use of simulation in applications that could not otherwise be economically justified. The experience in developing these systems has resulted in a number of new techniques that can nevertheless be applied to produce more sophisticated simulations. In the past there has been a tendency to design a simulator from a engineering functional specification rather than from user requirements. The result can be extremely expensive to implement and no more effective at meeting the training needs than a cheaper part-task solution. Although multimedia technology can enable lower cost simulators to be produced, it is still essential to keep the original requirements to the fore. If 90% of your needs can be achieved with only 70% of the functionality it may not be worth trying to simulate more, particularly if the cost to do so is significantly higher.

About the author

Stefan Nowak has a degree in Architecture, specializing in acoustics, and is a qualified teacher. After five years teaching in schools he moved into the computer industry where an interest in computer-based training developed. Over the 15 years since then he has combined his experience in education and computing to specialize in the emerging multimedia technologies. The development of part-task train driving simulators for Britisih Rail led to an involvement with virtual reality systems and the Dutch Rail project described in this paper.

Stefan continues to pursue his interests in multimedia publishing, simulation and virtual reality, most recently as a freelance consultant. He currently lives in south-eath London with his wife, three children and two cats.

8 The presentation of time in interactive animated systems diagrams

Detlev Fischer and Clive Richards

8.1. INTRODUCTION

The potential application of multimedia in the domain of technical documentation and training is one aspect of the work being carried out in the Visual and Information DEsign (VIDE) research centre of Coventry University. The work of the centre is concerned with the needs of designers and users and is mainly concerned with the "look and feel" of interfaces. One important strand of this work deals with the role interactive time-varying media can play in conveying information about complex processes.

Rolls Royce plc in Derby are collaborators in this research. The Department of Visual Communications at Rolls Royce has long been involved in producing large systems diagrams which show the layout and function of sub-systems of turbine engines. The multipurpose character, functional complexity and visual richness of the systems diagrams seemed to render them ideal candidates for the application of interactive animation techniques. We have therefore started developing a prototype of an interactive animated systems diagram, or cinegram, showing the oil system of the Rolls Royce Trent 700 turbine engine.

8.1.1. The application domain: technical documentation and training

Nowadays, more and more companies are following the trend of putting their technical documentation into digital form. In view of the growing complexity of products and accelerated production cycles, electronic (possibly on-line) documentation techniques offer a number of advantages. They are expected to reduce information access time, facilitate the creation and updating of documents, enable automation of repetitive and book-keeping tasks, and facilitate document exchange, conversion and the production of different versions.

MULTIMEDIA SYSTEMS AND APPLICATIONS
ISBN 0-12-227740-6

The existing applications in this area are mainly text-based. For the sake of consistency, they often retain the structure of printed documentation since both electronic and printed documentation are still expected to be used interchangeably. Pictures or technical drawings, if included in the application, are not usually interactive. The possibilities of animation and digital video have only recently begun to attract attention.

With the availability of animation and digital video for interactive computer systems, the design, implementation and expected usability of mixed-mode or active multimedia documents that can contain time-varying media have become research issues. Much current research is focused on the technical integration of time-varying media into space-based informational structures (Horn and Stefani, 1993). An important example is the development of the SGML-extension "HyTime" (Newcomb et al., 1991). Other topics include storage and compression techniques for multimedia applications (Worthington and Robinson, 1991) and performance-related issues, i.e. studies investigating the utility of motion pictures within learning environments (Faber et al., 1991).

8.1.2.   The research focus: presentational aspects of time-varying media

The way complex temporal relationships of some reference domain can be visually presented in multimedia documents by using interactive time-varying media has hardly been investigated. This is perhaps due to the fact that real-time digital video and animation, and more generally, time-based protocols have only recently become available for machines other than dedicated high-end workstations.

The prototype discussed in this chapter is currently implemented in HyperCard™. Through an external command, HyperCard can access and display chunks of animation and video saved as QuickTime movies. Therefore, the term "movie" will be used in the following to generally refer to sequences of digital video or animation. In most multimedia applications that use them at all, the movie is simply bolted onto the space-based structure. A mouse click on a button or still picture (or "poster", in QuickTime parlance) triggers the movie. Clicking within its boundaries rarely has any other effect than pausing the sequence; the implementation of click-sensitive areas for particular time segments is cumbersome and time-consuming. For fear of losing consistency, the rest of the environment is usually suspended while the movie is playing. At the end of the sequence, the environment is in the same state as at the time when the sequence was triggered.

In the domain of technical documentation, the practical use of time-varying media is still severely limited by pragmatic considerations regarding the hardware currently available to the customer. But in view of the rapid technical development of hardware, storage and compression techniques, development software and communication tools, time-varying media may soon be professionally used in many areas of technical documentation. This chapter focuses on interactive, animated systems diagrams (cinegrams). Cinegrams may be used for self-guided tutorials, as reference tools, or as visual aids to troubleshooting. They may also interface to large multimedia databases. It therefore seems timely to consider the visual information design characteristics of cinegrams.

8.2.   DIAGRAMS AND CINEGRAMS

Cinegrams are seen as the digital offspring of conventional systems diagrams. Since they are expected to reflect their respective reference domain in a dynamic way, they bear some resemblance to simulation models. It will therefore be useful to start out with a definition of the term "diagram", and to draw a distinction between diagram and model.

8.2.1.   Diagrams as reconstructions

All diagrams refer to some reference domain. This domain may be a genealogy of Greek gods, the human nervous system, election results, or, as in the example presented here, one of the sub-systems that make up an aircraft turbine engine, e.g. the ventilation system, the fuel system, or the oil system.

A diagram may be described as a visual construction of relations between those features of a reference domain that, for the intended purpose of the diagram, are expected to be significant. In other words, the designer aims at establishing a correspondence between what he or she perceives as being significant objects and relations in the reference domain and certain graphic elements in the diagram. Diagrams are "always graphical and explain or record for the future what is already known to the maker" (Richards, 1984, pp. 2–3).

Obviously, the way a diagram is actually constructed depends not only on its intended purpose and the knowledge, individual preferences and graphical skills of the designer, but also rests to a large extent on the diagrammatic conventions already used in the respective field.

In emphasizing diagrams as constructions, the use of the much debated term "representation" is avoided. Another term that readily comes to mind is "model". Both "model" and "representation" carry the notion of substitution, that is, both terms somehow suggest that the artifact can in some respect be taken for the real thing.

Mathematical models simulate selected system parameters within certain bounds. If the aim of a presentation is to reflect continuous changes of some parameters of a reference system, applications like the "Steamer system" (Cypher and Stelzner, 1991, p. 412) might be more adequate than a diagram. Numerical simulation models could also be integrated within a larger knowledge-based framework. However, real-world problems can be so complex "that there are no efficient means of solving them algorithmically, and stand-alone experts systems do not have the flexibility to deal with the myriad exceptions and special cases that arise in real life" (op. cit., p. 404).

For the purpose of this paper, a distinction will be drawn between simulation models and diagrams. While simulation models try to mimic and visualize selected physical properties of a reference system in order to simulate its intrinsic behaviour within certain bounds, diagrams often emphasise extrinsic and semantic relations between the reference system and its environment. They interpret rather than simulate the behaviour of systems and draw conclusions beyond the bounds of simulation. This interpretative freedom is reflected in the fact that the diagram elements do not necessarily stand for physical objects. They can stand for locations, functions, or be in themselves concepts that are treated as black boxes on some given level of conceptualization. Similarly, the use of a particular graphical attribute can vary greatly. Amongst other possibilities, an arrow between two elements of a diagram may indicate:

the temporal or functional transformation of the same object (both depicted objects being two instances of the same element);
the passing of a signal, energy, object or substance from one to another object;
a functional dependency of some sort between two objects; or
the feeding or integration of the first object into the second.

The respective meaning of the arrow (like that of any other element of a diagram) results from the semantic context of the diagram, which in turn rests on the conventions established in the respective tradition of diagrammatic expression. With the possibility of creating interactive, animated diagrams on the computer, the designer is now given expressive means that go beyond the known repertoire for traditional diagrams on paper.

8.2.2.   Cinegrams

The term "cinegram" has been coined and introduced here to refer to diagrams that are both interactive and include time-varying media such as digital video or animation. In other words, cinegrams may be defined as the subclass of multimedia documents that explicitly use mixed-media technology for diagrammatic purposes. In a cinegram (as in hypermedia in general) the designer can first of all translate his or her conceptual model of the reference domain into a network of interconnected nodes. The resulting structure can be dynamic and account for more than one decomposition. The possibility of tucking away large amounts of information reduces the information overload and visual noise found in many diagrams which compress a detailed view of a rather complex system into a single field (Plate 7, colour section).

In terms of the spatial layout, the recurring problem of interface design is how this complex network of information can be presented to the user on the very limited space of the computer screen. In addition to the usual hierarchical tree model, a number of suggestions have been made as to how the information load can be alleviated. Drawing on an example of aircraft maintenance data, Mitta (1990) discusses the use of fisheye views first suggested by Furnas (1986). Other suggestions employ the metaphor of a perspective wall (Mackinlay *et al.*, 1991) or cone tree (Robertson *et al.*, 1991).

While most of these suggestions deal with the spatial presentation of information and are neutral with respect to time, cinegrams are designed to present information about processes or causal interactions as processes. On top of, and closely linked with the spatial network of composite nodes, cinegrams feature animation sequences that dynamically illustrate temporal and functional aspects of the respective node content. These sequences may be automatically triggered according to the run-time system status when the node is accessed, or explicitly triggered by the user. Every animation sequence is broken down into small segments that can also be played separately. This degree of temporal granularity allows the presentation of the current state of a node content through an appropriate recombination of animation segments and other media, like text, graphics, or synthesized speech. (A more detailed description of the way cinegrams work can be found in sections 8.4 and 8.5.)

On a rudimentary level, passive temporal constraints are a common trait of computer-based training (CBT) material. A voice-over may explain a task and then tell the trainee to perform some related action, which in turn advances the session to the next step. These CBT modules are designed to teach a certain task in exactly the given order. This is often justified by the particular order in which such tasks have to be carried out, e.g. in the flight deck procedures that precede the starting of the engines. Requesting the trainee to identify the order of steps within a certain task is also an easy way to test training results. An unwelcome effect of this method may be that it seems to suggests that as long as things happen in the given order, everything will be alright. Given unusual circumstances, a person trained to do tasks by rote might not have the conceptual understanding to adapt to the new situation. Recent work on CBT therefore stresses the importance of "the range of feedback and ability to vary training interactively" (Smith, 1992).

Cinegrams are expected to provide such flexibility. They reflect the multiple interconnections and interactions found in the reference domain and dynamically assemble linear sequences of events, e.g. the downstream effects of a fault, in the wider context of the semantic relationships encoded in the document link structure. A look at the way conventional systems diagrams are used at Rolls Royce today will point to useful techniques cinegrams might employ to support users in their understanding of, and dealing with the reference domain.

8.2.3.   How are systems diagrams used?

At Rolls Royce, systems diagrams have quite a special role. In the development of an engine, hundreds of engineers co-operate in designing the various physical components, creating and using thousands of documents: scheme drawings, technical reports, technical illustrations and diagrams, test and simulation results, etc. The systems diagrams show all those components in their functional context. They provide the only available view of the overall process of a system. Therefore, systems diagrams have been used for many years by quite different departments for a variety of purposes, e.g. as reference tools for development engineers, in customer training, and as a visual aid in trouble-shooting.

The development of the concept of cinegrams may well benefit from looking at the the way paper-based systems diagrams are used in the context of technical documentation. Generally, people will consult systems diagrams in order to see their particular task in the system context. An engineer might investigate possible repercussions due to a change in the type of pumps used in the oil system. In the labyrinth of pipes, components, labels, and enlarged details, he or she would first locate the pumps' module. From there, he or she would follow each pipe to find out to which other unit they are connected. Thus one could say that the engineer translates the spatial information of the diagram into a functional sequence. The pipes act as pathways through the system. They also lead to the points where the oil system interacts with other sub-systems.

There are many such interactions within one engine: the high pressure shaft drives the gearbox, which in turn drives the oil pump which in turn lubricates both shaft bearings and gearbox. Another example is the fuel-oil heat exchanger which has the double effect of cooling the oil and heating up the fuel. The oil system diagram illustrates all those interactions with other sub-systems, helping the user understand the functional complexity.

While the oil system is dynamic, the conventional systems diagram is of course static. In working out how a cinegram might present the system and utilize its inherent capabilities, one needs to consider the ways in which temporal and functional aspects of the system can be graphically presented.

8.3.   EXPLICIT AND IMPLICIT PRESENTATIONS OF TIME

There are two different approaches to the graphical presentation of time. The first one is by explicit reference to some conventional metric or "time as pulse, striated time" (Boulez, 1986 p. 60), the second is implicit in the visible movement or change of objects in processes.

8.3.1.   Metrics and scales

The implicit space–time relationship can be seen as a precondition to the constitution of an explicit metric in that any metric relies on some formalisation of repetitive physical motion, e.g. as swinging pendulum or oscillating crystal. If the metric is moved through space, it results in a time-indexing scale, like the way the regular pace of footsteps leaves a trace on snowy ground. If the scale is bent back over on itself, it results in a clock face. The circular scale has no indication of start and end. It mirrors the repetitive pulse. The notion of progression must now be supplied by another linear scale, e.g. a calendar.

In scalar representations of time, duration is mapped onto the length of the scale. This mapping is arbitrary; e.g. in Apple's proprietory digital video protocol QuickTime (as indeed in most other digital video formats) the width of the movie's adjacent slide controller is simply derived from the width of the respective movie. The slider's thumb button acts both as an indexical "moving now" pointer (Horwich, 1987) travelling from left to right while the movie is played, and as a control device for interactively accessing the movie. As a result of the arbitrary nature of the time-to-space mapping relation, the actual speed at which the thumb button travels bears no semantic relation to the frame rate of the movie or the movie content. Also, there is no easy way of reflecting different states within of the movie's content through segmentation, flagging or annotation of the slide controller.

The mere technical correspondence between slide controller and movie becomes most obvious in single state fluid flow animations that play a short movie or movie segment in loop mode. Here, the thumb button keeps jumping from the end of the controller back to the beginning, belying the impression of continuous flow given in the movie. While the presentation of time is technically correct, it seems conceptually wrong. Fortunately, both controller and window frame can be easily hidden to embed the movie within the cinegrammatic context.

In what follows, this chapter focuses on ways of presenting time without reference to an external metric or scale. Such a technique is used to indicate the oil flow in the prototype of the oil system cinegram.

8.3.2. Flow animation as implicit presentation of time

The oil system is a relatively simple full flow recirculatory system. Under normal running conditions, the system is expected to operate in a state of equilibrium once the aeroplane has reached cruising altitude. Changes only occur under certain specific conditions (e.g. under cold starting conditions, when the fuel-oil heat exchanger is bypassed to make the oil warm up quicker).

At the outset, the cinegram prototype is organised hierarchically: from the overview map (Plate 8), the user can zoom in to any component, e.g. the pressure pump and filter (Plate 9 and 10), and from there, further down to component parts. All system components are rendered in normal operating mode as a default condition.

On the component level, the oil flow is presented in a simple animation loop. The illusion of flow is achieved through an old, but quite efficient and often used animation technique called palette cycling. By looping through a range of palette colours, it is possible to create moving wave patterns based on an arrays of adjacent stripes. The animated display immediately shows two things that are not always obvious in static displays like paper diagrams: it readily singles out the pipes through which the oil currently flows, and it indicates the direction of flow. These two parameters are binary, that is, the flow is either on or off, and it has – ignoring the subtleties of fluid dynamics – only one of two directions. The implicit presentation of other parameters, like flow speed, pressure, and temperature, is more difficult to handle.

One reason for this difficulty is that the number of sufficiently distinct colour parameters is limited. Since some hues are lighter than others, the technically distinct parameters of brightness and hue cannot be used independently for an analogue mapping of fluid parameters. Also, the current cinegram prototype attempts to comply as much as possible with the colour coding conventions established at Rolls Royce. In traditional oil systems diagrams, the distribution side of the system is generally rendered red, while the scavenge side is rendered green. High pressure is indicated through a higher saturation of the respective colour. So, how can temperature be expressed? Since the hue is already used arbitrarily to denote oil status, superimposing a non-arbitrary, analogue variance in hue to denote temperature is problematic. A variance in brightness would not be sufficiently distinct from the variance in saturation already used to denote pressure. Also, a dynamic variance in brightness is already used in the moving wave pattern that causes the illusion of flow.

In the current prototype, an increase in temperature is at some points expressed through a transition to a similar, but warmer hue. The problem is that this may lead to confusion since other parts of the oil system, e.g. the vent pipes, are arbitrarily rendered in a warm yellow. The compliance to colour codes is just one example of the general problem that in designing cinegrams, one will often be constrained by conventions already established for static presentations.

8.4.   EXAMPLES OF PRESENTATION POSSIBILITIES IN CINEGRAMS

Clearly, the aim of the current cinegram prototype is to go beyond a presentation of the normal operating mode. What are the information presentation possibilities of cinegrams? The following is an incomplete list of possible applications:

cinegrammatic spatio-temporal reconstructions of complex functions; task animation for maintenance;
the application of cinegrammatic techniques for the presentation of fault conditions;
presentation of normal transient system behaviour, e.g. at starting conditions;
document paths, combining any of the above animations into virtual training modules.

Examples of the first three points are given further on in this section. The last two points, transient system behaviour and document paths, are not yet included in the current prototype. An interesting discussion of scripted document paths combining various media into sequential presentations can be found in Zellweger (1992). She particularly points out consistency problems of paths that can be selectively browsed by users, "when actions earlier in a path may be prerequisites for either the branching decisions or the actions at a later stage of a path" (*op. cit.*, pp. 49–50).

8.4.1.   Cinegrammatic spatio-temporal reconstructions

The arrangement chosen in the overview diagram produced at Rolls Royce (Plate 7) attempts to combine a faithful rendering of the location of components and a functional view of all the connecting pipes, to some extent at the expense of functional clarity. In redesigning the overview map for the cinegram (Plate 8), the decision was made to emphasize the functional independence of components by placing them in a temporally ordered chain, neglecting topographic fidelity. However, on the component level, a more "realistic" spatio–functional arrangement is chosen.

The oil system can be viewed in three different modes (operational states, faults, and maintenance). First of all, the oil flow through the components is rendered in single-state animations corresponding to five common operational states (cruise, ground idle, take off, blocked, shut down). In the faults and maintenance mode, various sequences provide temporal reconstructions of fault conditions and maintenance tasks.

Each of the available component sequences is rendered in two complementary views (Plates 9 and 10):

1. An animated technical illustration, composed of a queue of technically separate media segments generated at runtime, demonstrates the transition between initial and final states. Initial and final states are mostly steady state animations, bracketing a number of transient state animations; in future versions, sequences may at their end trigger jumps to other causally related sequences. Additionally, particular parts of the component illustration (e.g. in the case of the scavenge filter, the main chip detector or the heat bulbs) are clickable and reveal additional information.

2. Additionally, the cinegram features a step window providing a more abstract and static sequence overview. The individual segments, roughly corresponding to identifiable states, are rendered as a vertical stripe of interlocking puzzle pieces. Sequences may be composed not only of animation segments, but also of other media, like text or static diagrams (displayed for a specified duration). The step window provides a visual index of the sequence, both by indicating the current state within the sequence and in providing a navigational device through which the user can override the sequential order of presentation in order to view any particular segment. Optional horizontal add-on puzzle pieces point to additional information related to the respective state, e.g. safety information or reference numbers to the illustrated parts catalogue, engine manuals, or schematics.

The most general animation sequence would include all system components and arrange them along a linear path in the order in which they are traversed by the oil flow: from the oil tank to the bearings and finally back to the tank. This is indeed possible, but there are problems related to the fact that the system can be decomposed in different ways. A temporal decomposition will encounter the problem that one unilinear sequence cannot cover the whole system, since the flow actually branches to lubricate the four bearings and three gear boxes simultaneously. Another decomposition, according to functionality, might suggest treating pumps as a generic concept, since they all work identically.

In decomposing the reference system and reconstructing it in a cinegram, design decisions are undeniably biased towards a particular kind of anticipated use (training, in the case of the current prototype). Not only is there an inverse relationship between efficiency and generality of multimedia systems (see Harrison, Chapter 4 this volume); radically different user requirements may only be reconciled at the expense of the clarity of design. Another constraint that has a strong impact on design decisions is the layout of the source material. For reasons of economy (and also in order to secure consistency with the printed oil system diagram), the cinegram designer would be ill-advised to attempt a complete redesign of the laboriously produced technical illustrations serving as the source material for the cinegram animations. An example may illustrate this constraint, and also show how the diagrammatic purpose can inform particular spatial reconstructions.

The technical illustration underlying the pressure pump and filter component animation (Plates 9 and 10) shows both pump and filter in one diagrammatic cross section. In fact, these two functionally independent components are again part of an even bigger ensemble also housing all scavenge pumps. For the design of the overview map (Plate 8), this poses an interesting question: should the overview emphasize spatial or temporal relationships? While pressure pump and scavenge pumps are far apart in terms of a temporal flow cycle, they are placed in the same case and even driven by the same gear shaft.

The technical illustration itself (Plates 9 and 10) is actually an ingenuous montage: the designer (Mark Johnson from the Department of Visual Communications at Rolls Royce) has combined two different cross sections into one image in order to emphasise the functional relation within the overall assembly of the pump casing. The view focuses on those technical details that contribute to an understanding of the function. While it is conceptually precise, it modifies the actual physical arrangement.

8.4.2. Task animation for maintenance

One sequence of pressure pump and filter component view (Plates 9 and 10) demonstrates the application of cinegrams for the instruction on maintenance procedures. The animation shows the functioning of an invention that makes life easier for the flight mechanic. When the filter element is removed, an anti-leak valve is automatically closed to prevent oil spill.

The scheme drawing of the component shows both states of the filter on each side of a vertical dividing line. Some technical imagination is required to complete the other half for each state and mentally perform an "in-between" between both states. A static technical illustration might show both states separately. An animation has the advantage of showing the transition between both states over time. This way, the functioning of the automatic shut-off mechanism becomes immediately obvious.

8.4.3.   The application of cinegrammatic techniques for the presentation of fault conditions

Under certain fault conditions, there are processes in the oil system where time is critical. Such fault conditions can cause cascade effects that rapidly propagate beyond the system boundaries to affect the whole engine. Regular maintenance ensures that those conditions rarely become reality. But the very fact that such conditions are rare and consequently rarely observed indicates that cinegrammatic presentations of those conditions and their effects may help the people who fly and maintain those engines to get a better conceptual understanding of the system.

One of the fault condition sequences shows the blockage of the scavenge filter through debris in the oil clogging up the filter element (Plate 11). This results in an pressure drop past the filter and pressure rise before the filter. When a differential pressure of 13 psi has been reached, a differential pressure meter sends a signal to provide flight deck indication of impending bypass (Plate 12). At 20 psi, the spring-loaded pressure relief valve is blown (Plate 13) to let the oil bypass the blocked filter element (Plate 14).

The entire fault sequence falls into two radically different stages on both sides of a peak in the sequence: the slow building up of pressure until the signal is sent, and the blowing of the valve shortly after. The first stage may take weeks of operation during which the filter gets increasingly clogged; the second may take only a fraction of a second until the filter bypass state is reached. The animation takes considerable license in its treatment of time. In order to accentuate the relatedness of both stages, it radically accelerates the first stage and to some lesser degree, slows down the second stage.

The above examples have given some indications as to the presentation of sequential information in cinegrams. The following section will look at some aspects of presenting time-varying media in more depth.

8.5.   CHARACTERISTICS AND PROBLEMS OF PRESENTING TIME-VARYING MEDIA IN CINEGRAMS

The task of embedding time-varying media in the interactive, spatial environment of cinegrams entails a number of problems:

temporal granularity (segmentation);
interactions of simultaneously playing movies;
the relation of time-varying to static media;
the presentation of embedded, timed links;
the design of embedded control structures.

8.5.1. Temporal granularity

A fundamental problem of handling time-varying media within a space-based framework is the temporal granularity. What the user perceives as one sequence actually consists of a number of segments which exist as separate files. This has the advantage of reducing redundancy: any segment can be accessed from any other stack/sub-system, and all segments can be re-arranged in any order by runtime operations.

Segments stand either for steady states (technically, they loop) or for transitions between two states. States are useful abstractions; e.g. if nothing much happens, one calls it "normal state", although in the real system, there will always be slight variations. Therefore, the extension of a state depends on the threshold corresponding to the respective level of conceptualization. The shorter the segments, the higher the temporal granularity and consequently, the resulting combinatory complexity.

Technically, meaningful sequences take the form of a movie queue in which several transitional segments are combined in a particular order. In the most primitive case, segments will simply play forward and at their end, call the next segment in the queue set by the sequence script. In more elaborate cases, timed movie call-backs may cause side effects in the environment, e.g. update text, play other movies, or even recursively set new call-backs.

Some of the parameters of temporal presentation, like duration, playback rate, and play mode (e.g. loop, palindrome, reverse) can be easily set. However, a reasonable playback rate will depend on sufficiently fast hardware. QuickTime supports a number of synchronized movie tracks, so that audio, video and even text tracks of a particular movie can be set according to runtime conditions.

Segments can thus be seen as flexible building blocks for the construction of meaningful sequences. Some problems arise if the system allows the user to override a given sequence and navigate to other components, while still maintaining the current system status. The greater the number of explicit links to related components, the greater the requirement for varying segments to show each component in the state that correctly corresponds to the respective overall system state. Soon the point is reached where some form of simulation model might be more appropriate.

8.5.2. Interactions of simultaneously playing movies

A fault sequence might progress through the presentation of a number of different components it affects. Since the fault condition also causes state changes in components not contained in the sequence itself, the choice of an overall sequence depends on priorities that depend on the explanatory context; e.g. the system could show the quickest way from the root cause to an in-flight engine shut-down. In another case, a clear presentation of the fault sequence might require that two or more components are shown simultaneously to demonstrate the way they interact over time. The design would have to accommodate a dynamic screen layout, where the currently selected sequence could run at full size, with related scaled-down sequences running next to it. There should also be indications as to the direction of causality. Movies could be made aware of, and adapt to, other simultaneously running movies. The sequence script could request priority information with regard to the particular mode and context of presentation from a knowledge base, and consequently set the movies appropriate audio, text, and video tracks.

8.5.3.   The relation of time-varying to static media

In analysing the different media used in the oil system cinegram, a general distinction can be made between time-varying and space-based, or static, media. While time-varying media unfold their content sequentially according to a time code, the dynamic aspects of static media are normally user-controlled; e.g. the user will activate links, scroll a text field, zoom into a graphic, open and close windows, etc.

Perhaps the closest possible relation between both media genres occurs when user interaction causes transformations from one into the other. A simple example might be the execution of a static element, e.g. when an icon representing static text is dropped onto a speech synthesizer icon. A roughly reverse transformation might be the dragging of static frames or "snapshots" from a playing movie.

The beauty of time-varying media is that they let the user experience the changes within a process as a continuous, transitional sequence. They can also express the character, speed and direction of movements in a graphical and immediately evident form. The drawback of the sequential presentation is that only one instance out of the series of all instances is visible at any one time. Comparisons between the current instance and earlier or later instances have to rely on the user's memory and/or explicit "rewinding" or "forwarding" to those other instances.

Static diagrams, on the other hand, allow abstraction from continuous processes by singling out discrete and semantically distinct stages. These stages can be rendered as separate graphical elements and shown simultaneously. Thus, by providing an overview, static diagrams can ease system conceptualization. For discrete processes like computation, diagrams can even become isomorphic notations of processes to the point that they are executable by some visual parsing mechanism (Golin 1991). Another important advantage of static process layouts is that they can incorporate and visualize control structures like "if – then" or "do while" clauses that are not directly presentable in time-varying media.

In a cinegram, both time-varying and static media may be used together to show simultaneously both a sequential animation and the corresponding static sequence overview. Cinegrams combine elements of different media types into composite nodes. The concept of composite node (Halasz, 1988) has been used to extend the node-and-link concept of hypertext. An important issue is how the static and time-varying elements within and between composite nodes relate. Michon (1992) refers to them a "streamy-things" and "chunky-things" and claims that "the association of a chunky-thing to a streamy-thing constitutes a fundamental primitive in synchronised multimedia information" (*op. cit.*, p. 362).

Mutual synchronization through timed call-backs or "triggers" (Ogawa *et al.*, 1991, p. 41) or user actions means that a movie may display or update a static element at a specified time, e.g. by highlighting a corresponding static graphic or displaying additional text, while clicking a static element may in turn play the corresponding movie segment. Any such update message may cause several changes, simultaneously or with a specified delay. In a similar way, the sound of a spoken text may highlight the corresponding words in a text field. Movies can also trigger, or act as indexes to, other movies.

The issue of synchronization is not only a technical problem, but entails difficult design decisions about the implementation of linking mechanisms in general. Several nodes may share the presentation of a single process, e.g. by animating the evolving status of a number of system components during a fault condition. When defining links between these nodes, the designer must decide if the elapsing time is treated as a global property of all nodes or if the temporal status of the node containing the link anchor is saved at link execution in order to enable a precise return (Muller, *et al.*, 1992).

8.5.4.   The presentation of embedded, timed links

The issue of synchronization must be seen in the broader context of user interaction. Typically, the user interacts with multimedia documents by activating links that may lead to other parts of the document, reveal additional information, etc. A particular application may use a number of different link types, e.g. up-and-down linking, cross-referencing, or annotation links (De Young, 1990). The issue of linking is very complex and cannot be dealt with in detail here. For the purpose of this chapter, it might suffice to say that for all links, some element of a node, e.g. a word, a button, or a part of a graphic, functions as a link anchor, which, if triggered through user interaction, will execute some piece of code that will cause the display of the link destination. The link code may be stored in the anchor or depend in some way on the current state of the document, the interaction history, or on additional specification through user input. The link destination is not necessarily another node; the link may simply change the status of the current node, i.e., scroll to another part of a text or jump to another frame of a movie.

While a node in a static network can be seen as a "timeless" location, a composite node must contain additional information about the temporal layout of any time-varying element that contains link anchors of specified duration or is itself contained in a time-specific link destination.

Ogawa *et al.* (1991, p. 38) have suggested a "scenario model" in which embedded hot links within composite nodes can be graphically defined. The model basically presents the multimedia scene as a 3D spatial layout in oblique projection. Individual screen objects, like text fields, windows, or anchor regions, are shown as solids. The screen layout of those objects is shown on the x,y-plane, while start and end points are mapped onto the z-axis.

While this model might ease the definition of links, it does not solve the problem of how the location and type of links can be communicated to the user. For static networks, a number of conventions have emerged that indicate the existence of links and provide visual feedback when a link is selected. In frameworks that explicitly define temporal aspects, the situation is more complicated. How, for example, could the existence of an embedded hot link within a movie be indicated? A simple and rather ugly solution would be to superimpose the outline of the link anchor permanently onto the movie surface. Such permanent outlines might distract from the information presented and may even be taken for an element that belongs to the movie content. Another possibility is that the system constantly evaluates the cursor position and, whenever the cursor is moved over a click-sensitive area, changes the cursor image or draws the outlines of the click-sensitive area. Alternatively, or in addition to the techniques already mentioned, the cursor position may trigger voice messages or "earcons" (Brewster *et al.*, 1993) that communicate the link or directly annotate the movie.

Whatever technique is chosen, the designer is well advised to use it consistently throughout the system. Generally, it seems appropriate to indicate embedded links in movies in response to some user action, e.g. when the cursor is moved over the movie area, or explicitly by providing a "show links'-button which would cause the drawing of the available link on the movie surface. Also, the system might evaluate the runtime status to provide and indicate only links which are meaningful in the context of the current overall sequence.

The problem of link indication gets more complex if the use of several types of embedded links within one movie are considered. In the example of the scavenge filter (Plates 11–14), one could easily imagine four functionally different links:

1. Clicking the magnetic chip detector might activate a goto-link to another node.
2. Clicking the strainer unit might expand the node to reveal additional information like part number, diameter, or pore size in an additional permanent window.
3. Moving the cursor over the heat bulbs may display a dynamic temperature read-out in a transient window.
4. Dragging the top of the bypass valve up and down might display an opening or closing the valve, i.e. jump to other movie frames while remaining at the same node.

While the implementation of these link types might be desirable, the appropriate presentation would have to reflect the respective nature of each link. Moreover, this presentation should interfere as little as possible with the display of the movie content.

8.5.5.   The design of embedded control structures

It is perhaps worth noting that the different link types described above are triggered by three different mouse actions: mouse click, mouse enter, and mouse down drag. It could be argued that the mouse down drag technique introduced above is actually not a link type in the proper sense, but rather an implicit, "tailored" slider control that works in a roughly similar way as the QuickTime movie controller. Embedded sliders can be seen as simulating object behaviour to some extent. The parallel with the direct manipulation interfaces of 3D applications is obvious. The difference, however, is that in embedded movie control structures, the location, constraints, scope and ratio of the structures can be defined independently of the object itself, and can even be changed at runtime.

Embedded slide controllers are not confined to the linear, horizontal orientation found in the standard QuickTime movie controller; e.g. a circular drag on top of the cross-section of a vane pump cylinder could trigger a pump rotation in either direction. Technically, some code would constantly evaluate the mouse position and drag offset over time and accordingly access the corresponding individual frames. Such an implicit control technique might well be implemented without explicit indication if it can be assumed that the users are familiar enough with the reference domain to infer which elements of an animation might stand for moveable parts of the system.

Other possible control techniques include mouse gestures and colour evaluation at mouse position. A mouse down drag on top of the presented fluid could trigger or accelerate the flow in the indicated direction. Given a precise analogue mapping of one of the colour values to any one fluid parameter, e.g. oil temperature, it would be possible to provide a generic parameter read-out at any mouse position.

It is too early to attempt any predictions as to the usability of such implicit control devices. The examples given may indicate both the possibilities and complexities of such presentation and interaction techniques.

8.6.   CONCLUSIONS

This chapter has discussed some of the possibilities of implicitly presenting time-varying system aspects in interactive, animated systems diagrams. The term "cinegram" has been coined to refer to these diagrams. The presentation of the cinegram prototype of an aircraft engine oil system has shown the potential of using interactive animation for presenting various temporal and functional aspects found within the reference system.

The discussion of the prototype has led to the identification of a number of problems related to the time-varying nature of the suggested presentation techniques. While the implicit presentation of temporal aspects can reduce the amount of external control structures needed to present the functionality of cinegrams, it also makes it more difficult to communicate this functionality to the user. The trade-off between explicit and implicit presentation techniques is to some extent unavoidable.

The work presented here is in its early stages. The concept is sufficiently general to allow application to a variety of other domains, but much further research into implicit presentation techniques is necessary in order to investigate the potential and scope of their application. So far, no formal usability study has taken place. However, the increasing availability of interactive time-varying media such as digital video calls for the development of information presentation techniques that can alleviate information overload. In this regard we believe the implicit approach to the user interface for the presentation of temporal and functional aspects has much to offer. As Zellweger (1992) has pointed out, interactive multimedia documents begin to overlap the role of user interfaces (p. 52). In developing the concept of cinegram, we intend to reformulate the wealth of information design techniques found in the diagrammatic tradition (Richards, 1984; Pedersen, 1988; Tufte, 1990) within an interactive and time-varying framework. Thus we expect that the concept of cinegram will contribute to the development of future interactive and highly dynamic mixed-media environments.

ACKNOWLEDGEMENTS

We would like to thank John Buckland, manager of Visual Communications, for arranging attachments to Rolls Royce for one of the authors which provided many insights as to the way technical documentation is used within the company. Frank Thomas was particularly helpful in giving expert advice, providing many documents, and arranging numerous meetings with other people at Rolls Royce. Much is also owed to Mark Johnson, the designer of the paper-based Trent oil systems diagram for frequent discussions. Rolls Royce plc is gratefully acknowledged for permission to reproduce the simplified oil system overview shown in Plate 7.

Thanks are also due to all those people from Rolls Royce plc in Derby who in some way contributed to our research. Amongst those who provided first-hand experience, helpful comments and critique are, in alphabetical order, Ted Bardgett, Patricia Barnes, Richard Barton, Mike Bowman, Xavier Buthun, Macolm Grayburn, Jeremy Laffan, Graham Lewis, Brian Lomas, Liam Murphy, Simon Pank, Paul Rees, Andy Smith, Simon Smith, and Ken Udall.

Finally, we also thank John Vince of Thomson Training & Simulation,

Don Hinson of Coventry University, Coventry School of Art & Design, John Lindsay of Kingston University, School of Information Systems, and Karl Longman of Attica Cybernetics for helpful comments and discussions.

The prototype makes use of a number of different XCMDs amd XFCNs: Hilite XCMD, GetGlobalToLocal XFCN, LocalToLocal XFCN, UpdateWindow XFCN ©Rob Bevan 1993; "say" XCMD ©Sam Deane 1993; QTmovie XCMD ©Ken Doyle, Apple Computer 1993; WindowScript™ 1.0.1 XFCN ©Heizer Software 1993; Textoid XCMD ©Frederic Rinaldi 1992.

REFERENCES

Boulez, P. (1986). *Orientations*. Faber and Faber, London.

Brewster, S. A. *et al.* (1993). An evaluation of earcons for use in auditory human–computer interfaces. In *Proceedings of the ACM INTER CHI '93 Conference on Human Factors in Computing Systems*. Association for Computing Machinery.

Cypher, A. and Stelzner, M. (1991). Graphical knowledge-based model editors. In Sullivan, J. W. and Tyler, S. W. (eds), *Intelligent User Interfaces*, pp. 403–420. ACM Press, New York.

De Young, L. (1990). Linking considered harmful. In Streit, N., Rizk, H. and Andrei, J. (eds) *Hypertext: Concepts, Systems and Applications*, pp. 238–249. Cambridge University Press, Cambridge.

Faber, J. Meiers, T. Ruschin, D. and Seyferth, A. (1991). The motion picture in interactive information systems: A necessary or facilitating component? In Bullinger, H.-J. (ed.) *Human Aspects in Computing: Design and Use of Interactive Systems and Work with Terminals*, pp. 344–349. Elsevier Science Publishers B. V.

Furnas, G. W. (1986). Generalized fisheye views. In *Proceedings CHI '86, Human Factors in Computing Systems, ACM Special Interest Group on Computer and Human Interaction*, pp. 16–23. Association for Computing Machinery.

Golin, E. J. (1991). Parsing visual languages with picture layout grammars. *Journal of Visual Languages and Computing*, 2(4), 371–393.

Halasz, F. G. (1988). Reflections on Notecards: seven issues for the next generation of hypermedia systems. *Communications of the ACM*, 31(7), 836–855.

Hinson, D. (1991). Computer-aided fault-finding documentation. *Communicator*, 9(2/3), 2–9.

Horn, F. and Stefani, J. B. (1993). On programming and supporting multimedia object synchonization. *The Computer Journal*, 36(1).

Horwich, P. (1987). *Asymmetries in time. Problems in the philosophy of science.* Bradford Books (MIT Press), Cambridge, MA.

Mackinlay, J. D., Robertson, G. G. and Card, S. K. (1991). The perspective wall: detail and context smoothly integrated. In *Proceedings of the ACM CHI '91 Conference on Human Factors in Computing Systems*, pp. 173–179. Association for Computing Machinery.

Michon, B. (1992). Highly iconic interfaces. In Blattner, M. M. and Dannenberg, R. B. (eds). *Multimedia Interface Design*, pp. 357–372. ACM Press, New York.

Mitta, D. A. (1990). A fisheye presentation strategy: aircraft maintenance data. In *HCI Interact '90. Proceedings of the IHP TC 13 Third international conference*, pp. 875–880. North Holland, Amsterdam.

Muller, M. J., Farrell, R. F., Cebulka, K. D. and Smith (1992). Issues in the usability of time-varying multimedia. In Blattner, M. M. and Dannenberg, R. B. (eds) *Multimedia Interface Design*, pp. 7–38. ACM Press, New York.

Newcomb, S. R., Kipp, N. A. and Newcomb, V. (1991). HyTime. Hypermedia/time-based document structuring language. *Communications of the ACM*, **34**(11), 67–83.

Ogawa, R., Harada, H. and Kaneko, A. (1991). Scenario-based hypermedia: a model and a system. In Streitt, N. Rizk, A. and Andrei, J. (eds) *Hypertext: Concepts, Systems and Applications*, pp. 38–51.Cambridge University Press, Cambridge.

Pedersen, M. B. (1988). *Graphics Diagram 1: The Graphic Visualisation of Quantitive Information, Procedures, and Data*. Graphics Press Corp., Zürich.

Richards, C. J. (1984). *Diagrammatics*. PhD dissertation. Royal College of Art, London.

Robertson, G. G., Mackinlay, J. P. and Card, S. K. (1991). Cone trees: animated 3D visualizations of hierarchical information. In *Proceedings of ACM CHI '91 Conference on Human Factors in Computing Systems*, pp. 189–194. Association for Computing Machinery.

Smith, C. S. (1992). New computer delivered training systems to support technical crew training programmes. In *Aerotech '92*, Congress seminar papers, The Aerospace and Airport Technology Exhibition and Congress.

Tufte, E. R. (1990). *Envisioning Information*. Graphics Press, Cheshire.

Worthington, W. and Robinson, B. (1991). The medium is not the message: mixed mode document technology. In Feeney, M. and Day, S. (eds). *Multimedia Information*. Proceedings of a Conference held at Cambridge Churchill College, 15–18 July 1991, pp. 13–66. Bowker Saur, London.

Zellweger, P. T. (1992). Toward a model for active multimedia documents. In Blattner, M. M. and Dannenberg, R. B. (eds). *Multimedia Interface Design*, pp. 39–52. ACM Press, New York.

About the authors

Clive Richards MPhil PhD(RCA) MCSD FISTC is Associate Dean of the Coventry School of Art & Design. His background is in both the practice and teaching of graphic information design. Early experiments in computer animation at Lanchester Polytechnic led to research work in collaboration with the CAD Centre, Cambridge, on the application of computer-aided drafting techniques to technical illustration. Later research on diagrammatics was carried out at the Royal College of Art, London. He is director of the Visual and Information DEsign (VIDE) research centre at Coventry University.

Detlev Fischer MA studied film and hypermedia at the Hochschule für bildende Künste in Hamburg and Electronic Graphics with an emphasis on multimedia at Coventry University. He has worked commercially on the design and production of multimedia products. He is a research fellow in the VIDE research centre.

PART 2

Applications: Education

9 Developments in multimedia technologies, learning environments, distributed access, and interactive perceptualization

R. A. Earnshaw

9.1. INTRODUCTION

Interest in multimedia technology and applications in academia, commerce, and industry is increasing rapidly due to a number of factors.

1. Functional advances in technology and falling prices are bringing benefits to everyone. Users can now buy a "PC with everything to go", i.e. add-ons, or integrated facilities, for CD-ROM, stereo speakers, software etc., at very competitive prices.
2. Spin-offs from the technology developments for the entertainment industry are resulting in benefits for other areas. For example, collaborative arrangements between Silicon Graphics and Time Warner will develop interactive digital facilities via domestic TV. This will provide remote VCR, interactive shopping, computer-based learning (CBL)/instructional courses, virtual books, and computer-supported cooperative working (CSCW).
3. Initiatives in UK higher education are seeking to develop and provide a curriculum which is enhanced by multimedia facilities, to enable the student to obtain a richer educational experience. The UK Universities' Funding Council (UFC) has recently initiated the Teaching and Learning through Technology Programme (TLTP) in order to provide the pump-priming developments necessary in order to move forward in this area.
4. The desk-top PC is now a "window on to the world", and users' horizons are no longer bounded by information and developments on the local campus. Facilities such as Gopher and World-Wide-Web (WWW) provide useful tools and information sources of current work and activity around the world. Increasingly, faster networks (e.g. UK SuperJANET) will enable interactive video sequences (and CSCW) to be accessed from the desk-top.

MULTIMEDIA SYSTEMS AND APPLICATIONS
ISBN 0-12-227740-6

5. A wide range of software tools and facilities is becoming available to enable users to handle video, animations, and audio just as easily as they have handled lines of text on a PC screen. The term "digital media" refers to the integration in a seamless environment of a variety of entities such as 3D graphics, video, images, audio, text, and animation, all linked in a manner that allows quick and easy interactivity on the local PC or workstation, across a network, or round the world.

6. Methods for storing and accessing published information are moving into the digital arena caused by the enabling capabilities of the new technology and the shortage of physical space in many libraries. Hence the terms "virtual books" and "virtual libraries" are entering into common usage. A UK review of university libraries has recently taken place, chaired by Sir Brian Follett, and a report has been produced (HEFCE, 1993). It highlights the increasing role that digital media, networks and information technology is expected to play in the future.

7. Digital facilities can provide a version of reality which in many cases is indistinguishable from the real thing. For example, in the recent Steven Spielberg film *Jurassic Park* the majority of the dinosaurs were created and animated entirely by computers. This work was done by state-of-the-art graphics and animation facilities at Industrial Light and Magic (ILM).

One author writes: "Over the next decade or two, digital media is likely to have an impact on nearly every aspect of creative endeavour – an impact that will rival that of the printing press, the telephone, and the motion picture – while incorporating aspects of all of them" (Cruickshank, 1992).

9.2.   A VIRTUAL WORLD

As the user's horizons are now no longer limited to the provision of the local computing facility, this means that a "virtual world" of information, software, facilities, demonstrations, and software becomes available via the network.

At the same time as functional capabilities increase, a new technology called "virtual reality" also appears to offer great potential, at least for high-end applications such as computational fluid dynamics (CFD), CAD, molecular modelling, and augmented reality for surgical procedures and applications. The new Boeing 777, currently at the design stage, is using virtual reality techniques extensively in order to reduce costs, speed up design and manufacture, and optimize design and manufacturing procedures.

Scientific visualization has enabled many researchers and users to explore their data and see their results from a new perspective (e.g. Earnshaw, 1992). Developments in visualization are now utilizing further modes (or channels) of information such as those provided by sound and touch. Although multimedia developments tend to be primarily concerned with technology and the ways in which such technology can be exploited in application areas, we need to ensure that technology is developed and harnessed with a human-centric perspective and with an approach that best fits the cognitive model. From this viewpoint, interactive perceptualization is probably the best term for multimedia.

Information access via Gopher and World-Wide-Web (WWW) enable users with network connections to access a wide variety of information from the desk-top. Electronic information is challenging the traditional role of publishers of journals and books, particularly for forms of information where speed of distribution and access is important or where digital information offers increased value to the user (e.g. for video, animations, or keyword searching).

9.3.   NETWORK FACILITIES

Multimedia applications are currently being used as some of the pilot projects to test out and evaluate SuperJANET in the UK in its initial phases of operation. SuperJANET has the planned capability for running at 140Mbit/s with two channels of video at 34Mbit/s.

The Joint Network Team in the UK has expressed strong interest in multimedia in the context of developments in SuperJANET for the areas of distributed functionality, interworking of standards, and the implications of network loadings. Some of the pilot applications in 1993 include computer visualization, supercomputer interconnection, medical scanning, and remote teaching. User applications are expected in the areas of distributed hypermedia systems, video conferencing, supercomputer support, and the use of X400 mail with video clips. The latter is likely to overload even a fast network! Multimedia applications may require a store and forward service (e.g. to send a text message with a video clip), or synchronous access (e.g. for pan and zoom across an image via the network).

Cambridge, Edinburgh, Imperial College, Manchester, University College, and Rutherford Laboratory were connected to SuperJANET in March 1993, and a further six sites joined up in late 1993.

9.4.   VIDEO AND COMPRESSION

Compression of video is essential because the lowest resolution (VGA) and lowest frame rate saturates an FDDI or high speed line. Compression of still images can be performed by non-image compression (e.g. Unix LZW), run-length encoding (which can give a 20:1 reduction), JPEG, or fractal methods (using area decomposition).

For JPEG, there are both lossy and loss-free methods, and also software and hardware implementations, with several modes of operation:

sequential encoding;
progressive encoding;
lossy encoding;
hierarchical encoding;
JPEG is fast and predictable in hardware.

Compression of moving images can be done by the H.261 teleconferencing standard, real time JPEG, MPEG, fractal methods, and DVI (Intel). Different application areas tend to prefer different compression systems – no single method is best for all applications. JPEG and MPEG provide symmetric, predictable results for compression.

Digital video enables video to be stored with electronic data, transmitted with electronic data, and manipulated on the computer along with electronic data. There is no clear vendor standard as yet – different manufacturers use their own systems (e.g. DVI, Photo-CD, CD-I, MPEG, MPEG11, Quicktime, and Video for Windows).

9.5.   EUROPEAN INTEREST IN MULTIMEDIA

The European Commission included many multimedia topics in its Call for Proposals for ESPRIT for 1993/94. The EC listed the following areas as being of interest: publishing and copyright protection, multimedia authoring, retailing, banking, security, mobile and portable assistants, tourist information services, education and learning environments, games and entertainment, home automation devices, and documentation of cultural artefacts.

9.6.   MULTIMEDIA AND THE TEACHING AND LEARNING ENVIRONMENT

The following are areas where multimedia tools are regarded as having something effective to contribute to the work of academic institutions:

teaching larger classes more effectively;
improving tutorial teaching;
benefits in easing lecturer loads;
more attractive learning environments for students;
teaching concepts or topics not possible by traditional methods (e.g. exploring virtual worlds!).

In the UK, the objective of the Universities' Funding Council (UFC) Teaching and Learning via Technology Programme (TLTP) is to:

cater for the large increases in student numbers;
address the high student/staff ratios;
modernize and enrich the learning experience;
promote flexible and computer-based learning.

Multimedia, networks, and computer-based learning offer the potential for the following transformations in the learning environment:

passive to active;
synchronous to asynchronous;
real to virtual;
static to dynamic;
audience to personal;
impassive to supportive;
single medium to multimedia;
unidirectional to interative;
from one location to the network.

All these factors have the potential for transforming the learning environment from one based primarily on 19th century techniques and methods, to one that is timely and relevant to the 20th century's needs and requirements.

9.7.   DEVELOPMENTS AND INITIATIVES AT THE UNIVERSITY OF LEEDS

In January 1992, the Dean for Academic Development, Professor Holdcroft, set up the Multimedia Group (Prof. French, Dr Earnshaw, Mr Brook, and Prof. Hartley) to address the following areas:

to audit current activities in the area of multimedia at the university;
to propose areas for development and investment;
to explore potential collaborative links with suppliers and vendors;
to produce medium-term and long-term plans for future developments;
to provide a framework to respond to the UK UFC TLTP initiatives.

The group undertook a programme of work with the above as the principal goals. Current work and activities were surveyed, and members of the group visited key groups in the university and prepared reports on their current activities. The group then invited bids for development funding and received proposals totalling £85 000. To provide a common basis for addressing many areas in these proposals a university summer school was set up for the period July–September 1992, where multidisciplinary developments in teaching materials could take place in a facilities rich environment well equipped with computing and multimedia devices. Projects were funded to work in this cluster of PCs and workstations. This work was also used as showcase for developing wider interest in the university as a whole, and a programme of staff development seminars and demonstrations was mounted. Staff who were new to multimedia, or even new to computers, were able to see the potential of the new approaches and offered "hands-on" demonstrations in the laboratory. Developers also benefited from the cross-fertilization of ideas.

At the same time as these developments were being progressed, the medium-term strategy for multimedia in the university was prepared, and this provided the context and background for the university's proposal to the UFC TLTP programme in conjunction with Silicon Graphics Ltd. This proposal was accepted and this programme of work is now underway, centred on a CBL/Multimedia Support Unit, with a manager and four development staff. This unit has strong links with other groups in the university (as demonstrated in Figure 9.1) and is governed by the Multimedia Board. The board now includes the Pro Vice-Chancellor (Information Technology) and Pro Vice-Chancellor (Teaching) in its membership. The university's TLTP project is primarily responsible for the developing and porting of multimedia courseware in core disciplines, providing information and advisory services to the university, providing staff training and staff skills update, and exploring the issues of

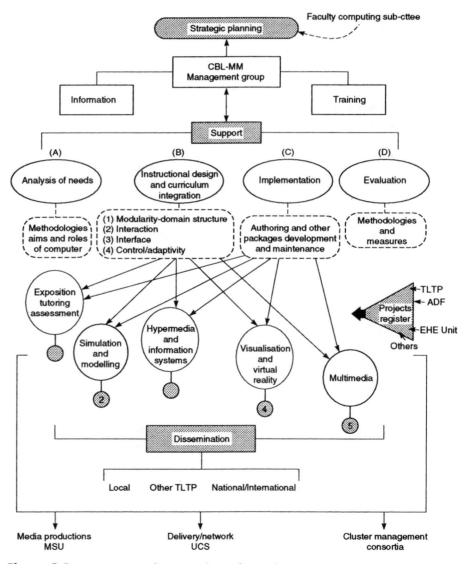

Figure 9.1.   Overview of CBL multimedia at the University of Leeds.

transportability and standards. The unit also has strong links with the other (discipline-specific) TLTP projects in the university where a university department is in partnership with other departments in other universities in the UK.

The university also has a number of pilot projects which are running to exploit and assess the functional capabilities of the SuperJANET networking environment in the UK. These include the following:

1. TLTP biological sciences teaching consortium;
2. library document delivery;
3. scientific visualization from remote systems;
4. physical chemistry teaching;
5. group work software;
6. remote access to real-time video for collaborative applications.

Projects 3 and 6 are particularly relevant for the work of VISINET, a European consortium which is being set up by the European Commission. In particular, Project 6 is investigating the feasibility of simultaneous collaborative working between three UK sites (Leeds, Nottingham, and Newcastle) via video and teleconferencing on SuperJANET – for the delivery and interaction with tutorial and demonstrator materials for the biomolecular sciences. Although this project is being initiated using high end Silicon Graphics platforms that have powerful computational and graphics capabilities, it is intended to migrate the technology down to more general computing platforms.

The above projects will provide very useful data on the performance of a high speed network in conjunction with visualization and video requirements, and can be seen as the preparatory stages to wider network connections between the UK and sites in Europe (and vice versa).

9.8. MULTIMEDIA ISSUES

A recent workshop in the UK (JISC/AGOCG, 1993) identified the following issues as needing further consideration:

greater coordination in the multimedia area is required;
new technology needs new skills for its effective use;
how multimedia can be best exploited in educational software;
copyright, IPR, and reuse of materials in electronic form;
vendor systems versus de facto standards versus open systems;
optimum ways of integrating new media, and interoperability;
measuring the effectiveness of utilizing new technology in learning;
guidelines for the capturing of images and multimedia components;
selection of storage formats;
discovery and dissemination of information over the network;
relative merits of different network solutions.

A series of recommendations and proposals were produced and it is hoped to progress these in the UK.

9.9.   MULTIMEDIA FUTURES

Digitally based information is the key enabling characteristic of today's information technology (IT) world. Experts currently indicate that digital information will become even more pervasive as it moves into homes via cables, TV sets, RF devices, and digital phones. Computing is set to become ubiquitous in the sense of being everywhere and always accessible. Intelligent agents and filters will protect us from information overload and will enable us to select just those items we need to know about, or interact with. We may expect to see further developments in electronic publishing (particularly to take advantage of multimedia functionality), virtual reality, CSCW, and digital video.

A number of companies have products in the pipeline which will offer facilites on the desk top for some or all of the following:

telephony;
video phone;
interactive CBL;
virtual VCR;
remote learning;
multimedia;
virtual books;
computer-supported cooperative working.

It is clear that the digital arena is going to experience major investment and expansion over the next five years. Information access and provision will follow this. Cable and telephone connections to offices and homes will increasingly offer access to wider ranges of information and new services, including digital libraries, videos, shops, and banks.

REFERENCES

Clark, J. H. (1992). A telecomputer. *ACM SIGGRAPH Computer Graphics*, **26**(2), 19–23.

Cruickshank, D. (1992). Digital Media, *IRIS Universe*, No. 20, 16–21.

Earnshaw, R. A. (1992). Scientific visualization at the University of Leeds, *ACM SIGGRAPH Computer Graphics*, **26**(3), 182–183.

Earnshaw, R. A. (1993a) Communicating with virtual worlds: accessing data, information and knowledge by multimedia technologies. In Magnenat-Thalmann, N. and Thalmann, D. (eds) *Communicating with Virtual Worlds*, pp. 29–40, Springer-Verlag.

Earnshaw, R. A. (1993b). Multimedia, networks, and the electronic publishing press. University of Leeds, Internal Report, November.

Earnshaw, R. A. and Haigh, A. B. (1993). The exploitation of new media for text, graphics, images and sound. AGOCG Technical Report No 23, October.

Earnshaw, R. A., Gigante, M. A. and Jones, H. (eds) *Virtual Reality Systems*. Academic Press.

HEFCE (1993). *Joint Funding Councils' Libraries Review Group Report*. External Relations, HEFCE, Northavon House, Coldharbor Lane, Bristol BS16 1QD, UK.

JISC/AGOCG (1993). Multimedia in higher education: portability and networking. JISC/AGOCG Report.

Obraczka, K., Danzig, P. B. and Li, S. (1993). Internet resource discovery service. *IEEE Computer*, **26**(9), 8–22.

About the author

Rae Earnshaw is Head of Computer Graphics at the University of Leeds, with interests in graphics algorithms, scientific visualization, display technology, CAD/CAM, and human-computer interface issues. He has been a Visiting Professor at Illinois Institute of Technology, Chicago, USA, Northwestern Polytechnical University, China, and George Washington University, Washington DC, USA. He was a Director of the NATO Advanced Study Institute on "Fundamental Algorithms for Computer Graphics" held in Ilkley, England, in 1985, a Co-Chair of the BCS/ACM International Summer Institute on "State of the Art in Computer Graphics" held in Scotland in 1986, and a Director of of the NATO Advanced Study Institute on "Theoretical Foundations of Computer Graphics and CAD" held in Italy in 1987. He is a member of ACM, IEEE, CGS, EG, and a Fellow of the British Computer Society. Dr Earnshaw has written and edited 17 books on graphics algorithms, computer graphics, and associated topics, and published 60 papers in these areas. He Chairs the Scientific Visualization Group at the University of Leeds, is a member of the Editorial Board of *The Visual Computer*, a Committee Member of the board of the Computer Graphics Society, and Chair of the British Computer Society Computer Graphics and Displays Group.

10 Multimedia in education

Colin Beardon and Suzette Worden

10.1. INTRODUCTION

This chapter is concerned with the use of multimedia in higher education and, more particularly, the development of new multimedia interfaces for this environment. This has been undertaken as an example of collaborative design, based upon the Scandinavian model of work-oriented design (Ehn, 1988), in which a computer specialist and a design historian worked together to develop software that fits naturally into a particular work environment. Developing educational multimedia differs from corporate, product-oriented research and development. Apart from obvious funding differences, it has different objectives. For example, whereas it may be of prime concern to a commercial developer that a system be user-friendly, there may be limits to this concept within an educational setting that aims to make students confront issues and think for themselves. Education is not only about ready access to off-the-shelf information, it is also about the development of a critical awareness and the ability to transform what one is given into something more meaningful.[1]

There is a need to recognize the increasing diversity of backgrounds of students entering higher education, who bring with them specific cultural values. The move towards student-centred learning implies an openness that enables students to enhance and share their heritage with other students and teachers. If students are to be active and develop discriminatory powers, an understanding of the social construction of knowledge and representations is crucial.

Given such developments, how should we approach contemporary multimedia applications? We have to place ourselves outside existing multimedia productions and review their qualities in terms of our own aims.[2] Multimedia needs the critical consumer and our work involves a

---

[1]This implies a deep rather than a surface approach to learning. The deep approach consists of understanding the material for oneself; interacting vigorously and critically with content and relating ideas to previous knowledge/experience. With the surface approach the intention is to reproduce parts of the content; accept ideas and information passively; memorize facts and procedures routinely (The Committee of Scottish University Principals, 1992, p. 5).

[2]Edward Said has identified "strategic location" which defines the location of the author in relation to the material about which she writes; and "strategic formation" which defines how texts acquire mass density and referential power among themselves and in wider cultural contexts.

critical review and evaluation of what is available. The relationship between the activity undertaken with the computer and activities in the social world must be continually reassessed as a contribution to the process of further development. The products and processes involved must be examined as artefacts and texts that are both a reflection of social activities and an influence upon them.

Our own review of material identified several metaphors for the organization of information. The encyclopaedia metaphor is very common, combining a factual database with structures giving multiple points of entry and associations of information. Magazine and book-related structures allow the development of localized styles more appropriate to the material. Less common, though we believe a particularly rich form, is the autobiographical narrative. The museum metaphor is one of the more complex, providing more radical possibilities as it suggests a richer mix of opposites: library and gallery; storage and retrieval; organization and dissemination; creativity and passivity; past and present.

Part of our research project involves teaching groups of students taking the second year of the BA in Design History at the University of Brighton. These students were asked to evaluate various multimedia systems and their response was not one of immediate acceptance. The relationship of form and content was questioned because the ability to read information from the means of delivery did not seem "natural". What was "fact", what was "opinion"? Technical expectations were high, so disappointment quickly set in if delivery was not reliable. Critical reflection was most useful when multimedia was seen in contrast to other traditional forms of reception and production of information. The value of the essay or seminar could be compared to a multimedia presentation and the particular values of each more fully appreciated. The students were also required to use HyperCard as a creative tool, and the new organizational rules that are central to the medium had to be discovered and implemented by the students. The structures they developed ranged from simple hierarchical catalogues, to non-linear explorations of particular topics, to the creation of a virtual world about the medium itself. Some students deliberately incorporated an opportunity for the user to add text to what the author provided, while others provided assistance to first-time users.

Initially, the richest and most satisfying examples appeared to be those that offered ease of use, well-chosen graphics and smooth navigation. Increasingly, as confidence grew, interactivity and authorship became more highly valued. This led us to focus our attention on some of the key issues in multimedia and to ask what specific opportunities it has to offer within an educational system that still espouses the principles of a liberal education.

10.2.   SOME EXPERIMENTAL SYSTEMS

The research programme with which we are involved has three elements. As indicated above, it combines a theoretical analysis of multimedia and education with the experience of teaching a multimedia course to groups of students. It also involves us putting our own ideas into practice and developing prototype systems that explore the ideas that emerge from this practice. We see these systems as important in bridging the gap between theory and practice, for they force our theory to have a practical edge without being overly restricted by the current features of multimedia systems. The systems are not aimed at particular practical uses but are to be seen both as "texts" whose design is open for discussion, and the source of practical ideas for radically different systems in the future.

10.2.1. CD-Icon

It is a problem to make sense in a world that is very complex. We wished to explore the question of whether we could use the fragmented graphical images that appear upon our screen in a way that communicates our thoughts or intentions to others. In a sense, the desktop metaphor does this with its language of clicking and dragging icons around the screen, but this is too restricted. We envisage a system in which intuitions and conventions combine to enable us to use the objects on the screen to say things: make statements, ask questions, state our wishes, arrange meetings, speculate about the future, and even tell jokes.

Within most multimedia systems there are two languages: the language of the subject matter, and an interface language that enables navigation. When using such systems one soon learns that a large arrow in the bottom right corner of the screen is not part of the subject-specific message, but is an interface symbol for going to the next piece of information. This design solution raises several questions: is the user always aware of the difference? is there always a clear distinction between the two languages? is the interface language sophisticated enough to allow the user to exercise any degree of initiative? For some researchers, the conspicuous interface is a problem,

. . . an interface is an obstacle: it stands between a person and the system being used (Norman, 1990, p. 216).

We developed a prototype system, called CD-Icon, which explored the use of text and image in a new form of iconic language (Beardon, 1992, 1993). Most iconic languages to date have been closed formal languages (e.g. programming languages), but CD-Icon set out to explore the possibilities of a general purpose graphical language. The first version used 32×32-bit icons and, by layout and animation, tried to enable users to both read and write messages without using words. Being text independent, its messages do not require translation into different natural languages. We are currently enhancing the system to enable it to use any graphical object where we currently use an icon.

The structure of messages in CD-Icon is based upon Schank's Conceptual Dependency (CD) representation (Schank, 1973). Schank held that underlying all natural language utterances there are messages that can be unambiguously represented in CD. At the lowest level are simple concepts which refer directly to objects and properties in the world. In Schank's work he represented these by words (e.g. "man", "car", "black"). In CD-Icon we represent them by icons from a scrapbook, as in Figure 10.1. If the reference is not clear, an icon can be interrogated, in which case an animated picture dictionary is accessed giving an explanation of its meaning. When we come to compose messages these icons are selected and pasted into the message.

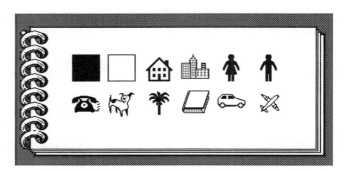

Figure 10.1.   Twelve icons in a scrapbook (representing *black, white, house, city, woman, man, telephone, dog, tree, book, car, aeroplane*).

These simple concepts are composed into structures that refer to objects (e.g. "John's black car"). An object is represented in CD-Icon by a window that shows an icon for the head term and icons for its qualifiers. As "John" refers to an object we would first create a structure for a male person with the name "John" (proper names are the only place where text is allowed). We would then create a second structure for the car, indicating that it is black in colour and is owned by the object we had just created (see Figure 10.2). There is a direct link between the man within the car description and the object window describing John. By such means it is possible to create static units that act as descriptive phrases referring to particular things.

Objects participate in events (e.g. "John drove his black car to London") which can have tenses applied to them. It is in the handling of events where Schank is at his most radical. All the verbs of natural language are reduced to a set of 14 primitive ACTs with associated case structures. For example, "John went to London" is represented in CD by an event of type

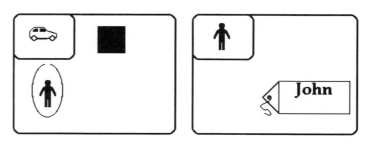

Figure 10.2.   Object windows: (*left*) a black car owned by a man; (*right*) a man named John.

PTRANS (physical transfer), with John as the AGENT and OBJECT, and London as the DESTINATION. In CD-Icon we use the head icon to stand for an object and exploit animation to help us convey meaning. Events are first shown as an animation in which the event is played out (e.g. for an ACT of type PTRANS, the object moves from one location to another across the screen). When this has been completed, the static window is available for interrogation (see Figure 10.3).

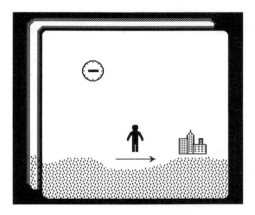

Figure 10.3.   An event window which superficially says that a man went to a city. Icons can be interrogated to find out which man and which city. The third icon represents past tense. The hidden window shows how the event was carried out (e.g. by car).

Within CD, events can be combined by logical and temporal relations into more complex messages (e.g. "When John drove his black car to London, it broke down"). There is a predefined set of such relations and each is given a unique icon (which can also be interrogated to see an explanation of its meaning). A complex message is shown in Figure 10.4 where icons representing two different events are linked by an icon representing the conceptual relation "at-the-same-time".

The system is written in HyperCard and, though it has limitations, it is possible for users to write messages and for untrained users to interpret them more or less correctly. The most complex message successfully communicated so far is, "When John went to the big house, how did Mary take her black and white dog there?".

If the system is to develop we must escape from the world of John, Mary and their various domestic arrangements, and be able to request that all information that is to do with John be copied and placed in a new

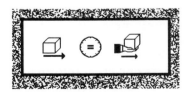

Figure 10.4.   A complex message indicating that a physical transfer took place at the same time as somebody moving something.

folder. Before we get to this point, there are one or two problems to be overcome. While CD-Icon is relatively straightforward and successful when handling physical concepts, it becomes much more stylized and problematic when dealing with mental and abstract concepts, and with chains of events.

This is not completely unexpected. Alan Kay argues that human cognitive facilities are made up of, at least:

a *doing* or *enactive* mentality, which is best suited to orientation and manipulation and utilizes devices such as the mouse;

an *image* or *iconic* mentality, which is best suited to dealing with concrete objects and to tasks of recognition, comparison and configuration and utilizes icons and windows;

a *symbolic* mentality, which is best suited to dealing with abstract objects and long chains of reasoning.

Kay concludes that "no single mentality offers a complete answer to the entire range of thinking and solving" (Kay, 1990, p.197).

Kay's analysis strengthens our belief in the value of a multiple modality language, utilizing user actions, icons and windows in a way similar to that described. The limitations of CD-Icon are concerned with its clumsiness with those aspects of language that Kay argues are better served by symbolic systems. This may be true but we feel that the occasions when people wish to convey formal or abstract information are fairly rare and that many of the problems encountered in CD-Icon concern the rhetorical, discourse or narrative structure of the message rather than its formal or logical structure. We are already planning further enhancements in which an entire message would be displayed as a developing animation while still incorporating the interrogation of objects as described above.

Experience of creating messages in CD-Icon suggests that, though initially messages are conceived in English and then implemented in iconic form, very quickly the medium is used in its own right without comparison. This led to the observation that the meaning of the messages exists in its clearest form in the iconic version and that natural language interpretations are, like all translations, slightly lacking. Whilst the meanings thus generated may not be as precise as natural language statements, the juxtaposition of images creates a richer field of meaning which, we believe, deserves further exploration.

10.2.2.   The Virtual Curator

We use multimedia in the teaching of the history of art and design, a subject for which the museum metaphor is particularly relevant. The museum is both the source of much information and interpretation and a place where finished work can be displayed. For some, the computer serves primarily as a database of factual information about the objects in the museum (Arts Council, 1992). For others, multimedia technology can be used to simulate a visit to a museum (Garvey and Wallace, 1992).

The restriction to factual information is becoming increasingly problematic. Scott (1988) shows how difficult it is to provide indisputable textual information for objects of art. Traditionally, secondary sources about a painting would indicate what is represented in the painting but with a work that does not attempt to be directly representational, such as Picasso's Three Musicians, this becomes unclear[3]. Others have argued that any attempt to recreate visual information in textual form is bound to be inadequate (Hogan *et al.*, 1991).

The idea that museum objects have only one authoritative interpretation is also being questioned.

The notion that material objects 'speak for themselves' honestly, a principle that guided museum professionals of a more positivistic cast is definitely obsolete (Hein, 1993, p. 77).

Exhibitions, it is argued, are also to be seen as spaces that use objects "to tell a story", and museums "must learn to listen as well as to speak".

The Oakland Museum takes this on board in a system that aims "to highlight the role individuals play in history" and to "present differing interpretations of the past" (Cooper and Oker, 1990). While accepting the need for multiple viewpoints, the system still distinguishes between the authoritative expert and the passive user. The curator acts as a controller and validator of material within the system and this is embodied in the concept of a "curator's file" which can only be edited by museum staff. There are different interpretations but they are all given by eminent scholars.

Larry Friedlander also realizes the importance of counterbalancing the attempt to recreate authenticity in multimedia. In the plans for the International Shakespeare Globe Centre are a number of technology-supported experiences. Friedlander, while excited by the possibility of "planned authentic recreations" of the Elizabethan period, wishes to supplement these with a more radical approach to multimedia in the museum:

I believed it would be possible to create a museum environment that blurs such categories as exhibit and user, past and present, entertainment and education (Friedlander, 1990, p.119).

He suggests surrounding the central authentic experiences with "islands" of contemporary space where users could play with scale, colour and texture.

The concept of the virtual museum has been developed by several authors (Garvey and Wallace, 1992; Hoptman, 1992; Tsichritzis and Gibbs, 1991). It is an attempt to recreate, in electronic form, not just the contents of a museum, but also the institution of the museum. It attempts to recreate the aura of the object, the ordering imposed by the physical layout, the prestige of the public gallery and the authority of the information presented. Technically brilliant, it fails to address the central issue of education – how students can critically analyse material and transform it into something new. To do this the student must become an interactive author, but at present she has to make a leap from using minimally interactive CD-ROMs to becoming competent in at least six distinct general purpose software tools for multimedia production. This is not only very time consuming but, because there is no subject-specific context, is seen as a digression from the main themes of her education.

In a deliberate attempt to pose an alternative to the concept of the virtual museum, we developed authoring software which we call the Virtual Curator. It is also built around the metaphor of a museum, but this museum has no objects on display. The user is put in the position of a curator with a store room of objects which needs to be explored, and the objects examined and understood (see Figure 10.5).

Facilities are available so that more objects (e.g. scanned images, sound or video recordings) can be added and text-based links made between objects. The task is to mount an exhibition on either a given theme or one chosen by the students. Objects can be copied from the store, assembled into groups (e.g. a poster, or a display cabinet) and arranged within a virtual exhibition space (see Figures 10.6 and 10.7).

The Virtual Curator represents a clear alternative to the current line of multimedia development. Objects do not try to "honestly speak for themselves" but are puzzles, to be explored and appropriated by the user and transformed into the elements of a new composition. The student has to be sensitive to the process of creating history and criticism, as well as to work towards a finished product dependent on technical and manupulative skills. The system has an underlying human activity that is difficult for students to perform in the real world, yet can be meaningfully transposed onto a computer. People using the system are aware at all times that they are dealing with representations and not real objects.

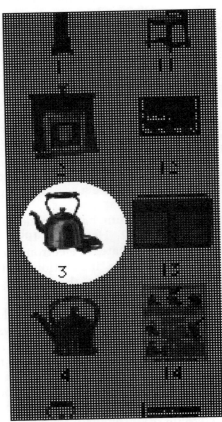

Figure 10.5.   Objects in the store of the Virtual Curator.

Figure 10.6. A poster assembled in the Virtual Curator.

Figure 10.7. An exhibition constructed in the Virtual Curator.

Meaning and understanding are constructed by author and reader (i.e. student and tutor) in an act of human–human communication. The Virtual Curator does not aim to replace the tutor in education, but rather to provide a context within which students can work on realistic complex tasks which give rise to directed and constructive discussion. It is such objectives which, we believe, should guide the development of multimedia systems for serious educational use.

10.2.3. Other systems

One of the major challenges to educational multimedia is the reality of living in a multicultural, pluralist world. CD-Icon goes some way to addressing the issue of multilingualism, but it does not address the issue of multiculturalism. The Virtual Curator provides the environment for users to speak for themselves, but says little about how they should do so. We are concerned that approaches to multimedia based upon the concept of a single factual database enforce the description of the world from one perspective and that such an approach fails to initiate processes of understanding. In a project entitled "Maori-Pakeha" we are exploring the complex question of how people from a white European cultural background can approach and gain some understanding of objects created within a different culture, in this case that of New Zealand Maoris.

The project raises many important issues. For example, the "ownership" of images has different meaning in the two cultures. For Europeans, the reproduction of an image is negotiated as an economic transaction with its legal owner. For Maoris, an image can be a sacred object and, some believed, reproduction of the object reduces the stature of the person depicted. Furthermore, as they are cultural and sacred objects, some images can only be used if certain customs are observed.

In real life there are two ways to approach artefacts from a very different culture. Superficially, one can simply appropriate them into one's own culture and see them simply as aesthetically pleasing objects. Alternatively one can try to understand the culture from which they emerged. In trying to build a multimedia system from this latter perspective, we have found that the issue of user-control needs careful planning. In most multimedia systems the user is given maximum freedom to roam around the material, but very little freedom to interact meaningfully with it. In the system we are developing, simply giving the user freedom to roam around material is not always appropriate. We want to simulate the experience of confronting a different culture and understanding something about it from its own perspective. As in real life, the user has to listen, watch and come to respect a different culture that seems at first alien. Within the system the user is at first given very little degree of freedom to navigate. As he or she builds up experiences, so the degree of freedom offered by the system increases.

History is often as distant as other cultures. In another project on Modernist carpet design we are exploring the issues of making history rather than consuming "facts". The presentation of specific historical subjects should suggest to the user that they are experiencing contexts and clusters of information that have a coherence that is historically specific. The historical specificity is the product of the act of writing history, the act of authorship: the objects do not speak for themselves. Clusters of information make more sense than isolated facts, and objects or representations have multiple meanings. The constructed nature of the argument should be visible. The material must be presented in a way that suggests its "pre-virtual" state. If this is achieved then the ability to integrate images and texts in a multimedia environment will emerge as a constructive device.

For example, in this project a photograph of a showroom in a factory is collaged with carpet illustrations from trade catalogues (Figure 10.8). These illustrations have been reconstructed in perspective and can be interrogated visually in the showroom. They can also be seen as part of a

Figure 10.8.   Layout for carpet project.

series in the reproductions of the pages of the trade catalogue. The image of the showroom brings together several stories and can be the starting point for several divergent themes, both before and after this episode in the history of the carpet's production and its consumption. It is possible to move to the trade catalogue or to contemporary illustrations of the factory.

10.3.   CONCEPTUAL ISSUES

The term "multimedia" is unfortunate because the technical phenomenon of multiple media is not new. Thirty years ago we spoke of magnetic tape and magnetic discs as two different "media" for the mass storage of data, and it is the same usage that led to the term "multimedia". Technically, we have new input and output devices that handle images, sounds, video, force feedback, etc., but this is not a new idea in itself, and it would be better if we referred to these as different modalities of expression. What are new, and do deserve a new name, are devices that we relate to directly through our senses, rather than indirectly through symbolic text. When computer output was entirely in terms of the ASCII character set, understanding that output only required knowledge of the formal structures within which various pieces of information appeared. One could recognize the printed output as a sales report (or as an invoice, a payslip or a core dump) and provided that one knew the structural rules for the format one could derive meaning from what was presented. The feintness of the print, the tone of the paper and the speed at which the output was produced, were all irrelevant to the meaning of the product.

The present-day multimedia computer can no longer be seen solely as a symbol processing machine but as one that deals directly with the stuff of experience–sight, sound, touch, motion. This has enormous implications, not least of which is the greater opportunity to affect meaning. The information content of the output is much higher, attention must be paid to connotations as well and denotations, and the speed of delivery is integral to the product. We can no longer read computer output as a set of formal symbols arranged according to a precise syntax, but rather as a field of signifiers constantly changing in real-time. To comprehend the meaning of such an artefact we need something more powerful than formal systems, we need an enhanced science of signs, or semiotics (Andersen, 1990).

Multimedia systems' design requires a paradigm shift in our conception of what a computer is and how it relates to a world of active human beings. We are concerned that thinking about multimedia is dominated by concepts that have arisen from contributing technologies, whereas what is needed is a set of user-driven concepts. The real challenge of multimedia is to subvert its very name; it is to integrate different modalities of input and output and to create a single medium of expression.

10.3.1. Text and Image

To anyone brought up in the computing tradition, the first difference between text and image is one of representation: text is anything represented in the ASCII character set, whereas images are held in TIFF or PICT. Secondly, they are different because we process them differently: we can click with the cursor placed between letters of text and add a space, whereas we cannot within the same software click between pixels and add a blank pixel. Thirdly, we believe that the meaning of text is constructed from the elements of the text (letters, morphemes or phonemes), whereas the meaning of a picture is either derived automatically using feature recognition or neural network techniques or, more usually, is left to the user.

We are not the first to question whether this rigid distinction has outlived its usefulness (see Hogan *et al.*, 1991, p. 217). Typographers and graphic designers have long recognised the importance of the visual appearance of text, while many images can be read according to a syntax and a semantics that is just as precise as any natural language.

Not only are texts read as images and images read as texts, but we find situations where the combination of text and image creates something greater than the sum of the parts. A prime example of this is found in collage where images are reused to create new meanings or where images and other media are put together so that the content opens for the viewer to create "their" final meaning.

In some contexts it is important to break cultural codes through ways of combining image and text. From a feminist perspective, combinations of text and image have presented a way forward for women artists to represent themselves. Although some women artists have found ways of using images of themselves, or other women, to explore the "feminine" and gender issues, others wish to break with the way meaning is given to the female body through the male gaze (Mulvey, 1988, p. 62). The artist Mary Kelly works in a way that creates

a text working its materials to produce meanings, not merely to picture already formed meanings (Pollock, 1988, p.171).

In "Corpus" she combines various media and text, creating an open structure of several intersecting narratives and signifying systems (Figure 10.9). It is up to the spectator to create meaning from experiencing this work.

Our work on CD-Icon in particular indicates that it is worth exploring what is textual in images and was is visual in text. In the Virtual Curator we push this further, and begin to challenge the closed, formal meaning systems that have grown up around computing systems, and ask whether it is not time for an exploration of more openness.

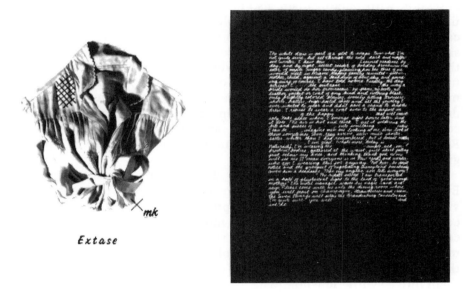

Extase

Figure 10.9.   Mary Kelly Interim (1984–   ) Part 1: Corpus, detail of Extase.

10.3.2. Virtuality

The concept of *virtuality* is central to our thinking about multimedia. Virtuality has two aspects: we must believe that what we experience is real, but we must also secretly know that it is not. Ted Nelson makes this clear:

The virtuality of a thing is what it seems to be, rather than its reality, the technical or physical underpinnings on which it rests (Nelson, 1990, p. 239).

Many multimedia systems strive for what has been described as a "believable magic", or what Alan Kay calls "user illusion" (Kay, 1990, p.199). The idea of virtuality means that we, the designers, create a believable world inside the machine and that users will enter that world, experience it and somehow meet the objectives we have set for the system as a whole.

Much of our thinking about virtuality is based upon the desire to use the technological means we have. In virtual reality, it is through the power of photorealistic images and a seamless means of interaction that we seek to overpower the senses and force the subject to believe in the world that we have created. While such experiences may be relevant in certain areas of training, we seriously doubt the relevance of this model for multimedia in education, the point of which is to end up wiser about this world.

It is not difficult to see how this happened. The construction of photo-realistic images is largely a question of geometry, and computers are excellent at handling large amounts of mathematics. The industry is naturally interested in exploiting this capability to the full, but the resulting obsession with photorealism also has a cultural meaning. It requires a fixed viewpoint from which the whole scene is viewed and the significance of all objects (their position on the plane, their orientation, their size, the extent to which they are hidden) is determined by the location of this single viewpoint. Objects are not displayed according to a conceptual understanding of their construction or significance, which is why for many diagrammatic purposes photorealism is inappropriate. In technical drawing, for example, we use orthographic projections, while in maps we combine abstractions (e.g. contours) and symbols (e.g. for a church). Reading such images can yield information superior to that in a photograph.

In art, particularly following the development of photography in Europe in the 1830s, there have been many attempts to use different visual codes (Benjamin, 1968). The Impressionists, for example, were concerned less with subject matter and more with the effect of light and colour, the result being to reduce the significance of space and present a relatively flat image. The Cubists broke from the single point perspective, showing many different aspects of the same object but combining them into a synthetic whole. The Vorticists and Constructivists tried to represent temporal aspects of an object within one single image. One commentator has said of this period that there was a

complete dismissal of the convention that the picture surface should appear to the viewer like a window pane through which he looks into an illusory space (Lynton, 1980, p. 64).

Nelson and Kay argue that we should see the computer as a virtual world in which we act. The act of communication takes place between the user and the world inside the machine. Within the same context, Brenda Laurel has provided a new approach to multimedia application design with her invitation to see the computer as theatre (Laurel, 1990). She does, however, adopt an aesthetics that is consistent with her view that the computer contains a virtual world. She adopts an Aristotelian view of drama which sees it as mimesis (the imitation of action) through which the audience empathizes with the characters and are purged via the emotions of pity and fear in the process of catharsis. This theatre, and for Laurel the use of computer systems, is not a critical exercise but one in which the audience willingly suspends belief in order to be healed and strengthened.

The German dramatist Bertholt Brecht was directly opposed to the idea that drama provided cathartic illusion and wanted the theatre to be an experience that enabled users to better understand and act in the real world.

> Where the realist theatre relying on illusion actually invites the spectator's gaze and encourages him to read the proffered text naively, as a mirror-image of a pre-existing world, the self-referential theatricality of Brecht's theatre, with its constant reminders of the illusory and hence changeable nature of the world, produces an engagement with the theatrical in life (Wright, 1989, p. 56).

Brecht developed several techniques to achieve this. Events were to be represented in as ordinary a manner as possible so that the audience feels instantly at home (the *gesture*). The text is fragmented into a number of discrete episodes that are interrupted and do not form a continuous unbroken narrative. The stage is designed in such a way that it is not naturalistic (sometimes no curtain is used). Brecht's ideas centre around two key concepts: *Verfrumdung*, which can be translated as "distancia-tion" or "estrangement", refers to the distance that is deliberately cre-ated between the audience and the play so that the audience is aware that it is watching a play; and *Lehrstücke*, which can be translated as "learning or teaching plays", refers to the fact that the audience and the actors are involved in a learning situation and come to understand things about real life. Through not totally successful (maintaining a balance between familiarity and estrangement does not always work) Brecht's idea of didactic theatre raises important ideas for educational multime-dia software that the cathartic virtuality currently in vogue appears to ignore.

In some respects the more successful aspects of multimedia systems do reflect Brechtian ideas. Brecht used collage and montage in order to create distance, so that the act of understanding involved action by the audi-ence. Multimedia systems that use different modalities to approach an object from different directions, create spaces between the different modalities in which the viewer must exercise their own understanding.

10.3.3. Interactivity and Authorship

To computer scientists, interactivity is defined technically as a user-driven interrupt to the system. Every time a user moves a mouse, types a key or speaks into a microphone, a message is sent to the processor, and the user has interacted with the system. From a technical point of view this is well understood, but from the designer's point of view there are so many different types of activity that end up as interrupts that the simple label "interactive" lacks precision. Hence we get "interactive" HyperCard stacks that make the single demand upon the user to click on a right-pointing arrow to go to the next card. Interactivity needs a richer analysis which we resolve by asking whether the user is an author who is able to create something that was not there before.

In both CD-Icon and the Virtual Curator we sought to give the user the right to be the author but we are aware that the empowerment of users is not simply a matter of giving access to an authoring system. The form of the language within which people are allowed to express themselves also controls what they can say. Different languages allow different degrees of closure or openness. Highly formal languages, such as first-order predicate logic, attempt to establish complete closure between syntactic form and meaning content, to the point where one can be systematically derived from the other. Natural languages, it is now recognized, are different in that they are naturally evolving phenomena with inbuilt ambiguities and vagueness, some of which we need in order to express our emotions, tell jokes, be innovative, be evasive and choose our degree of precision.

A similar argument can be provided for visual codes, from the highly controlled meanings derivable from technical drawings and maps, through the more ambiguous photographs, to the more open meanings that can be expressed in works of art. What is noticeable is that the more closed the meaning system, the narrower the bandwidth needed by the language – formal logic can be expressed in highly compressed form and technical drawings can be expressed in terms of a few graphics primitives. The advent of multimedia, which if nothing else means much greater bandwidths, means that we have the opportunity to use less closed meaning systems. More than this, the wider the bandwidth that is used the less possible it is to control the meaning.

What this suggests is that a strict dichotomy between the user as author and the author as consumer of products is not a helpful one. If we think in terms of multimedia development environments and authored multimedia products then we find that the immediacy of the authoring environment is taken as a model for the qualities considered desirable in the product. Multimedia is considered successful if it is experiential, tactile, immediate, has directed narrative qualities and provides interactivity. The values from the implementation system are expected to be mirrored in the final product.

In contrast to this, *hypermedia* is described as virtual, with meaning only coming from the interpretative acts of the user:

> . . .hypermedia without users are as dead as print media without readers or movies without viewers. Without such an interpretation they are simply galleries of wisdom without visitors (Jonassen & Mandl, 1990, p. xix).

The concept of hypermedia suggests interaction through pathways, access structures and chains of association. There is, however, a tension, even a contradiction, within hypermedia between the attempt to provide freedom of access and equality of status to all information, and the methods provided by developers for users to retrieve information. If you want to say something you cannot avoid taking control and cutting out options and the concept of hypermedia seems to avoid this issue. The real question is not whether you exercise control, but quite where and how you do so to encourage other participants to develop.

In our own work we are finding the distinction between authorship and product to be a distraction. CD-Icon is an authoring system but we have discussed it here as a text. Messages can be created in it, read by other people in their own way and then taken over and added to or amended. The Virtual Curator is an authoring system but it says something about design history. It attempts to create messages that are not closed but need to be actively understood, perhaps in the context of person-to-person discussions. In Maori-Pakeha the issue of control is negotiated between the developer and the user in order that certain objectives are paramount. In all these cases the issue of control requires careful articulation rather than blanket categorization.

10.4. CONCLUSIONS

This chapter contains a double message. On the one level we provide an example of collaborative design as applied to multimedia educational products. This approach requires the technologist to work alongside the subject specialist and pay particular attention to their "professional language". It is this that should be reflected in the finished product if it is to fit naturally and usefully into the working environment. We have done so within the specific context of design history or, to be more precise, design history education. We would be wary about drawing too many general conclusions from this work, as every area requires a unique study if we are to develop the best systems. Some of the issues, however, do apply more generally to education particularly in the arts, humanities and social sciences.

At a second level we have set out to review multimedia critically and to challenge some of its most fundamental ideas, but that does not mean that we doubt its significance or its value. We believe in its potential and our concern is only that, if we wish to pursue social goals such as encouraging participation, making it part of popular culture and achieving new levels of cross-cultural communication, then languages have to be developed in order to create sophisticated meanings. Only if this is done will we be using the technology to its full potential. We do not know where these new languages will finally come from, but we do believe that multimedia developers must look to both professional practices, to understand the particular objectives different groups have and their different work practices, and to all forms of culture where meanings are created and communicated in a manner that utilizes the capacity of the multimedia stations we now envisage.

REFERENCES

Andersen, P. B. (1990). *A Theory of Computer Semiotics*. Cambridge University Press, Cambridge.
Arts Council (1992). *Very Spaghetti*. Arts Council, London.
Beardon, C. (1992). CD-Icon: an iconic language based on conceptual dependency. *Intelligent Tutoring Media*, **3**, 4.
Beardon, C. (1993). Computer-based iconic communication. In Ryan, K. and

Sutcliffe, R. (eds) *AI and Cognitive Science '92*, pp. 263–276. Springer-Verlag, London.

Benjamin, W. (1968). The work of art in the age of mechanical reproduction. In Benjamin, W., *Illuminations*, pp. 219–253 Collins & Fontana, London.

The Committee of Scottish University Principals (CSUP) (1992). *Teaching and Learning in an Expanding Higher Education System*. Edinburgh.

Cooper, D. and Oker, J. (1990). History information stations at the Oakland museum. In *Hypermedia and Interactivity in Museums*, pp. 90–113, Archives and Museum Informatics Technical Report no. 14.

Ehn, P. (1988). *Work-Oriented Design of Computer Artifacts*. Swedish Centre for Working Life, Stockholm.

Friedlander, L. (1990). Electrifying Shakespeare: modern day technology in a renaissance museum. In *Hypermedia and Interactivity in Museums*. pp. 118–125. Archives and Museum Informatics Technical Report no. 14.

Garvey, G. & Wallace, B. (1992). From "Le Musée Imaginaire" to Walls without Museums. *Computer Graphics*, **26** (2), 391–392.

Hein, H. (1993). Review of "Museums and Communities" and "Exhibiting Cultures". *Journal of Aesthetics and Art Criticism*, **51** (1), 75–77.

Hogan, M., Jorgensen, C. & Jorgensen, P. (1991). The visual thesaurus in a hypermedia environment: a preliminary exploration of conceptual issues and applications. In *Hypermedia and Interactivity in Museums*, pp. 202-221. Archives and Museum Informatics Technical Report no. 14.

Hoptman, G. (1992). The Virtual Museum and Related Epistemological Concerns. In: E. Barrett (ed.) *Sociomedia: Multimedia, Hypermedia and the Social Construction of Knowledge*, pp. 141–159. MIT Press, Cambridge, MA.

Jonassen, D.H. & Mandl, H. (1990). *Designing Hypermedia for Learning*. NATO ASI Series, Springer-Verlag, Berlin and Heidelberg.

Kay, A. (1990). User Interface: a Personal View. In Laurel, B. (ed.) *The Art of Human-Computer Interface Design*. pp. 191–207. Addison-Wesley, Reading, MA.

Laurel, B. (1990). *The Computer as Theatre*. Academic Press,

Lynton, N. (1980). *The story of modern art*. Phaidon, Oxford.

Mulvey, L (1988). Visual pleasure and narrative cinema. In Penley, C. (ed.) *Feminism and Film Theory*, pp. 57–79. Routledge, London.

Nelson, T.H. (1990). The right way to think about software design. In Laurel, B. (ed.) *The Art of Human-Computer Interface Design*, pp. 235–243. Addison-Wesley, Reading, MA.

Norman, D. (1990). Why interfaces don't work. In Laurel, B. (ed.) *The Art of Human-Computer Interface Design*,w pp. 209–219. Addison-Wesley, Reading, MA.

Pollock, G. (1988). *Vision and Difference: Feminity, Feminism and the Histories of Art*. Routledge, London.

Schank, R.C. (1973). Identification of conceptualisations underlying natural language. In Schank, R.C. & Colby, M.C. (eds) *Computer Models of Thought and Language*, pp. 187–247. W H Freeman, San Francisco.

Scott, D.W. (1988). Museum data bank research report: the yogi and the registrar. *Library Trends*, **37** (2), 130–141.

Tsichritzis, D. and Gibbs, S. (1991). Virtual museums and virtual realities. In *Hypermedia and Interactivity in Museums*, pp. 17–25. Archives and Museum Informatics Technical Report no. 14.

Wright, E. (1989). *Postmodern Brecht: a Re-presentation*. Routledge, London.

About the authors

Colin Beardon is a Reader in Computer Graphics at the University of Brighton. He obtained his PhD in artificial ingelligence from the University of Essex in 1976 and worked in industry and academia in Australia and New Zealand before returning to the UK in 1987. He currently manages a research centre concerned with the use of multimedia technologies in art and design.

Suzette Worden obtained her PhD in design history in 1980. She has researched historical and cultural aspects of furniture production and early electrical appliances and has also published on the work of women designers and on feminist approaches to technology. For the past three years she has been involved in a collaborative research project evaluating and designing software for use in art and design education.

11 Animated icons and visual help

Claire Dormann and Colin Beardon

11.1. INTRODUCTION

Help systems are traditionally seen as detachable additions to software products, appearing either as a printed book or as on-line text accessed by key words or phrases. As multimedia environments become more sophisticated and the immediacy of the experience of using them increases, users will find that they are more engrossed in using applications and they will not want to leave them to find on-line help or, worse still, leave the machine altogether to go to the bookshelf. Help will have to be an integral part of a product, be accessible naturally from within it and be delivered within the same environment as the application operates. While multimedia may thus place greater demands upon help systems, the exciting new possibilities for expressiveness that it offers provide a richer context for the development of multimedia on-line help systems. No longer restricted to textual explanations, multimedia help can exploit text, drawings, photographs, videos, animation and sound. We conjecture that the future acceptability of much multimedia software will depend upon the sophistication of the on-line help that is offered. This chapter explores the question of how such help systems might look in the future and how we should set about designing them now.

11.2. SUPPORTING THE USER

There are various ways in which support can be provided to users (see Figure 11.1). In a *tutorial* system a new user is introduced to major features of a package by the presentation of special examples rather than in the course of normal use. The advantage of an animated tutorial system in this context is that it gives the user a broad understanding of the functionality of the package in a form that is consistent with the interface language. However, a real beginner often learns a package by discovery: clicking on icons, pulling down menus and generally trying things out; experienced users who have never seen the particular software before, but have experience of using similar packages, will typically require a quick look at the new software and want to focus on novel functions.

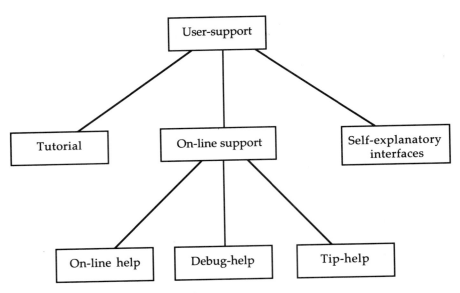

Figure 11.1.   Different types of user support.

In various forms of *on-line support*, specific help is provided to the user in the course of their normal use of the package. We identify three distinct types of on-line support: *on-line help*, *tip-help*, and *debug-help*. The role of on-line help is to provide direct access to particular information that may be new but will often serve to refresh the user's memory; it aims to provide reference information of the sort one might discover in a user's guide or reference manual. It is usually accessed through a specific object, and one expects to receive a limited amount of descriptive information relevant to that object.

Tip-help introduces new information about an object to the user, or shows more complex uses of the object. Most people only use a fraction of the functionality offered by software and always tend to do things in the same manner. For example, within some applications, to copy text from one field to another can be a complex operation (requiring a number of discrete operations such as: select text, copy, go to second field, unlock text, etc.). The same effect might be achieved by a single function invoked by pressing a combination of two keys but a novice user would not realize that this existed and thus would never find it. The purpose of tip-help is to watch for occasions when unnecessarily complex approaches are taken and to intervene with advice on more efficient approaches.

Debug-help aims to help users in situations where there are unexpected outcomes. A possible scenario would be the confusion experienced by a novice user who clicks accidentally in a background window or the desktop when clicking near to the border of the active window. The dramatic changes that can occur can be extremely disorienting, particularly because they happen so quickly. Displaying in slow motion what really happened will help the user understand the cause of this event.

We also include *self-explanatory interfaces* as a third kind of user help, in which the design of the interface itself aims to provide explanatory help to the user; for example, the use of the wristwatch to indicate that it is necessary to wait and to show that the system is still working.

We believe that animation can be used to advantage in all areas of user-support, though in this chapter we are primarily interested in on-line help systems. The approach we propose is to build on-line animated help systems which will be easily accessed, will provide easily understood, pertinent and attractive explanations, and will use different explanations for different kinds of help situation. In order to make the help system attractive and engaging as well as easily understood, the explanation will be provided as a visual animation. In the system we propose there will be no separate help manuals associated with a product. By avoiding the use of text one help system will be sufficient for all users, regardless of the natural languages they know. The animation itself need not be complex and could be based around an average of, say, 15 key frames thus limiting storage requirements.

11.3.   SHORTCOMINGS OF PRESENT HELP SYSTEMS

Many novice users approach a new software product without having received any formal introduction to it or having read any introductory tutorial material. They approach it as they might approach a computer game, trying to learn what it can do simply through a process of exploration. Draper and Barton, in their study of novice Macintosh users learning MacPaint by exploration, report that this is not a particularly efficient way to learn about a product (Draper and Barton, 1993). Even when users have discovered the meaning of a particular command it is not always remembered and it is often revisited several times within a single session before a lasting understanding of its functionality is achieved.

Some of the difficulties experienced with traditional help systems are:

switching between the application and the help system;
finding the appropriate information;
distinguishing relevant from irrelevant material;
understanding the explanation given;
extracting the relevant information.

Being frustrated at not understanding a particular command, the frustration can be compounded by problems using the help system.

By way of example, consider a novice user of HyperCard who may wish to know what the pencil tool (Figure 11.2) represents and what it does.

Figure 11.2.   HyperCard "pencil" tool.

Ideally, of course, such a user will use a tutorial package first, but if they do not then how useful is the help information?

The on-line help system is accessed by selecting "Help" from the "Go" menu which leads to the main menu card of the "HyperCard Help" stack being displayed. This explains the main sections of the stack but, even for more experienced users, does not offer much direction for this particular query.

Selecting "Find topics" users would face an immediate problem in that the help system requires the use of words. To proceed it is necessary to recognize the icon as a pencil before more information can be accessed. Assuming the user enters the term "pencil", he or she will be directed to two related topics. "General tools versus Paint tools" produces a card that explains generally about the painting tools with respect to the tools palette, but gives no information concerning particular tools. The alternative option, "Draw freehand", reveals that drawing with the pencil is one of three ways to draw freehand. Instructions on how to use the pencil tool will be provided, followed by instructions on how to constrain the pencil to a horizontal or vertical path and how to use the pencil to either draw or erase.

Various additional information can be accessed via buttons. "Troubleshooting" indicates what to do if none of the painting tools can be used. "List of tips" gives some general information, only some of which is relevant (e.g. turning Fat Bits on and off) while irrelevant information is also provided (e.g. choosing different patterns). The "Related topics" button gives access to three other cards, none of which contains information directly relevant to the use of the pencil.

The "HyperCard Reference" manual has similar problems to the on-line help system in this situation. Again one has to know that the tool is called a "pencil", and looking this word up in the index points to four pages in the text. The first of these, "Drawing lines and shapes", gives a brief explanation of the effect of using the tool and refers the user to the second page which is mysteriously titled "Drawing in inverse". This page actually provides the clearest explanation of the pencil within the help systems. It describes the effect one might achieve by using the pencil tool, indicates how to use it, explains about the effect of different colours at the starting point, informs how to draw straight lines and states the things that it cannot do as well as those that it can.

This experience suggests that very basic help information of the sort that might be relevant to a real novice user is not easily accessible through the use of the on-line help stack. Users need to know the appropriate word or words to start the process; there is no simple and direct access to the required information, and relevant information is fragmented into different locations while relevant, irrelevant and even misleading information is sometimes placed together. These comments are not a criticism of HyperCard's on-line help system as compared to any other existing product, but rather comments about the viability of this kind of help for novice users learning by exploration. We suggest they would not find it easy to access or simple to use when learning a new application.

11.4.   ANIMATION AND HELP MODELS

Animated help seems a very promising medium but its successful development will require a simple mechanism whereby the user invokes the appropriate help sequence. The help system should be initiated by means of a standard operation on an object. This could be similar to Apple's "Bubble help" in System 7, or by means of a clearly identified action such as holding down a special key while clicking on an object. As we envisage different responses depending upon such things as the sophistication of the user and the operation being performed, simply selecting "help" on an object will not be sufficient. There are various automatic systems that could be explored to determine the precise nature of the help required. For example, user profiles could be used to infer which explanation is most relevant, given the user's familiarity with the system and application, or an analysis of the latest operations performed by the user might give clues as to the nature of the particular problem being faced. However, we believe that users should not be denied a role in selecting the type of help they require, and keys labelled "What?", "Why?", "When?" and "How?" might be introduced. It is clear that this topic will require further investigation once the range of help options is better understood.

Once initiated, a short animation will provide the user with a purely visual explanation relevant to a selected object and the type of problem the user is facing. We believe that different users require different types of support and that different classes of problem can be identified which require different types of explanation.

As we have noted, a particular problem is caused by novice users who, though we might prefer that they use a tutorial system first, inevitably prefer to learn by exploring the package for themselves. From their study of learning by exploration, Draper and Barton distinguish two types of user goal: "experimenting with a command to learn what it does, and looking for the appropriate command to achieve a specific effect" (Draper and Barton, 1993). Sellen and Nicholl extend this classification when they look at user-centred on-line help systems, distinguishing five kinds of problems that lead users to approach a help system (Sellen and Nicholl, 1990).

Goal-oriented: "What kinds of things can I do with this program?"
Descriptive: "What is this? What does it do?"
Procedural: "How do I do this?"
Interpretive: "Why did that happen? What does this mean?"
Navigational: "Where am I?"

Goal-oriented requests relate mostly to tutorial assistance; descriptive and procedural requests relate mostly to on-line help; and interpretive and navigational requests relate mainly to debug-help.

Baecker is interested in all uses of animation that make interfaces more comprehensible (Baecker and Small, 1990) and describes eight possible uses of animation.

Identification: "What is this?"
Transition: "From where have I come, to where have I gone?"

Choice :	"What can I do now?"
Demonstration:	"What can I do with this?"
Explanation:	"How do I do this?"
Feedback:	"What is happening?"
History:	"What have I done?"
Guidance:	"What should I do?"

We can see clearly that Baecker's and Sellen's models complement each other. Animation as history is a navigational type of help; demonstration is a type of descriptive help; explanation is a procedural type of help; and guidance is an interpretative kind of help.

In addition, feedback consists in providing information about the current status of the working environment and tends to take place at the system interface level. For example, if the system is "busy" then, instead of having a single animation such as the rotating watch, an improvement would be to have different animations for different processes that might be taking place. A small printer could be shown with paper passing through it to indicate that the system is waiting for printing to take place (Figure 11.3). Another example is showing a truck with spinning wheels when data is being loaded.

Figure 11.3.   System waiting while printing takes place.

Animation as identification tends to run when the program is being loaded. The interface metaphor can be briefly explained by displaying key elements of the software and relating them to the application metaphor, stressing the important relation between the objects. Thus in the desktop metaphor, the page icon would be related to a sheet of paper and the folder icon to a document wallet. In addition to showing the representational meaning, it must be shown that just as sheets of paper are kept in wallets, so the page icon can be put into the folder icon. As another example, the function of a painting package can be explained by showing an animation of a set of painter's tools, or an animated picture of a person working at a painting (Figure 11.4).

Figure 11.4.   Animated graphic for a paint package.

Other uses of animation include displaying the interface structure and the semantics of the interface. It has been noted that users are often initially confused by the handling functions of icons, e.g. click, double-click, click-and-drag. In a tutorial sequence, these can each be demonstrated by means of a short animation. We can also show such things as how a particular menu is concerned with object manipulation, whereas one set of tools are drawing tools while another are selection tools.

11.5.   ON-LINE ANIMATED HELP

By way of illustration we will demonstrate aspects of an on-line animated user-support system for Macintosh paint packages. Though our primary aim is to develop the on-line help module, we will first describe a short tutorial animation which presents an overview of the set of icon-tools. In most Macintosh paint packages this set consists of both painting and drawing tools and selection tools (Figure 11.5).

The following help animations are designed to address particular user problems with the painting tool set and, particularly, the pencil tool.

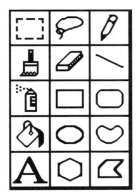

Figure 11.5.   A typical set of Apple Macintosh painting icon-tools.

11.5.1.   "What kinds of things can I do with this program?"

The objective in this type of animation is to identify the program metaphor and the role of each tool within it. We identify the painting and drawing metaphor and explain how the metaphor works with the particular set of tools. As important as showing the metaphorical status of each tool separately, it is important to stress the differences between them.

To address this task an animation is shown in which a person is seen sitting at a drawing board with a piece of paper and a collection of drawing and painting implements in front of them. The person works at a drawing and as each tool is used, or each shape is drawn, so the scene freezes and the relationship between the activity and tool panel is illustrated. Figure 11.6 shows an extract from the animation where the pencil tool is used. The advantage of such an animation is that not only does it show the utilization of each tool in the application context, but it also helps to clarify the intended representation of each icon. For example, it is not always obvious at first glance that the eraser icon refers to an eraser and not a cube. The semantics of the set of icons will also be clarified. A similarity of shape between the rectangle and the dotted rectangle might lead to the erroneous conclusion that they are both drawing tools, whereas the latter is in fact a selection tool.

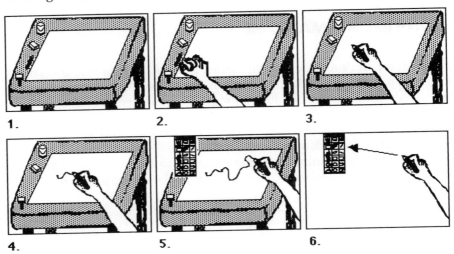

Figure 11.6. Keyframes in an animation to explain the role of the pencil within the drawing metaphor.

11.5.2. "What is this?"

The objective in this type of help-animation is simple identification: to enable recognition of a particular icon in terms of the real world object to which it refers. To address this type of help problem, one or more pictures of a pencil could be shown as in Figure 11.7. In a simple case such as this, one image is probably sufficient. It is perhaps easy to underrate this type of help but with more complex examples such as a regular polygon or a lasso there is not only a greater need, but also more complex explanations will be required.

Figure 11.7. Identification of the pencil icon.

11.5.3. "What does it do?"

The objective in this type of help-animation is to explain the typical use of the tool within the application. Each animation starts with displaying the icon and ends with displaying the icon. In some cases the animation could fit within the icon frame, but in our system all animations are shown in a small help window. As opposed to the animation in Figure 11.5 which explained the tool in terms of the real-world metaphor, this animation will show the relevant actions within the computer-world (Figure 11.8).

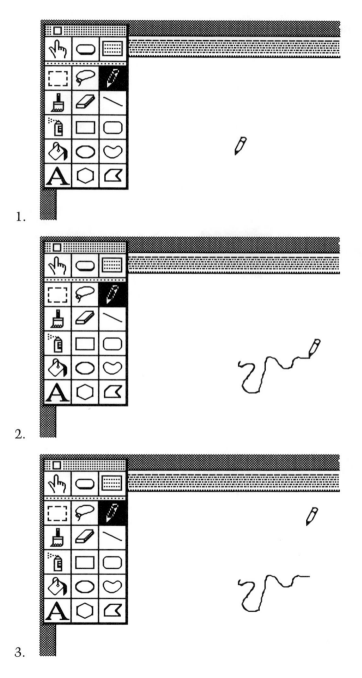

Figure 11.8.   What the pencil does in the computer-world.

11.5.4.   "Why did that happen? What does this mean?"

The objective in this type of help-animation is to explain what may appear to the user to be exceptional behaviour. For example, the pencil has initially been explained as a device that draws a black line on a white background but eventually the user will discover that the pencil may sometimes draw a white line, or it may appear to be erasing. The animation in Figure 11.9 explains the effect of the starting pixel.

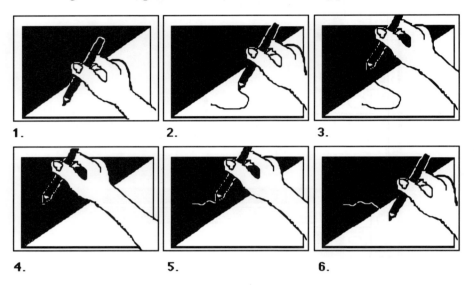

Figure 11.9.   Key frames in an animation to explain the effect of the colour on which the pencil starts.

11.6.   ISSUES IN THE DESIGN OF ANIMATED HELP

The examples to date have been based upon what is probably the simplest tool to explain. When approaching other tools in the set we face more complex problems of visual explanation. Consider a slightly more complex example: the sprinkler (Figure 11.10).

The on-line help animation starts with the selection of the sprinkler, followed by the effect produced by this tool using plain black ink. The question is raised whether the animation should be stopped at this point. Baecker, Small and Mander's experimental evidence suggests that

Figure 11.10.   The sprinkler icon.

animated icons improve user performance, and we therefore believe it preferable to include the total range of effects that can be obtained with a tool somewhere in the help animation (Baecker *et al.*, 1991). In this example, different sprinkler options produce different designs so the animation could continue with the selection from the sprinklers's menu of a different sprinkler showing the result obtained when using it. A few other options are also shown without repeating the menu selection sequence, which would become boring and distract from the main purpose.

There are other elements which we could introduce into this animation, most notably the colour of the ink and the pattern. As these affect the behaviour of most of the painting and drawing tools, and as animations are to be developed for each tool, these parts of the animation would have to be repeated many times at the global level. The essential problem here is that all paint packages are based on an underlying graphic definition language (GDL) which has functional attributes, such as linewidth, fillpattern and pencolor, which are applicable to many drawing and painting operations. While some packages represent these as menu items others represent them as explicit icons. Thus it might be better to accept three types of icon tool: drawing, selection and attribute, and to ensure that cross-reference is made whenever appropriate, rather than to continue with the view that attributes are not tools.

The "lasso" tool is a particularly complex tool to explain visually. For those unfamiliar with its operation, it is used to select areas of the screen for further operations such as "copy" or "invert". It is primarily used to select one or more irregularly-shaped objects for which the selection rectangle (the dotted rectangle in Figure 11.2) is inappropriate. Having chosen the lasso tool, the cursor will allow a freehand shape to be drawn around all the objects to be selected, and will then "shrink" that shape to ignore any white space, stopping only when it comes upon a non-white pixel. The metaphor of the lasso is surprisingly relevant: it is like casting a lasso onto the drawing board and tightening around a particular object which is then "captured" for further work.

Though the metaphor is appropriate in isolation, it is completely at odds with the prevailing metaphor of drawing and painting at a drawing board. To introduce it into a tutorial sequence, such as Figure 11.6, will require special techniques to overcome the obvious shift of metaphor. It is most likely that humour is the best approach, with the animation showing a cowboy lassoing an object in the drawing and dragging it away. Having identified the lasso in terms of the general world metaphor, there is still the task of explaining what it does. Again humour may be the best approach, appealing to some other agent which shrinks around objects, such as a boa constrictor snake (see Figure 11.12). Explaining selection tools in general is difficult because they have no effect on a drawing but merely set the scene for a large number of other tools. Thus there is a need to explain the concept of selection first and then to explain the set of selection tools. In the case of HyperCard there are only two selection tools (the lasso and the dotted rectangle) and it is necessary to stress the difference between them.

Whilst we can imagine specific solutions to some more complex cases, we do not envisage that all animations will be individually crafted.

Techniques need to be developed to enable the efficient production of animations that reliably communicate to their intended audience. If possible, these techniques should build upon the better explanations currently developed by technical writers, not least because these are the people whose working practices would be most affected by such a development as animated user-support systems. If they cannot adapt their working processes to produce them, then there is little chance of their being commercially accepted. Having argued for techniques, we do not want to over-regiment the design process so that one of the major advantages of animation, its ability to engage the user in a light-hearted way, is lost in a purely functional design.

We can adopt a more systematic approach to the design of animated help by borrowing from the world of animation design. We adopt a technique whereby to realize an animation of, say, a running man a film is shot of the desired action. Key frames of the sequence are traced directly from the film and the resulting frames are linked to produce an animation. A similar method could be adopted for animated help which consists in filming a user performing a sequence of actions in which a particular icon is used. The problem with such an approach is that it would be necessary to alternate between hand movements and the screen, and this would become too repetitive and cumbersome. An equivalent computer technique has therefore been adopted: the *snapshot* technique in which a digital "snapshot" is taken of every change in the computer environment during a sequence of actions when someone is using a specific tool. It has to be noted at this point that some judgement has to be exercised concerning the selection of key frames in the sequence. Also, within the snapshot approach the mouse movements and handling functions that lead up to a change in the environment are not represented. Since an understanding of the role of the mouse has been seen to be a problem experienced by some users, this must be conveyed in the animation. The solution adopted is to present the handling information in an auditory fashion so as not to overload the user by excessive graphic information.

11.7. ANIMATION AS A CREATIVE TOOL

The help space is at a secondary level, thus it is a space where an element of creativity and humour can be more flexibly introduced without the formal requirements that may apply to the primary (drawing) space. This is also true for some explanatory animations that do not use a separate window to indicate the secondary space but occur directly on top of the primary space (e.g. animations within the interface). The use of humour is not a minor consideration if we wish our systems to be used and well understood. Apart from making systems more pleasant and attractive, humour can directly address emotional responses to using the computer such as surprise, frustration and achievement which do not appear within any more formal analysis. By addressing these emotions, it is hoped that the system can be viewed as being more sympathetic and understanding to the user, and that therefore the user is more likely to persist with using the system.

If we review some of the preceding examples, we can see how they could involve more humour in the animation. In the feedback animation, a sequence representing a laser printer in action (as in Figure 11.3) could be replaced by a sequence of an old metal printing press. In animation as identification, instead of representing the painting tools in a realistic fashion (as in Figure 11.7) a friendly and smiling pencil, or a dancing eraser (Figure 11.11) or fat dancing paint brush could be shown.

Figure 11.11.   Humorous identification of an eraser.

One advantage of using humour in such circumstances is to focus attention on the crucial aspect of explanation. If we simply show animations for the lasso and the dotted rectangle then their essential difference may be lost. If we use traditional highlighting techniques such as arrows or inversion then there is still danger of misunderstanding, and even if the correct point is understood, it may not be remembered. In this case, by concentrating attention on the contour of the selected objects within the animation and using a striking image it is hoped that the function will be understood and remembered. Having used the lasso tool to mark an area, the dotted flashing line marking the selected space fades to a dark green then, more strikingly, for a few seconds the line transforms into a boa constrictor that tightens around the object before returning to the normal animation (Figure 11.12).

To boost the creative and humorous elements of a computer interface, the field of visual comedy and jokes is briefly explored in search of techniques and principles underlying the making of humour. Three basic principles of visual comedy are summarized by the propositions: an object becomes funny by behaving in an unexpected way, by being in an unexpected place, or by being the wrong size. Examples are numerous: an enormous sandwich being thrown at someone; a person behaving like a lamp shade which can be switched on and off; a bus falling over after being tripped up by an old lady with a stick; speeding up animations, etc.

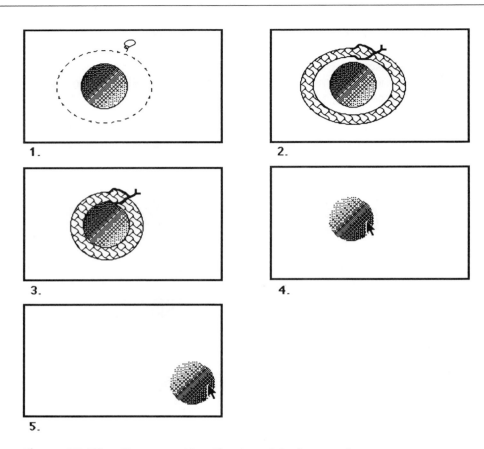

Figure 11.12.   Humorous identification of the lasso tool.

The comic effect functions on pairs of opposites such as normal/unusual, plausible/impossible, surprising/normal.

Of particular relevance to our work are those comedians who work silently, particularly comedians such as Laurel and Hardy and Charlie Chaplin. Their humorous sequences are often very good at describing situations where the normal becomes abnormal. For example, the closing of a door is taken as normally sufficient to secure a house. In a scene from *Shoulder Arms*, Charlie Chaplin is being pursued, and carefully locks the gate in the front wall even though the wall is in a bad state of repair and will give way to his pursuers. In *Don Jose* he is about the fight a duel, and instead of doing the gentleman's salute as we might expect from the situation he puts his opponent on the floor. He then circles around like a muscular body builder having knocked out his opponent in the boxing ring. In another scene, from *Apprentice*, he uses a woodworker's file not like a carpenter but like a manicurist. In another scene, instead of listening to the sound of the alarm clock with his ear, Charlie uses a stethoscope as if he were a doctor listening to the heart. In these few examples, Charlie is behaving and using objects in unexpected ways, but each scene is not built using the same construction principles. In the first example, the effect of "securing" a house is wrongly anticipated as the consequence of "locking the door". In the scene from *Apprentice*, the shown object and the gesture call to mind the absent object through a common function: filing. In *Don Jose*, a few specific gestures call to mind the world of boxing, its actions and place.

A simple example where this could be used is in explaining the effect of the starting pixel when using the pencil tool. Simply showing the two sequences as in Figure 11.8 does not draw particular attention to the crucial difference, nor does it identify with the user's sense of shock when this first happens. The size of the change (a black pixel instead of a white one) is completely disproportionate to the size of the effect (it is forever more a white pencil instead of a black one). An alternative humorous animation is suggested which addresses these issues (Figure 11.13).

Visual puns are a second relevant example of visual humour (Lessart, 1991). A visual pun is a drawing in which a line or shape has two meanings at the same time, so that the element can be perceived as part of two different systems of meaning. There are different possible constructions for visual pun: one example is found in a poster for road safety which contains a face in which the two eyes are represented by two head lamps. Thus the same circles belong to both the car and the face, and take two meanings. Another case of visual pun is the metaphor where one object is

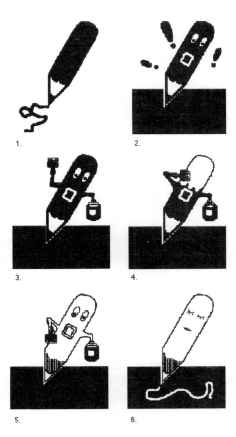

Figure 11.13.   A humorous explanation of the effect of the starting pixel when using the pencil tool.

surprisingly compared with another: for example, a drawing where an intestine replaces a pipe underneath a sink. There are other visual jokes based on different principles such as irony, satire, parody and caricature. Satire is based on criticism, parody depends on prior knowledge utilizing the familiar in such way that we recognize both the original and the departure of the original. Parody relies upon a frame of reference to be truly effective.

Some of the techniques we have seen so far belong to the world of visual rhetoric: for example, exaggeration, anthropomorphism, metaphor, synecdoche (the boxing ring), metonymy (the locked door), etc. They are used in the design of the computer interfaces but are also employed in a more amusing and creative fashion. For some artists and designers, humour is a natural point of view reflecting the feeling one has about things, but for less fortunate authors, the world of visual comedy provides ideas from which we can draw and visual rhetorics give us guidelines from which we can transform and improve the expressiveness and attractiveness of our message.

11.8.   CONCLUSIONS

We have argued that the future acceptability of much software will depend upon the quality of the help environment provided, and this will lead to a new generation of help systems that fully exploit the potential of multimedia. To many novice users, current help systems appear inappropriate and, being text based, they require translation into different languages. Attractive, general purpose, on-line and text-free animations can be provided within multimedia environments, but require a range of design techniques beyond those used for traditional software design.

Though we concentrate in this chapter upon functions that are represented iconically, the same techniques can be applied to other representational forms such as menus. For example, reference manual explanations of items that appear in the transformation menu of a paint system (e.g. perspective, rotation) consist of a series of diagrams and short sentences of the form "choose X" or "select X" followed by a short summary. It is easy to see how a short animation together with a short explanatory text could lead first to a hypermedia help manual. From here it is a short step to complete animated help.

One topic that we have not considered here, but which can be particularly effective, is the development of appropriate cartoon characters. In many instructional books a cartoon character is used to guide the users through the material, and cartoons are also used to stress a point or give a secondary information as they can relax the reader and enhance the delivery and presentation of the material. A cartoon "guide" can provide a unifying factor for a body of instructional material, it can add a trademark to the help system and, most importantly, it lends itself to endless humorous possibilities suggested by visual comedians and the comical code. If we compare the two sources of comical effect, we find that Chaplin plays on gestures and objects rather than on images and the cinematic gesture evolves slowly by small touches.

To summarize, an animated help system is not only consistent with the format of multimedia and promises to be easy to use but, by introducing an attractive and less rigorous element into the software, it encourages novice users in their effort to become familiar with the world of computing.

We have described some basic techniques and shown, by example, how visual help can be provided for different identifiable situations. On-line animated help of this kind could be shown in a small help window that includes simple controls, such as play, slow, pause, rewind, etc. Features would be needed linking the information together, as in the case of the sprinkler where it is necessary to link to help information concerning changing colours. In the same way that we have to balance carefully the help animation, so the humorous elements must not interfere with the explanatory message and must be suitably tailored to the target audience. The complexity of the help system would also have to be kept in check so that it does not defeat the main objective of making the system easy to use.

This chapter is an exploration of the area of multimedia help system, and clearly much work needs to be done, both gathering techniques and methods for the design of such systems and empirically testing help systems on groups of users. Multimedia help is, however, a very important topic if we wish future products to be accepted and used by an increasingly demanding public.

REFERENCES

Baecker, R. and Small, I. (1990). Animation at the interface. In Laurel, B. (ed.) *The Art of Human–Computer Interface Design*, pp. 251–67. Addison-Wesley, Reading, MA.

Baecker, R., Small, I. and Mander, R. (1991). Bringing icons to life. In *CHI'91 Conference Proceedings*, pp. 1–6.

Draper, S. and Barton, S. (1993). Learning by exploration, and affordance bugs. In *INTERCHI '93 Proceedings*, pp. 75–76.

Lessart, D. (1991). Calembours et dessins d'humour. *Semiotica*, **85**, (1/2), 73–89.

Sellen, A. and Nicholl, A. (1990). Building user-centered on-line help. In Laurel, B. (ed.), *The Art of Human-Computer Interface Design*, pp. 143–53. Addison-Wesley, Reading, MA.

About the author

Claire Dormann is studying for her PhD at the University of Brighton into animated icons and animated help systems. She obtained her first degree in psychology from the Université de Paris V – Sorbonne and her Masters degree in computer graphics from the University of Middlesex in 1990.

Colin Beardon is a Reader in Computer Graphics at the University of Brighton. He obtained his PhD in artificial intelligence from the University of Essex in 1976 and worked in industry and academia in Austrialia and New Zealand before returning to the UK in 1987. He currently manages a research centre concerned with the use of multimedia technologies in art and design.

PART 2

Applications: Publishing

12 CD-ROM and interactive multimedia publishing

Howard Sloan

12.1. INTRODUCTION

The development and evolution of the compact disc has become one of the most important factors behind the rapid growth of multimedia applications. Today, with estimates of an installed base of 10 million drives worldwide and with nearly 10,000 consumer titles available, the compact disc has become the medium of choice for many electronic publishing efforts.

Prospective multimedia publishers might wonder how deep an understanding of this technology is necessary in order to employ it successfully. In an ideal world, technology would be all of the things that its purveyors suggest: simple, easy to use, and reliable. Of course, although it provides people with wonderous and useful things, computer technology is not perfect, and to benefit from the opportunities that it has created, as with the electronic publishing of ideas and information, we need to be aware of imperfections.

Because every technology has its strengths and weaknesses, an understanding of what these strengths and weaknesses are is desirable so that we may realize our objectives through the use of a particular technology. Regardless of whether that objective is to programme a VTR or to calculate the amount of lift required for a spacecraft, the deeper our understanding of the principles upon which something is based, the greater our ability to evaluate merit and limitation; making informed predictions about how its use will impact upon the achievement of our objectives.

Facing the prospective publisher of electronic media who recognizes the need to learn, is the challenge of simply finding information on the many different subject areas that combine to make up this brave new world of interactive multimedia. As we will mention later on, one of the most exciting aspects of this development in communications is the convergence of several disciplines, each requiring unique skills. Ultimately, it must be said that specialist skills will continue to remain distinct within the multimedia production team: there cannot be an equal understanding of each task by everyone. Nevertheless, it is essential to the success of a project for each team member to acquire knowledge of diverse subjects to a greater or lesser degree.

MULTIMEDIA SYSTEMS AND APPLICATIONS
ISBN 0-12-227740-6

The aim of this chapter is to provide an introduction to the subject of one such technology: compact disc, and also to discuss some of the considerations involved in the development and marketing of interactive multimedia products for that format, and in general. It cannot be an in-depth study of the subject, but the interested reader can consult the references that appear at the end for further information. Overall, this chapter intends to support the view that the compact disc is a valid choice for the delivery of multimedia information and, at the risk of making a prediction, will continue to be in some form for the forseeable future.

12.2.   BACKGROUND

The digital compact disc (also known simply as the CD, but more accurately as the CD-DA or compact disc digital audio) that has achieved such a high degree of success in the music industry, began as a gleam in the eyes of its parents, Philips and Sony, in the late 1970s. Once the potential to store other kinds of information in addition to music was recognized, many variants of the original specification, including the familiar CD-ROM specification, were defined. These variants are described in considerable technical detail in a series of "books", each distinguished by having a different colour assigned to them. For those who are interested in exploring the colour book specifications further, these books are available from Philips. As an introduction to the subject, Table 12.1 lists the main variants and provides a description of their purpose.

Table 12.1.   Compact disc colour book formats.

Book	Acronmym	Purpose	Date
Red	CD-DA	Defines digital music format	1980
Yellow	CD-ROM	Defines error-corrected and raw computer data	1984
Green	CD-I	Defines multimedia data, OS, formats, etc.	1987
Orange	CD-R	Defines multisession appendable formats	1992
White	VideoCD	Defines linear format for digitally-encoded films	1993

As can be seen from the table, when referring to CD-ROM for example, we are also referring to something known as the Yellow Book standard. Almost from the beginning, the engineers of the colour book standards envisaged the compact disc as a storage medium for still or moving images, in addition to audio and character-based data. But it was not until Sony and Philips announced the Green Book standard, known as CD-I or compact disc interactive, that the medium became more closely associated with the message, and that message was meant to be embodied in the term "multimedia". CD-I directly targets the potential consumer market for interactive multimedia, and specifies not only a revised format for the compact disc, but also a complete processing environment, based on the 68000 microprocessor family from Motorola. This "dedicated" system approach by Philips and Sony has been perceived by many within the industry as something of a commercial gamble, the success of CD-I titles being inexorably linked with the success of the CD-I hardware platform.

Leaving the colour books aside for a moment, two other developments in the life of the compact disc that are not included in our chart are also worth mentioning, as reference to them is made frequently. These two developments are called High Sierra and ISO 9660, and again refer to further enhancements to the specification. The High Sierra specification was defined in 1985 by representatives from Apple Computer, Microsoft, Digital Equipment and others, with the purpose of extending the Yellow Book standard to better meet the needs of the computer industry. The name 'High Sierra' was, unglamorously, taken from the name of the hotel where the meeting to formalize the specification took place. The resulting specification was then adopted by the International Standards Organization, slightly modified, and released by them as the ISO 9660 specification. This specification was a significant step forward towards achieving greater standardization between hardware devices, as the format described an hierarchical file and directory structure commonly associated with computer storage media, such as the hard disk.

Following the chronological development of compact disc to the year 1989, Microsoft joined Sony and Philips to introduce CD-ROM XA (CD-ROM Extended Architecture). Microsoft, enthusiastic about the potential for the compact disc format as a delivery mechanism for multimedia information, but unwilling, not surprisingly, to be restricted to the hardware constraints of CD-I, retained the multimedia characteristics of CD-I while broadening, in theory, the compatible hardware base.

Despite Microsoft's participation, CD-ROM XA is perhaps best represented currently by products from Sony and Kodak. Kodak adopted the XA format for its Photo CD technology, which requires an XA-compatible compact disc drive and the appropriate Kodak software in order for an application to read a proprietary file format. The commercial intention of Photo CD is to encourage the consumer to have their photographic negatives "developed" (in fact, scanned) onto compact disc, rather than prints or slides. Kodak's efforts simultaneously resulted in a number of important advancements for compact disc technology: the pursuit and realization of the Orange Book format (otherwise known as CD-WO for "write once") and the ability eventually to append write to a compact disc, whose contents would otherwise remain only half-filled with photographic images. Currently, Philips is also employing CD-ROM XA as the compact disc format for VideoCD.

What is commercially available today as CD-R, or CD-recordable, has already revolutionized the process of interactive multimedia authoring. CD-R, in conjunction with the appropriate formatting software, allows the production of a master compact disc image on a desktop device attached to a personal computer by SCSI (small computer systems interface). This has brought the ability to publish information on compact discs within the reach of millions of personal computer owners. The cost of CD-R units has dropped dramatically over the last two years, to an average level of about £500, and a reasonably wide choice of manufacturer's models now exists.

12.3.   THE DEVELOPMENT PROCESS

Having established a basic technical framework around our subject, we want to look more closely at some of the practical considerations regarding the development and marketing of multimedia products on compact disc.

In any creative process, producing the desired result is often a question of striking a balance; of reaching the best possible compromise. In the case of interactive multimedia, there are many decisions that need to be made at each step of the planning, development and production process which should aspire to achieving the right balance. Many of these decisions will be concerned with how to reconcile the creative opportunities presented by a blank canvas and the availability of multiple artistic media, with the limitations of technology, the commercial demands of a particular market, and budgetary constraints.

One of the decisions most likely to impact upon the production budget will be the choice of hardware and software. Multimedia production often involves everything from bespoke software development to audio engineering, graphic design, video editing, animation, and more. The basic hardware and software requirements are shown in Figure 12.1.

It is common for a production team to decide upon a cross-platform development strategy. Although this decision increases both the complexity and the cost of developing a product, market considerations often dictate that a product needs to be available on more than a single hardware platform. Fortunately, developers of multimedia software tools are addressing this need through their attempts to tackle the incompatibility issue.

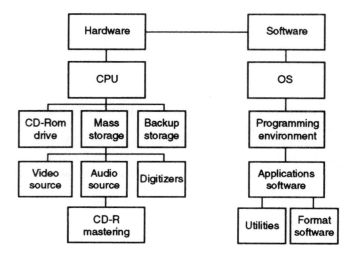

Figure 12.1.   Basic hardware and software requirements for multimedia production.

12.3.1.   Development Tools

The name "multimedia development tool" refers to a software application or high-level scripting language, or a combination of the two, that has been written especially with the task of multimedia creation in mind. Although dedicated programming languages, such as C or Pascal, offer unrivalled power and flexibility to the multimedia *programmer*, development tools ordinarily attempt to provide functionality while maintaining a degree of simplicity, and are therefore aimed at the multimedia author who is not necessarily an experienced computer programmer.

The choice of multimedia software development or "authoring" tools as they are commonly known, is determined to a large extent by the choice of delivery platforms. This is because no single tool exists that supports all of the major CD-ROM-based delivery platforms. It is possible to work with tools that will allow a multimedia CD-ROM project to run across both Windows and Macintosh environments, for example, but if a developer wants the same project to run on the CD-I platform, that developer will need to "re-engineer" specifically for that platform.

The holy grail for both the developers and users of multimedia authoring tools is true cross-platform capability, where one tool allows for the creation of a single work that can run across diverse manufacturer's proprietary hardware, without significant modification. In aspiring to this goal, Apple Computer and IBM formed an independent development company in 1991 named Kaleida, based in Mountain View, California, whose purpose is to design and develop just such a tool. The development of that tool, ScriptX, is proving to be an enormous undertaking in respect of the time and effort required to overcome the complexities of creating a true cross-platform authoring environment. Just as difficult for Kaleida engineers deciding on what hardware platforms ScriptX should support today (currently Macintosh and Windows, with plans for UNIX and possibly, CD-I), is the question of how to keep the environment open to the extent that it will allow support for tomorrow's hardware.

12.4.   A MARKET OVERVIEW

In addition to the compatibility issue, several historical problems have been sited as preventing the compact disc from achieving greater success in the market. One of the most persistent was the question of the lack of an installed base. There are now, however, many factors fuelling the growth for multimedia which have had a positive effect on the market position of compact disc technology.

12.4.1.   Positive market factors

Some of the most significant are:

the decline in the price of hardware;
the proliferation of CD-ROM drives;
improvements in performance;
aggressive marketing by manufacturers;
the games market move to CD-ROM formats;
the participation by new arrivals in investment and development of
CD-ROM product;
intensive media coverage.

Let us look at each of these in greater detail.

Price decline

On average, the cost of a multimedia-capable personal computer has
declined from between 25%–35% over the last two to three years. The
same is also true for the price of CD-ROM drives, video and audio digitizers, compression boards and computer-related hardware, generally.
Reduced cost has meant that, potentially, the technology can become
accessible to a much wider audience.

Proliferation of CD drives

Until fairly recently, it was extremely difficult to obtain reliable sales figures for either CD drives or interactive multimedia titles. Estimates often
varied wildly. This was due in some part to the early reluctance of manufacturers to provide accurate sales information. As the interest in multimedia has grown, market research companies have moved very quickly
to exploit the absence of reliable data, and there is now a reasonable body
of research available on the installed base of CD-ROM drives, in addition
to other pertinent market information, such as the number of multimedia titles that have been produced and their breakdown according to
delivery platform or target market.

These data give the prospective multimedia publisher considerable
scope for optimism, as the chart shown in Figure 12.2 suggests.

Better performance

The original data transfer rates for CD-ROM of 150 kbps have now been
superseded by drives capable of twice that rate, with several manufacturers producing drives with data transfer rates of four times the original
speed, or 600 kbps. Newer drives commonly make use of a data cache
which further improves the playback performance of the system.

Marketing

Major industries with a stake in the multimedia market, and particularly
personal computer and electronics manufacturers, are encouraging the
market for CD-based products in a number of ways:

Worldwide installed base of CD-ROM drives

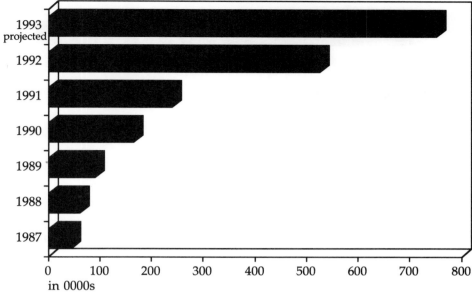

Figure 12.2.   Worldwide installed base of CD-ROM drives.

discounting;
bundling of titles;
more hardware models shipping with internal CD drives as standard or
as an option;
organizing multimedia trade shows, exhibitions and conferences;
through the creation of wholly or partly owned electronic publishing
divisions;
by commissioning market research studies.

Games market

Michael Spindler, CEO of Apple Computer Inc., once said that Nintendo,
the Japanese games manufacturer, posed the single, biggest threat to his
company. Sega, chief rival of Nintendo, has outsurpassed every other
proprietary system, including CD-I, Photo CD and Data Discman, in
terms of the installed base of CD-ROM drives attached to their Sega
Genesis game system. Estimates by the Optical Publishing Association of
the installed base for these consumer formats in the United States, to the
end of 1993 are shown in Figure 12.3.

New arrivals

This last, and perhaps most recent development, is of particular interest,
as it is generally acknowledged that the skills and experience of other

Optical Publishing Association estimates for year end, 1993 (USA only)

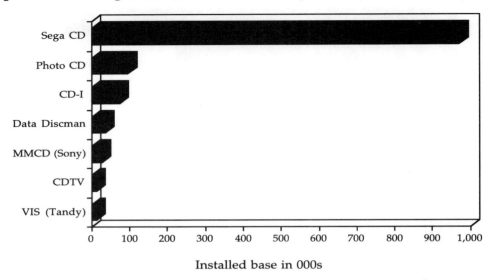

Figure 12.3.   Optical Publishing Association estimates for year end, 1993 (USA only).

disciplines would help to improve the quality and broaden the appeal of multimedia products. Conversely, companies who are newly involved in defining applications that exploit opportunities in this area may find that they do not possess all the requisite specialized technical skills needed to develop applications themselves. A range of possible options exists for the business who needs to address this issue. The correct choice will vary according to many criteria, but here are some common possibilities:

building an in-house development and design team;
outsourcing the necessary skills through the use of third-party development and project management teams;
licensing the electronic publishing rights, rather than participate directly in the production process;
forming a partnership or alliance with another company whose skills are complementary.

In-house development.   Building an in-house development team implies making a very strong commitment to the creation and production process. Start-up and running costs can be quite high and are therefore normally perceived as part of an overall business strategy that will focus on medium to long term returns.

Outsourcing.   There is a trend in business today to speak of the importance of outsourcing or leveraging outside resources, allowing companies to focus on their core business and remain small enough to be flexible in the face of continual change. Outsourcing specialist skills in particular, like those required for the development of interactive multimedia, makes sound business sense for many companies.

Electronic publishing rights.   Another route into the world of multimedia publishing that is finding favour with individuals and companies that own the electronic publishing rights to content is licensing. Licensing the electronic rights of selected material to a third party developer is a prudent approach to achieve revenue from assets without making a direct investment in development resources. The issues of rights licensing are beyond the scope of this chapter, but many intellectual copyright and entertainment law firms are extending their expertise to advise clients in this area. Indeed, most major companies seeking to license the electronic rights to their assets are gaining expertise on the subject within the legal departments of their own organizations.

Alliances.   The interest in multimedia production and publishing on the part of companies that were not previously technology oriented has also created an opportunity for the formation of beneficial, cross-industry alliances. Two excellent examples (among many) of this kind of alliance-making, whereby in multimedia terms the whole is greater than the sum of the parts, are the relationships between Dorling Kindersley, book publisher, and Microsoft, software company; and Random House, US publisher, and Brøderbund, software development company and creator of the entertaining Living Books series of children's titles on CD-ROM.

In addition to the obvious creative and development strengths of such alliances, it is anticipated that long-standing arrangements with retail and distribution operations that were perhaps enjoyed previously by one partner, might now become a shared channel by both the previous product line and also the new, jointly-developed electronic products. Taking the publisher and software developer partnership as an example, both printed books titles and interactive multimedia titles might be made available through retail bookshops. Identifying the right sales and distribution channels is an issue that will obviously influence the potential for success of any new product. In the case of CD-ROM, this issue has yet to be resolved completely, although there is a growing awareness (and in some areas an actual commitment) of the need to re-examine sales channels for electronic media.

12.4.2.   Negative market factors

The subject of sales and distribution leads us on to take a look at some of the obstacles preventing the wider acceptance and use of compact disc technology. Some of these are:

    development and production costs;
    format proliferation rather than consolidation;
    relatively complex personal computer technology;
    performance;
    uncertainty about sales and distribution channels.

Development costs

Interactive multimedia has often been compared with television and film production in terms of the amount of time, effort and finance required to create a quality product. That is not to say that in the course of preparing the budget for an interactive CD-ROM project, a producer should use the cost of the summer blockbuster as a general rule-of-thumb, but a realistic budget for a CD-ROM project could easily equal those of many small, independent films.

Too many standards

From the perspective of both the developer of CD products and the consumer, this is perhaps the most significant obstacle facing the industry. To achieve broad acceptance of the technology will require a greater move towards unification and simplification. The impetus for these developments has already begun with the work of organisations such as the International Multimedia Association, whose aim is to encourage both software developers and hardware manufacturers to adopt the same standards for implementing multimedia technology. In addition, the development of cross-platform tools and programming environments, as was discussed earlier, is a positive force for change.

Performance issues

Although, as mentioned above, the performance of the compact disc itself has improved considerably, there are several contributing factors which, when measuring the overall performance of a CD-based multimedia computer system, negatively effect the quality of the result and consequently, the user experience. As technology continues to evolve, however, personal computers or perhaps a new breed of powerful, portable devices, will gradually minimize the current importance of this issue.

Distribution channels

If we were to compare the ease with which it is possible to find a book on a particular subject with finding an interactive multimedia title on the same subject, what would the comparison tell us about the availability of multimedia titles? Of course the fact that distribution and retail channels for these products are narrow and specialized is not the sole reason for the lack of availability, but it is a major factor effecting market awareness of the technology, particularly where the consumer market is concerned. For interactive multimedia to succeed, an established and visible chain of distribution will have to be created.

12.5.   CABLE AND SATELLITE SYSTEMS

Although it was mentioned at the beginning of this chapter that CD-ROM has a secure future as a medium for publishing multimedia information, there is some speculation as to whether it may be ultimately surpassed by cable and satellite delivery systems. No one who has even so much as glanced recently at the newspapers could fail to have noticed the frenetic activity within the global telecommunications and cable television companies, apparently intent on allying themselves (or otherwise) with everyone from entertainment and publishing interests, to computer software developers and hardware manufacturers. In view of the fact that cable and satellite delivery systems overcome many of the obstacles that are listed above and in consideration of the tremendous financial resources of telecommunications companies, it is tempting to conclude that most multimedia information will be delivered via these means. Undoubtedly, the convergence of the telecommunications, entertainment, publishing and computer industries signifies the beginning of a powerful, dynamic influence on the future direction of interactive multimedia, and on our future relationship with technology.

12.6.   CONCLUSIONS

The compact disc is a portable, robust and efficient means of storing and distributing multimedia information. It is technology that can be held in your hands; a tangible product. Several clouds remain persistently on the horizon, however, that may serve to confuse both the prospective developer and the market to a point of apathy. In spite of these, there continues to be a number of very positive initiatives, such as the work being done by the International Multimedia Association (most recently regarding digital video) on the problem of standardization, and the push to develop more comprehensive cross-platform authoring tools. The compact disc will also benefit from the fact that multimedia technology in general continues to progress with respect to system performance and in terms of its ability to convey a higher degree of realism, thanks in part to the improving quality of full-motion, full-frame video display. Combine these positive signs with the present industry conviction that prices will continue to fall, and the compact disc seems likely to continue to grow in popularity for multimedia applications, at least for the remainder of this decade.

REFERENCES

(1986). *CD ROM–The New Papyrus*. Microsoft Press, Redmond, WA.
(1986). *CD ROM–Optical Publishing*. Microsoft Press, Redmond, WA.
(1993). *Demystifying Multimedia*. A Guide for Multimedia Developers. Apple Computer Inc., Cupertino, CA.

Burger, J. (1993). *The Desktop Multimedia Bible*. Addison-Wesley, Menlo Park.

(1992–93). *European Multimedia Yearbook*. Interactive Media Publications Limited, London.

IMA Compatibility Project Proceedings. Annapolis, MD.

InfoTech (1992–93). *Optical Publishing Industry Assessment*. InfoTech, Woodstock, VT.

Morph's Outpost on the Digital Frontier. Technical Magazine for Builders of the Information Superhighway. Orinda, CA.

Optical Publishing Association. Columbus, OH.

Apple (1993). *Optical Storage Media Market Research Report*. Cupertino, CA. Apple Computer Inc.

About the author

Howard Sloan is a leading authority on the subject of multimedia technology and electronic publishing. He was responsible for heading Apple Computer Europe's business development efforts in this area for several years, and has lectured and presented extensively on the subject of multimedia at computer and related industry exhibitions around the world. His consultancy company, Big Idea, was recently formed to provide an independent source of expertise with respect to the design, development, implementation and management of multimedia communications and electronic publishing projects. A native of the United States, Mr. Sloan has been working in the computer industry in Europe, primarily in the United Kingdom and France, for the past ten years.

13 Future developments in information publishing

Stewart McEwan

13.1. INTRODUCTION

As the market demand for quality multimedia product continues to grow, we have started to witness the expected covergence of the traditional media and computer industries. Through the integration of television, video, and interactive computers the consumer has now come to expect a more immediate and easier access to all types of information. With the sales of powerful multimedia platforms outpacing current manufacturing capacities, it would seem that these new and exciting developments of the "information age" have finally been coupled to the driving forces of the consumer market.

Although a great deal of the investment interest is being focused on the delivery methods promised by the provision of new broadband cable networks services, also known as "super data highways", there has also been a great deal of market comment on the development and acceptance, by the consumer, of the graphical user interfaces provided by most modern computer operating systems.

With the ever increasing power available to the software designer, coupled with the decreasing cost of high-performance personal computers, these graphical user interface (GUI) paradigms are providing an environment for the design and development of captivating and, therefore, entertaining multimedia titles.

The earliest multimedia products were criticized by many users as being in the main inaccessible, frustrating and limited. With many of these developments derived from traditional mainframe text databases or even laser disc computer-based training (CBT) products, the slow evolution of the associated interface may explain at least some of these shortcomings. The problems of mapping between these dissimilar environments were further compounded by the under-powered and expensive delivery platforms then available.

Although some interesting work has been accomplished within the academic and educational environments using hypertext, hypermedia and derivatives such as HyperCard stacks on the Apple Macintosh, these developments have generally faced similar limitations due to a lack of both computing and information resources.

MULTIMEDIA SYSTEMS AND APPLICATIONS
ISBN 0-12-227740-6

With most basic personal computers now offering relatively inexpensive access to much larger data storage via smaller and faster CD-ROM drives, complemented by high-quality sound and image display, this type of multimedia offering has now been almost entirely replaced by a more consumer-oriented second generation of product, purposely designed to take advantage of proposed specifications published by such bodies as the MPC council.

In this chapter, various aspects related to the design of such a consumer multimedia product are investigated, and the variety of emerging delivery methods and the recent advances in the associated technology are discussed.

13.2.   PRESENTATION OF INFORMATION

It is of critical importance that the designer of a multimedia product continues to respect the mental attitude that a novice user will adopt, when confronted by an unfamiliar product interface. Unless an easily identifiable metaphor is instantly established, and the underlying navigational functionality is rendered consistent and efficient, the user will quickly become reluctant to explore the product further.

By adding quality characteristics through attention to detail in typography, icon design, colour and dynamic and effective interactive sequencing etc., the look and feel of the product can be greatly enhanced.

Many of these concepts are directly related to traditional graphic design rules observed and employed in other, non-computer, related fields such as the methods used in the structuring and display of the large amounts of detailed information required in the publication of modern reference books.

In fact, development of appropriate methods to represent information via the computer platform have an earlier parallel with the evolution of modern information print publishing.

Not so long ago it was inconceivable to expect colour plate photography or illustrations on every page of a reference book. A reference publication employing a limited amount of illustration material can severely restrict the reader's attempts to access the important information quickly.

Correctly employed, graphic design can greatly enhance the textual information and provide help to the reader in understanding complex facts and data.

13.3.   DORLING KINDERSLEY AND LEXIGRAPHIC DESIGN

In 1982, Dorling Kindersley (DK) launched the first publication under its own imprint, *The First Aid Manual*, produced in association with the British Red Cross, St John Ambulance, and the St Andrews Ambulance Association. This adopted a completely new style specifically created to empower the reader with information through the copious use of graphic illustrations.

Other pubications that followed developed this theme by including large-scale use of colour photography and a carefully planned layout of text to *support* the illustrations and photographs. With the publication of *Eyewitness Guide: Bird* in 1988, a new and compelling style was successfully developed that would at the same time both inspire and captivate a young and enquiring mind, and still appeal to the adult reader (Plate 15, colour section).

Through the use of techniques such as the "exploded" photograph, subject matter was literally taken apart and laid out on a neutral white background with closely integrated text annotations, to enable the reader to receive the information in a truly non-linear fashion.

The challenge was undertaken by the many designers, editors, photographers and specialists at DK to find a means of making both the words and the pictures work together to enable effortless and enjoyable communication of information. At DK the name adopted for this philosophy was "Lexigraphic Design", with this word "Lexigraphic" encapsulating the principle of making words and pictures work together on a page.

The *Eyewitness* series now includes more than 70 titles and has become a modern publishing phenomenon with sales reaching over 15 million world-wide. The choice of topic for each publication has always been selected very carefully in order to appeal to the widest possible audience.

13.4.   THE MULTIMEDIA TITLE: MUSICAL INSTRUMENTS

Due to a common interest in developing multimedia products, 1991 saw a strategic agreement reached between DK and the Microsoft Corporation. With both companies eager to exploit their relative strengths, the synergy of a joint relationship in the development of consumer multimedia titles proved irresistible.

The first of these joint products was developed in London during 1992 by the newly formed Multimedia division at DK and was based on the successful *Eyewitness Guide: Music*.

The Lexigraphic style proved to be a perfect precursor to the required multimedia design, and the resultant product greatly expanded on and enhanced the original book by introducing high-quality digital audio to accompany the over 200 musical instruments featured.

Important considerations were given to the design of a "point and click" interface. The user is encouraged to explore the product using the mouse as the main navigation tool.

Beginning with a short musical introduction, the program quickly presents the main "Contents" panel. This offers the four main access points to the product and can be re-selected at any time or place within the program by using the mouse to select the "Contents" button available at the top of the screen via the permanently displayed button bar.

The four main choices available on entry to the product are as follows.

Families of instruments.   The user can select from classes of instruments such as brass, woodwind, percussion or strings and then move on to explore each selection in ever-increasing detail through successively narrowing the criteria of choice, until reaching the required individual instrument article page. At this level it is now possible to hear a uniquely commissioned "solo" performance of the selected instrument by clicking on the sound icon.

Musical ensembles.   This presents the most common associations of the many featured instruments in various groupings such as orchestras, jazz bands, pop groups, rock bands, etc. Many diverse audio examples are provided to accompany the illustrated selections. As each group is presented, the individual instrument illustrtations remain active to the click of a mouse to zoom down instantly to the individual instrument.

Instruments of the World.   This section superimposes many of the instruments on a series of colour atlas pages of the world to establish the ethnic and regional background of those represented. Each instrument includes a speaker icon to enable the immediate play-back of the associated sound, and this can be used to great effect to illustrate the range of the many different tonal qualities of instruments that have originated throughout the world. Once again, a direct jump can be made simply by clicking on the small thumbnail image represented on the map to further detail presented on the base-level article page.

A to Z of instruments.   A complete thumbnail-picture-based A to Z is available, with the user invited to select only the first identifying letter.

All of the instruments are illustrated through the use of a large horizontally scrolling picture and sound icon menu display. This technique was an attempt to provide an easy access to the complete contents of the product, and an overview of what the title contains.

As most consumers are used to evaluating the amount of information available within a book by both surveying its thickness and browsing through the pages, the designers at DK Multimedia wanted to represent this in providing a scrolling contents list that can be used to provide either a short sound sample of each instrument or, by clicking as before, a pathway directly to the main individual instrument article page.

A fully comprehensive text-entry index is available by selecting the "Index" button presented on the button bar. As each character is entered via the keyboard, the system is programmed to narrow down a user's choice continually and automatically, to enable the required selection to be found quickly and easily.

Almost all navigation is via picking with the mouse on graphical picture elements. The only exceptions are the "Back" button, which allows users to retrace their most recent path through the product, the "Next" button, which links you automatically to the most relevant associated instrument, and lastly the "Random" button which enables users a random choice of instruments to be selected with the automatic accompaniment of the associated sound.

The layout of a typical "Lexigraphic" page in a DK book involves a number of important parts. The main centre-piece is usually a large colour photograph known as the *Icon* (Plate 16). This is used to attract the reader's attention and to engage their curiosity. This level combines with the heading and a short piece of introductory text to signal the main topic of the spread. This is further supported by the second level of information which supports and amplifies the central theme. Both of these levels can usually be represented on a typical computer display at a resolution of 640 by 480 pixels.

A third level used on the book page layout to provide even further associated information must usually be converted to a series of "pop-up" windows on the computer. This allows the multimedia user to overlay the main article screen with supplementary information if they wish.

All of the text in *Musical Instruments* is displayed using an anti-aliased font to provide for a higher quality display, with certain key words being highlighted in red to indicated "hot text" associations, or hypertext links that further expand by calling up the previously mentioned pop-up windows to overlay the main display page.

Each of the main *Musical Instruments* article pages also provides a number of "icons" which can be selected by the mouse to access even further information, including sound.

Many of the hundreds of "pop-up" windows will offer further detail or additional options for the user to experiment with the sound of the instruments.

The feature on the Fender Stratocaster electric guitar, for example (Plage 17), has a set of effects pedals waiting to be selected and heard, and each of the strings has been individually recorded from the original instrument so that they may be "plucked" using the mouse, with the result that the user will be hearing *exactly* what each string on this specific guitar sounds like!

As a further clue to the user in the use of the product interface, the mouse cursor has been programmed to change from an arrow pointer to a pointing hand when it moves over a hot region. This cursor may also become a "drum stick" if for example, the instrument selected is of a percussion type, inviting the user to click on the mouse button to beat a drum skin (Plate 18).

The quality and attention to detail shown by the editorial, design and software teams at DK Multimedia has resulted in *Musical Instruments* receiving a number of awards from such distinguished bodies as the British Interactive Media Association (Gold Award for Information) and the European Multimedia Association (Best Information and Reference Title) among others. Furthermore, the resultant press coverage throughout the world has generally acclaimed *Musical Instruments* as a leading benchmark title in this medium.

This vote of confidence inspired both the management and staff at DK Multimedia to push on with the development of other information titles.

13.5.   DELIVERY PLATFORMS

Currently the multimedia platforms of choice for most consumers are the Microsoft Windows MPC and the Apple Macintosh. As both of these systems require relatively high-resolution computer displays, they do not exhibit the immediate screen-related problems of television-based systems such as CD-I or the newly proposed, more powerful games machines such as 3DO.

As most television graphics designers quickly discover, there is a finite limitation to the amount and size of readable text that can be displayed on a standard television receiver.

There is also a prevalent consumer attitude that sets televisions and computers apart. The television is seen as an entertainment device that is viewed on a "sit back and watch" basis. The traditional computer system assumes a more intimate, more interactive "one-to-one" relationship with the user.

This would suggest that until there is a union formed through the adaptation of, for example, an all-digital HDTV system, the television and the computer will continue to play differing roles in the consumer multimedia industry.

There still exist however, many limitations for the computer-based multimedia designer. Although manufacturers are continuing to offer ever more powerful hardware, the majority of existing systems adaptable as multimedia platforms are based on older and much less powerful processors. This will be one of the main limitations in the use of digital video within current CD-ROM multimedia developments. With software-only play-back of digital video being the only feasible solution for the large-scale acceptance of this new technology, further advances in both the system software, (possibly true 32-bit operating systems like Windows '95 may help), and data-compression techniques such as Motion-JPEG, MPEG Fractal and others, will be required.

The original CD-ROM bandwidth specification of 150 Kbyte/s has now been upgraded by most manufacturers. By doubling the rotational speed of the disc and providing a larger memory buffer, the result is an increase in the available bandwidth to approximately 300 Kbyte/s. A number of manufacturers have gone even further in offering four times the original bandwidth, resulting in data retrieval throughput of approximately 600 Kbyte/s.

In combination with the previously mentioned compression methods, this may result in an adequate drive specification to support the first generation of titles and systems based on the newly announced Video-CD format.

Unfortunately, although these advances will eventually become the norm for most users, it will be some time before the multimedia developer can justify adopting these most recent attributes as a minimum specification for product development.

13.6.   THE FUTURE

As the largest and leading players in the fields of telecommunications and cable TV forge strategic alliances with equally important members of the traditional media and computer industries, there is a growing expectation of a more standard approach in the offering of "on-line" interactive multimedia products and services.

With a growing base of newly installed, high-bandwidth, fibre-optic based networks becoming available, and with the financial community behind the required investment, these large consortia have the opportunity to increase their available bandwith still further, through the use of digital compression techniques similar to those previously mentioned.

This will enable the program providers the network capacity to offer a new generation of interactive services.

Computer-based cable converter boxes will replace current cable-television "head ends" that sit atop the TV set and these will enable access to 500 or more possible channels of programme material. With so many choices, the new "black box" and smart TV will require filtering and control software; this is the focus of a great deal of current development by the computer software community.

In addition, the processor inside the "black box" must be powerful enough to handle the decompression required to display in real-time the material selected and to offer support for such services as movies on demand, interactive home shopping, and interactive selection of the camera views at live sports events etc.

Television viewers are also expected to benefit through the added assistance of online information available via a linked CD-ROM platform or multichannel cable reception. This will offer the consumer the capability to "call-up" statistical facts related to the on-screen presentation, such as the performance details of individual golf players during live broadcasts.

Other related developments are now beginning to appear in the form of intelligent personal data assistants (PDAs). These systems aim to replace the mouse and keyboard on computers with the use of a pen-based interface, using powerful character and handwriting recognition software and complemented with enhanced high-resolution A4-sized flat panel displays, built-in high-speed mass-storage devices, such as PCMCIA flash RAM, and possibly the next generation of smaller, high-speed CD-ROM drives.

Plans are already under way to provide connectivity via cellular radio to enable many of these systems to have cordless access to existing network-based email and fax services, and even to some of the previously discussed specialized on-line services. Although many of the current systems available are expensive, heavy and require all too frequent battery changes due to their excessive power requirements, these problems will be removed over time to provide the basis for easily accessible, but incredibly powerful, electronic books of the future.

13.7.   CONCLUSIONS

The combination of high-bandwidth on-line services providing a possible new high-technology library of the future, and the smaller, lighter and highly powerful new generation of inexpensive portable multimedia systems, will provide a unique environment for the new age of electronic publishing.

As the first HDTV systems begin to appear, the timing will most likely coincide with the release of the complementary high-performance "black box" units that will provide further accessibility for the early adopter-consumer. Schools may soon have unimaginable access to vast electronic resource libraries whilst education and entertainment will continue to merge to make for a more exciting learning experience. Information publishing has now entered a new and immensely exciting phase of development, which will benefit both publishers and *consumers*.

ACKNOWLEDGEMENTS

I would like to express my thanks to all of my colleagues at Dorling Kindersley Multimedia who have established an innovative and exciting environment for the development of quality multimedia titles.

A special thanks is due to Alan Buckingham and Nick Harris for their support and assistance in the preparation of this chapter.

Finally, I could not conclude without reference to Peter Kindersley, who has contributed his inspiration, vision and drive to all of these developments undertaken at Dorling Kindersley.

About the author

Stewart McEwan has been involved in the design and development of software and hardware systems for over twelve years. He has been a member of ACM Siggraph and BKSTS since 1983 and has presented a number of previous papers with respect to his work in parallel processing and computer graphics. As Technical Director at Dorling Kindersley Multimedia his responsibilities include the management of the software engineering and technical support requirements of the division.

14 Multimedia and copyright: some obstacles on the Yellow Brick Road

Julian Dickens and Mark Sherwood-Edwards

Toto, somehow I don't think we're in Kansas anymore. (*The Wizard of Oz*, 1939).

14.1. INTRODUCTION

The brave new world of multimedia is here; or nearly. But before it really arrives, there are a number of legal problems which will have to be resolved. This chapter looks at two of the problems facing multimedia developers, suggests some possible solutions, and then goes on to discuss the structural issues that underlie the legal side of multimedia development.

Section 14.2 looks at the problem of underlying rights, and how the administrative cost of acquiring rights clearances is hindering the growth of multimedia. Section 14.3 looks at the problem of look and feel, which arises from the attempt to fit new technologies into old legal concepts, in this case copyright.

Section 14.4 is intended for the multimedia operator who, undeterred by the problems set out in Section 14.2 and 14.3, decides to carry on regardless. It provides a strategic analysis of the structural and legal issues which underlie the production of multimedia products.

14.2. TOO MANY COOKS?

CD-ROMs have three distinguishing characteristics. First, they can handle nearly every sort of medium – music, words, numbers, programs, images. Secondly, a CD-ROM is (or can be) interactive. Thirdly, a CD-ROM's capacity is, by present standards, huge. A CD-i can hold 300 000 pages of text, 19 hours of level C audio, 72 minutes of full screen video and thousands of colour images. The obvious thing for an entrepreneurial CD-ROM producer to do, therefore, is put all sorts of words, images, music, and information on CD-ROM; add some software which allows the user to manipulate the data; and finally, market the disc and retire rich and happy.

Unfortunately, this is exactly where the problems begin. The sort of material CD-ROM producers would like to put on CD-ROM is generally protected by copyright (pictures, music, words) and/or performing rights (performances by musicians and actors), and copyright (and to an extent performing rights) are property rights. This means that if you incorporate someone else's copyright material on your CD-ROM without their permission – however small a proportion of the CD-ROM that person's material takes up – that person can prevent you from selling the CD-ROM, and in many jurisdictions, have a court order the destruction of the CD-ROMs. The potential consequences for a CD-ROM producer whose CD-ROM infringes someone's underlying rights (as copyright and performing rights are collectively known) are financially very severe.

And quite right too, you might say; the CD-ROM producer *should* obtain permission before using a copyright work. But from whom? The complexity of the present rights system means that obtaining the necessary clearances (as permissions are usually called) can be difficult, time-consuming, and expensive. An example will illustrate the problem. Let us assume that you want to produce an interactive CD-ROM. As subject matter for your product, you choose the recent Hollywood film, The Bodyguard, starring Whitney Houston and Kevin Costner. You want to be able to show some footage from the film, play the theme tune "I will always love you", which is sung by Whitney Houston, display the lyrics onscreen, and allow the user to print hard copies of the lyrics. And because it is an interactive CD-ROM, you want to allow your customers to re-mix the song to make their own version. The first thing you have to do is get permission from the rights holders; to keep things simple, we will concentrate on the song.

To include the existing recording of the song on the CD-ROM, you will need permission from the performer (Whitney Houston) in respect of the performing right, and the record company (BMG), in relation to the recording of the song. Usually the record company will control both the performing right and the right in the recording, so you will need to contact only one body. On the other hand, the record company may not have the worldwide rights, in which case you will have to approach the record companies in the other territories for permission to distribute your product there (though this is subject, in the EC, to the effect of articles 30, 36 and 85 of the Treaty of Rome).

The backing musicians will have performing rights, and their permission will also be needed to make reproductions of their performance. They are likely to have transferred their rights to the record company as well, but they may or may not have consented to the use of their work on CD-ROMs. Because each territory will operate under different musician's union agreements, this will depend, largely, on where the recording took place.

However, the record company's permission is only one of the permissions that have to be obtained. The record company controls the rights for that particular recording as a recording, but to reproduce the composition on CD-ROM (or any other medium) you will also need permission from the composer of the song. Since the rights in the music and words are separate rights, this can be two people – the composer and the lyricist – and require two separate permissions: luckily, Dolly Parton wrote both the words and the music to "I will always love you". She will have transferred her copyright in the composition to her publisher who, in the UK at least, is Carlin Music. For other territories, it may be another publisher or sub-publisher. For the mechanical right (the right to press recordings of the composition) Carlin Music is likely to (though it need not) have transferred the mechanical right to the MCPS, the society in the UK which collects the revenue from licensing the mechanical right. However, although the MCPS will be able to grant the rights for records and CDs (and usually videos too), it is not always the case that it has the right to grant the rights for CD-ROMs: this will depend on each publisher's agreement with the MCPS.

Moreover, this mechanical right only covers the song played as a song. If you want the song to play in conjunction with the film footage or any other visual image, you need synchronization rights, and these you will generally have to get from the publisher (though they may be delegated to the MCPS or local equivalent), whose permission you will also need to display the lyrics on-screen and print hard copies (and the publisher may have assigned the graphic rights, as the right to print lyrics is called, to someone else). Again, the publisher may be able to give you the rights only for particular territories. If you want the right to distribute the CD-ROM throughout the world, you may have to approach a number of publishers.

Remixing of the song (this is an interactive disc, remember), may be a breach of the composer's moral right of integrity. Although some publishers may claim to have obtained waivers of moral rights from the composer and lyricist, moral rights are unwaivable in some territories (notably France and other European civil code jurisdictions), and a licence from a publisher may not provide sufficient protection. To be on the safe side, you may need to have the moral right waived directly by Dolly Parton herself.

All this for just one song. If you wanted to clear the underlying rights on a worldwide basis, the complexity of your task increases substantially. Furthermore, having just one song on a CD-ROM seems a poor utilization of the medium: as a producer, you would want to put many songs on the disc and, perhaps, produce a compilation of Hollywood theme tunes.

The complexity and, more importantly, the cost in time and money, of obtaining the requisite permissions for copyright works and performing rights can be so high that it acts as a brake on the development of a multimedia industry. It seems therefore, that if multimedia technology is to be able to deliver all that it promises, the legal structure for the licensing of underlying copyrights and performing rights will have to be re-evaluated.

What are the alternatives? First, we can carry on as we are. This may restrict the development of multimedia products, but maybe there are more important things to worry about. Secondly, the industry could set up a collective licensing system. Each rights holder could delegate his power to grant licences to the collecting society, and all producers obtain permission from, and pay the appropriate fee to, the collecting society. This provides the simplicity of one-stop shopping, particularly if backed by an electronic database system. The greater the number of territories covered by the collecting society, the more useful it is, and a collecting society licensed to grant clearances for all the EC would be something really worth having.

A third possibility would be to move away from the present system of copyright as a property right – which carries with it the idea of being able to use injunctions to prevent unauthorized dealings with the material – to a conception in which all that is protected is the right to receive fair payment. The problem with this system is defining what is "fair". The usual solution is to appoint a tribunal to fix prices. This is in itself an expensive overhead, but there is a more fundamental objection, and that is that price fixing has little place in a market economy (and all Western states are now, more or less, market economies). In a very real sense, property is merely a bargaining counter. If you pay me enough, I will give you access to my property, but unless I have a right to exclude you from my property, how can I oblige you to negotiate?

Moreover, a system based on property operating in a free market frees us from the problem of determining a fair price, because the price determined by the market is, almost by definition, fair. And compared to a tribunal-based system, allocation by the market is not only likely to be more efficient in both the short and the long term, it is also very cheap to run. (Market distortions, such as monopolies, can be controlled by competition laws.)

Therefore the second option, a collective licensing system, seems to be the best option. By acting as a central clearing house for sellers and buyers of rights it would create a market where, otherwise, the administrative cost makes many transactions uneconomic. Buyers would benefit because it would enable them to buy more easily and with reduced administrative costs. Rights holders (authors, artists, actors, musicians etc.), would benefit because it would enable them (through their representatives or assignees) to earn revenue from, or obtain higher prices for, rights which would otherwise be under exploited. One can even imagine the development of rights brokers who would package together those rights that most usefully go together.

Similar collective licensing schemes already exist (for example, the Performing Rights Society licenses broadcasting and performance rights for music in the UK), so the principle itself is sound. Moreover, the technology now exists (databases, digital highways, EDI) which will make feasible a rights clearing house on a much larger scale. To be successful, it would need to attain quickly a critical mass. This could be achieved by providing that unless rights holders deliberately opt out, they will be presumed to be in the system. Clearly, the realization of such a system requires a corresponding political will, but this may not be a major obstacle. The EC Commission is carrying through, one step at a time, a programme of harmonization whose logical outcome is a single, community-wide, copyright and performing right (though, where these rights remain nationally based, the bundling of rights referred to above might prove a workable substitute). Having set up a harmonized legal structure for the protection of underlying rights, the Commission might well turn its attention to the setting up of an EC-wide organization which would permit the most efficient exploitation of these rights: in so doing, the Commission would probably be supported by rights holders themselves. In the US, the Warner Music Group, recognizing that the complexity of rights licensing is hindering the development of multimedia CD-ROM, has recently set up a one-stop shopping facility for 3DO producers (Time Warner is an investor in 3DO).

Until then, however, we are stuck with the present situation. CD-ROM producers will continue to face a situation where they can incur greater costs in arranging the clearance of rights than they do in paying for the rights themselves and, despite technology and creative desire, realization of the full potential of interactive CD-ROM will be held back by a lack of usable material.

14.3.   LOOK AND FEEL

One of the more esoteric areas of computer-related law is the protection of look and feel. But esoteric or not, look and feel is important: it is not only one of the main factors in making a multimedia product successful, a successful look and feel is also one of the first things that competitors will imitate. This section takes a look at the developing UK (and inevitably, US) law on look and feel and assesses the protection it offers producers of multimedia products. However, you should bear in mind that laws are geographical things, and what holds good in one country will not necessarily hold good in another.

14.3.1.   What is look and feel?

Why, you might ask, is look and feel an issue? After all, there is copyright in the music, copyright in the film, copyright in the illustrations and photos, copyright in the text, copyright in the computer program, there are performing rights and a number of ancillary rights, and last but not least, there is copyright in the whole work as a compilation. Do not these rights adequately protect look and feel? Well, not exactly.

There are three main problems. Firstly, a product's look and feel is built up out of the interrelationship of screens, command structures, functionality, response times, colours – in short, a disparate collection of features and details, tangible and intangible, which define how a particular program appears and responds to the user. Unlike music, text or image, there is no single thing you can easily point to and say "that's mine".

The second problem is this. Copyright is an old-fashioned institution based on an old-fashioned paradigm, the book, and the traditional view of copyright is that it protects the expression of ideas, not the ideas themselves. The classic example is Mrs Beeton's recipe for yorkshire pudding:

Mrs Beeton might have had copyright in her expression of the recipe for yorkshire pudding ("take two generously heaped spoonfuls of flour" rather than "take two spoonfuls of flour") but she would have had no copyright in the recipe itself nor in the Yorkshire pudding produced by the recipe. Copyright protects Mrs Beeton's expression of the recipe as a static, one-dimensional, literary work, but not as an interactive, functional, capable-of-doing-something, set of instructions. This book-based paradigm is effective where the actual code of a program is copied because, in such situations, the analogy to the copying of a book is clear. But, as everyone knows, the instances of "literal copying" (legal jargon for copying of code) are rare. Much more significant commercially are the cases of non-literal copying, where the copier copies the look and feel of a program without referring to the code at all. But if copyright is extended to protect the non-literal aspects of the program – i.e. what the program actually does – is this not tantamount to giving Mrs Beeton copyright in the making of Yorkshire pudding? The fear of extending copyright beyond its established boundaries has made the courts reluctant to protect look and feel in its own right.

The third problem relates to the scope of the public domain. There has always been an argument that the elements that make up a user interface – key allocations, pull-down menus, and so on – are, like words in relation to language, basic building blocks which should stay in the public domain: giving copyright to such elements would stifle the development of software and make it impossible for new software companies and multimedia producers to compete. This issue has reached a critical stage in the US with the recent spate of litigation between Apple and Microsoft. In its Windows program, Microsoft had used a number of icons and associated functionalities which resembled Apple's icon-based operating system (Hewlett Packard was alleged to have done the same thing with "New Wave"). Apple argued that it had copyright, not only in the code of its operating system, but in the individual elements of its user interface. Microsoft argued that Apple could not have copyright in these individual elements because, *inter alia*, they were in the public domain. (Like the dog that did not bark, the whole Apple/Microsoft saga was notable for the absence of the creator of the icon-driven interface, Rank Xerox.)

14.3.2.   Present trends

How are these issues likely to be resolved? In the US, Apple has (for the time being, as it intends to appeal the decision) lost its case against Microsoft. There is therefore, in the US, no general copyright in icon-driven and windows-based interfaces, though there may be copyright in specific implementations of those techniques (for example, in a particular design of a trash-can icon).

As for non-literal copying, the UK has recently had its first major case on the issue. The case of *John Richardson Computers* pitted a company against an ex-employee, and concerned a stock-keeping program for chemists: on leaving the company, the ex-employee, who was a programmer, had written a rival program. The two programs were very similar in the way they appeared to the user but, because the programmer had written his version from scratch, no issue of literal copying arose. The case therefore turned on look and feel, and the judge listed 15 similarities in the user interfaces: they included key use (e.g. both programs used the Escape key in a similar way), on-screen messages (the message "operation successful" followed by a double beep), screen layout (e.g. both programs displayed the label outline towards the top left corner of the screen) and functions (e.g. the option to reset the daily figures): of these 15 elements, only eight had been copied and could therefore be claimed to be in breach of copyright. On a traditional view, there could be no infringement of copyright in the program because no code had been copied. The judge, however – and this is where the case breaks new ground – preferred an alternative approach: he held that this collection of user interface elements could be protected not just as a computer program, but also as a compilation (i.e. a collection).

To understand the judge's reasoning, you have to know a bit about the UK law on copyright in compilations. Generally speaking, for something to be copyright, it has to be original: "original", in most copyright systems, does not mean that it has to be new or unique, only that it must be the product of the creator's intellectual efforts (like a book). This entails that in most systems of copyright, things which are not created, like facts, cannot be copyright. The UK has always taken a slightly different view. According to the UK's law on compilation, it does not matter if the individual elements of a work are, like facts, unoriginal: what matters is whether you have put a minimum of skill and effort (the latter often being interpreted to mean the expenditure of money) into collecting together those unoriginal elements. If you have, then that collection is a compilation and you will have copyright in it.

As far as the judge was concerned, that was exactly what had happened here. The individual elements of the interface might have been unoriginal, but together they were copyright as a compilation. And precisely because the user interface was being protected as a compilation and not as a computer program, there was no need to show literal copying of the code. By this ingenious route, the judge had managed to lay the theoretical foundation for effective protection for look and feel (theoretical, because on the facts the company lost the case), while still paying lip service to the previous case law.

How did the judge reconcile this approach with the scope of the public domain? Are not key allocations, beeps on the occurrence of certain events, and so on, by their nature the property of everyone? Well, yes and no (and this is where the ingenuity of the judge's compilation approach becomes really apparent). Although the individual elements of the interface may well be in the public domain, the selection and arrangement of these individual elements into a unitary whole (i.e. the look and feel of a program) was the specific creation of the program's producer and was therefore not in the public domain. Therefore any substantial copying of the product's look and feel would be a breach of copyright in the compilation.

14.3.3.   CONCLUSIONS

What conclusions, however tentative, can multimedia producers draw from the developing law on look and feel? Firstly, and reassuringly, the present UK trend (and so far it is only a trend) is towards an acceptance that non-literal copying can be an infringement: copyright will not only protect the code of your program, but also its effects on-screen.

Secondly, in relation to the elements in the public domain, it seems that the UK may be taking a different route to other countries such as the US. Although commonplace elements of a user interface (such as the use of the Escape key to cancel or exit an operation) may not be copyright in themselves, a number of such individual elements grouped together to form a user interface may well be protected as a compilation. This, in general, is a welcome development in the law. It protects the designer of a user interface, while still giving competitors sufficient room to compete: for there to be an infringement of copyright, you will remember, copying must have taken place. If two poets independently write exactly the same poem, each poet will have copyright in his or her version of the poem, and neither poem is an infringement of the other.

Thirdly, what can a multimedia producer do to maximize the protection of his or her user interface? Frankly, not a lot. True, the more distinctive the interface, the easier it will be to establish copying, but commercially it makes little sense to design an idiosyncratic product purely to maximize the scope of legal protection. As soon as you become aware of a product that you suspect is a copy of your product, you should consider taking legal advice on possible action. Until then, however, your legal efforts are much better spent ensuring that you have acquired all the rights you need, that your production and distribution deals provide the right balance of risk and reward, and so on.

14.3.4.   A European postscript

What does the future hold for look and feel? Potentially the most important developments for multimedia producers are to be found in the proposed European Community Directive on Databases, issued by the EC Commission. This Directive (which is still in the draft stage and slowly grinding its way through the EC machinery), provides that databases are to be protected by copyright. It then defines a database as "a collection of works or materials arranged, stored and accessed by electronic means..." – as good a definition of a multimedia product as any – and includes in its definition of a database the "system for obtaining and presenting information" – again, as good a definition of user interface as any. However, the Directive then goes on to exclude expressly from its protection any computer programs used in the making or operation of the database. Given that it will inevitably be computer programs that operate the database, what can this mean? It is possible, though speculative, that this exclusion refers only to the code implementation of the system (i.e. its literal aspects), and not to the system's non-literal aspects (i.e. its look and feel). If this is the case, then the Directive on Databases may provide solid, and pan-European, protection for the look and feel of multimedia products.

14.4.   THINKING STRATEGICALLY

Players in the multimedia industry come from a variety of backgrounds and have different objectives. There is a good argument that one of the major inhibitions to rapid development of the industry for the good of all players is the frequent mismatching of the expectations of different parties trying to do business together. This lack of understanding manifests itself at many different stages – at the stage of acquisition of underlying rights for a multimedia product; at the stage of finance-raising by a producer; at the stage of distribution.

In a market characterized by unpredictability and immaturity, those players who spend a little time and resource trying to learn about and take into account the fears and aspirations of those with whom they are dealing will find it that much easier to find a way to close a successful deal. In this chapter we will identify some of these problem areas from the perspectives of different industry sectors, and suggest ways in which a better comprehension of the practices adopted in analogous media industries can help turn confrontation into resolution.

14.4.1.   The rights owners

Publishers, record companies, stills libraries and film and television producers all own completed works. A multimedia product is a copyright work which incorporates a number of such preexisting copyright works such as text, photographs and drawings, film clips and music, together with the software required to turn the underlying information into an accessible, interactive product. For rights owners the multimedia market thus offers a new opportunity for the repackaging and exploitation of their existing investment in catalogues and libraries. The emergence of the mass market for multimedia products will hopefully see this opportunity turn into a substantial source of revenue – but the rights owner sitting across the table from an eager multimedia producer will first want to see a number of concerns properly addressed.

(a)   How is the multimedia product going to be sold?

A key concern here for the rights owner is to ensure that the multimedia product will be sold in such a way as to tie in with other agreements entered into by the rights owner for more immediately profitable ancillary exploitation of the underlying product concerned – such as spinoff videos and books etc. If the rights owner is a television company being asked to grant multimedia rights in a successful programme, another key concern will be to ensure that use fees and residuals payable to contributors to the original programme will either be met by the multimedia producer or can be cleared in some other way.

(b)   How long should the licence last?

In an unpredictable market a rights owner will not want to licence his "crown jewel" product for an unlimited period of time. The multimedia producer may therefore find himself in a position of either having to agree a sizeable licence fee up front, or accept a term so short that he may not be confident of his ability to generate enough income from sales of the product to recoup his production costs. A useful solution here is to try to tie the licence period to the economic life of the product in some way – for so long as the rights owner is seeing a reasonable return from sales revenue, the licence should continue in force.

(c)   Will it be a quality multimedia product?

Given their own relative lack of knowledge about the multimedia industry, some rights owners are worried that they may be licensing a valuable title to a producer who may produce a second rate application. This in turn may have a damaging effect on the reputation of the original work, as well as make a good return from the multimedia product unlikely. Multimedia producers should not be afraid of offering references from satisfied customers, evidence of industry awards, or agreeing (as with the bespoke software industry) regular and defined stages of consultation. On the other hand, it is only fair that the rights owner should appreciate the reluctance of a multimedia producer to grant the rights owner any form of approval over the finished product. A multimedia producer will be very reluctant to see a rights owner, who may be relatively unsophisticated in his ability to analyse the strengths and weaknesses of a given application, have power of life and death over whether or not a product goes to market.

(d)   What is a fair price for a licence?

This is perhaps the most common and most intractable problem in rights negotiations. Where there is as yet no mass market distribution structure, it is very difficult to estimate with any degree of accuracy the standard means and costs of distribution and manufacture that will eventually become a recognized and predictable feature of the industry. Most compromise solutions involve an element of an upfront fee and some form of backend participation – although whether this is best cal-culated on a royalty basis, a net profits basis or in some other way will vary. Rather than try to adopt a familiar, but probably inappropriate, rev-enue structure from a neighbouring industry, the parties will generally do better to look at the multimedia product concerned and try to make a rea-sonable projection as to its possible future exploitation given the nature of the specific product. In a high risk market the joint venture structure is traditionally regarded as a fair way of sharing risk and reward. Not unreasonably, however, a multimedia producer will be reluctant to share control of a product with the licensor of rights in materials which will only play a minor part in the finished application.

14.4.2.   Hardware manufacturers

Hardware manufacturers are keen to ensure that exciting applications will be available for use on their kit from the moment it can be found in the shops. As such, they sensibly regard the commissioning of good prod-uct as a crucial part of their overall marketing and development budgets. However good a piece of hardware may be, nobody will buy it if there is nothing good to run on it. Producers, seeing the possibility of receiving part or full funding for their long-cherished projects, are therefore initially attracted by what the hardware manufacturers have to offer (i.e. cash) but are often upset to find that the cash comes with one or two strings. Whether these strings are fair, or an acceptable compromise can be negotiated, again depends on both parties understanding the implica-tions of the deal in the longer term.

a)   Platform specificity

The hardware manufacturer will often want to ensure platform exclusiv-ity for the product he is paying for, whilst the producer will often want to be able to version the application to run on as many platforms as possible so as to maximize revenue. A useful test of fairness here is to establish who is *really* taking the risk. It is of little interest to the producer of the application if he is only getting his out-of-pocket costs paid for – produc-ers, like everybody else, have to pay their own overhead and hopefully turn a profit at the end of the day. If the producer is being offered a sum which includes reasonable fees and a profit share if the product sells well, however, the hardware manufacturer's position seems much more rea-sonable. Between these two positions lies a wide range for possible com-promise. For instance, some form of holdback is often acceptable to both parties. Producers will also want to have some ability to go to market on another platform if the hardware manufacturer suffers an unexpected and significant delay in the launch of the hardware or decides not to publish the product at all. Conversely, it is not too unfair for a hardware producer who is financing the major proportion of a product to receive some share of the revenue from sales on other platforms.

(b) Ownership

Who should own copyright in a commissioned multimedia application? A multimedia product, unlike many of the other forms of copyright work, is easily divisible into separate components. There is copyright in the application as a compilation work – i.e. in the selection and arrangement of underlying copyright works (including the retrieval software) which, when taken together, constitutes the specific product. There is a separate and identifiable copyright in the retrieval software itself, and in the separate picture, sound and text elements incorporated in the database. All of these can be owned separately, provided the proper licensing structure has been identified and secured. Where the multimedia producer is being fully commissioned by a hardware company, it is not unreasonable for the commissioning entity to want an exclusive licence or even to acquire copyright in the finished product as a compilation, provided the producer can retain copyright in the retrieval software which can then be used on future products. Again, it is crucial to look at the question not in terms of arbitrary principle, but from the point of view of what the parties really *need* out of the arrangement in the long term. Joint ownership can be a good solution. As with any joint venture, however, it is crucial to ensure that each party has the same motivation. Where two parties so structure their affairs that they own a product through a joint venture, they have to consider what their motivations are likely to be when considering, e.g. licensing the product to other platforms in the future. If the joint venture is between a producer and a hardware manufacturer the co-owners risk finding themselves back in the "platform specificity *vs* maximizing revenue" argument discussed above. Where there is not likely to be a long-term community of interest, a joint venture is best avoided.

14.4.2. The producers

They are the prospectors of the multimedia industry. They have got used to the calloused palms, the luke warm coffee and the cold hard ground. But they know there is gold in "them thar hills" *somewhere* – so they have kept their operations lean and hungry, knowing that when there *is* a big strike, they will be there to stake their claims. For producers, two areas of problem are of particular interest – the wish, where possible, to keep their costs down by avoiding expensive rights clearance payments, and the need to ensure that the products that they *have* produced will be sold as effectively and profitably as possible.

(a) How can producers avoid having to pay fees for underlying rights?

Rather than face the clearance costs for underlying rights which remain in copyright, it is open to multimedia producers to save money by the use of public domain works – older, often classic, works in which the copyright has expired. The key point to remember here is that copyright is a nationally based right, and that a work in the public domain in the UK may still be in copyright in, for instance, the USA. The use of public domain works can be a valuable way of saving money, but it is therefore important to bear in mind the use to which the multimedia product will be put, and its likely range of distribution. A similar moneysaving measure sometimes taken by multimedia producers is to rely on the fact that, under the Copyright Designs and Patents Act 1988, there is no infringement of copyright unless the "whole or any substantial part" of the underlying work concerned is copied. This may appear to be an attractive money-saving ploy at first, but it is in practice a very high risk strategy, since the courts have consistently interpreted "substantial" not just by reference to volume but also by reference to significance. One can infringe a "substantial" part of a 500-page book by merely reproducing one page if that one page is of particular importance in relation to the work as a whole. There is no clear line here, and informed legal advice must always be taken.

(b) Who should control the distribution and marketing?

This is a critical issue. Reference to analogous industries tends to support the view that those who control distribution will ultimately become the dominant force in the marketplace. Distributors know best what the market will pay for a given product and know best (or believe they know best, which *de facto* often amounts to the same thing) which products the market will want to buy. Control of distribution and marketing should not therefore be given away lightly – especially when high volatility in the early years of the mass distribution market is generally regarded as a certainty. A key determinant to the answer to this question is to identify who bears the loss if distribution is not effectively carried out. Where a product has been fully commissioned and paid for by a hardware manufacturer, that manufacturer will, not unreasonably, want the major say over distribution. If no other party has an interest in distribution revenue there is unlikely to be any major resistance to this. Where a producer or rights owner *does* have an interest in continuing revenue, however, a demand for absolute control on the part of the hardware manufacturer is unlikely to be received sympathetically. A classic conflict tends to arise in the area of establishing pricing structures. A hardware manufacturer expects to make his profit out of sales of hardware. In budgetary terms, if the production cost of a disc has already been written off as a marketing expense, the manufacturer will be keen to see the disc sold for as low a price as possible. This is unlikely to be very satisfactory for a producer or an underlying rights owner with a vested interest in seeing maximum revenue. One solution here is to establish a floor on the basic calculation for royalty payments to the producer.

In other circumstances, where the owner of a product is negotiating terms with an unrelated third party distributor, it is the guarantee of distribution performance which must be the subject of critical analysis. Finally, particular attention should always be paid to the level of distribution fees and heads of distribution expenditure which may be recovered. In other media industries, reporting and verification procedures for distribution expenditure are the norm. There is no reason that multimedia distribution should be the exception.

14.5.   CONCLUSIONS

A comprehensive list of problem areas and possible alternative solutions would fill a book. We hope that the above examples are nevertheless enough to support our belief that when the mass market begins to emerge, and there is consequently rather more to be both won and lost, better deals will be concluded by those players who can identify their own needs in terms of defined strategy. For the market to grow, new players will have to enter it. Those new players will come from the more established but related industries of software, television, film, music and print publication industries into which the multimedia industry will be integrated as, in their turn, those industries are integrated by multimedia.

New entrants to the industry should ensure that they take appropriate legal and business advice from those who better understand the risks and rewards that multimedia has to offer, whilst those in the industry already must realize that they are more likely to conclude the long-term deals which they need to grow if they can understand the motivations of the record company, film or television producer or book publisher sitting across the table, and can rely on their advisers to help them to structure an agreement based upon mutual understanding.

About the authors

Julian Dickens has been advising clients active in all aspects of multimedia production since 1987 and founded the Olswang Multimedia team.

Mark Sherwood-Edwards is a member of Olswang's Multimedia Team, and advises in all areas relating to Multimedia.

PART 2

Applications: Futures

15 Multimedia futures

Carl Machover

15.1. INTRODUCTION

Multimedia is getting hard to ignore. As the 27 September 1993 *Computer Resellers News* points out, almost weekly, there is news of a new mega-deal involving consumer-electronics giants, telecommunications multinationals and high-tech hardware and software firms announcing alliances in preparation for the day when multimedia will be an integral part of every business and every household. The current USA administration's support of a high speed data highway further fans the interest in multimedia and its role in such areas as interactive TV.

15.2. IMPACT ON WORKSTATIONS

The promise of multimedia affects our workstation purchasing strategies. Over the past few years, almost no one would purchase a graphic workstation without a colour monitor. One recent survey found that over 95% of recent corporate workstation purchases were for colour units. Evidence for productivity gains using colour workstations is contradictory. But users like colour better, and since the incremental cost between a colour and monochromatic unit is small, most users opt for colour.

Similarly, we are now entering an era when users will begin to be reluctant to purchase a workstation that does not have multimedia capability. All major, and many minor, workstation vendors (including laptop suppliers) have incorporated various levels of multimedia capability into their products. At a minimum, today's workstations include sound capability, and provisions to play CD-ROMs. Live video capability is also often provided.

Recently, the Multimedia PC Marketing Council announced an upgraded multimedia specification whose PC requirements include:

25 MHz 486SX, or compatible;
4 Mbyte of RAM;
160 Mbyte of hard drive;
16-bit VGA graphics;
16-bit audio;
3.5 inch floppy drive;

double-speed, CD-ROM drive;
two-button mouse;
local bus (not specifically required, but system design virtually mandates it).

In the not too distant future, we can expect workstations to feature voice recognition, and voice output, higher resolution displays moving toward HDTV standards, built-in video cameras for teleconferencing, and increasingly common real-time full-motion video capture and playback. In the near-term, multimedia formats can be expected to proliferate. Users are now confronted with multiple standards like CD-ROM, CD-I, MPC, Ultramedia, Commodore, Atari, 3DO, laser-disc interactive and Nintendo. However, one can expect "shaking out" to occur in the next three to five years. Further, software is now being developed to make CD-ROMs essentially platform independent. Also, as is occurring in the workstation arena, we can expect more cross-platform capability, just as today we can move data and software fairly easily across DOS, Apple and UNIX platforms. Looking out a bit farther, say in five years or so, we can expect workstations and consumer television sets to merge, and the merged resource exhibiting extensive multimedia capability. This, in fact, was the basis for the USA interest in being a major HDTV player–many felt that if we lost HDTV as we had lost commercial TV, we would also lose the PC/workstation market.

15.3.   VIRTUAL REALITY

Virtual reality (VR) can be considered the ultimate multimedia experience. Presently, home and arcade video games increasingly use VR elements such as stereo viewing, helmet mount displays, surround sound, and gesture input devices. While VR now is quite costly, as applications proliferate, particularly in the consumer area, we can expect prices to be driven down dramatically.

15.4.   HARD COPY

Often ignored in the flush of the electronic home and office is the issue of hard copy. Each year, the death of hard copy is soberly proclaimed – and each year, we produce about 15% more hard copy than we did the year before. The author believes that as the cost of good colour hard copy continues to drop (especially those units using ink jet and thermal technologies), we will begin to see more hard copy units built into the multimedia workstations, satisfying the users' need for an instantly available "snapshot" of what is on the display.

15.5. APPLICATIONS

Much of our current experience with multimedia comes from business, education, and consumer applications – video games, product kiosks in stores, information kiosks in museums, reference works on CD-ROM, and in a variety of training situations. Certainly, such applications will continue to grow. Often overlooked, however, are the significant applications for multimedia in science, engineering and manufacturing. These applications are growing and include:

    analysis;
    design modifications;
    documentation;
    human factors analysis;
    maintenance simulation;
    manufacturing assembly instructions;
    research;
    teleconferencing;
    training/simulation.

For example, some CAD systems, such as ACCUGRAPH'S Mountaintop include the capability of voice annotation as part of the "red-lining' function.

Toshiba has loaded on the hard drive of their T4500 notebook computer a show that combines on-screen text and 2-D animation to introduce buyers to their new purchase. Dressed as a lab techician engineer, an animated character travels over a 3-D modelled computer back-drop, explaining each feature in a text balloon.

Bethlehem Steel uses multimedia to teach employees about the operation of a casting machine. Multiple windows of graphics and multiple audio streams with motion video are used. For example, in one part of this application an overview of the entire steel making process is shown. Using the mouse, the viewer can select an area of the process and see it in action. The torch cutting process sequence has a sound track, and text which says "Upon completion, the solid strand is torch cut into specified slab lengths and shipped to the hot strip mill or plate mill". The viewer can select the word "strand" with the mouse to see and hear a full motion video explanation of this aspect of the steel-making process.

Anderson and Company has developed a multimedia Manufacturing Process Analysis Workbench to capture shop floor procedures in full motion video and quickly integrate them into a process analysis. The application keeps track of individual operations while the user creates a flow chart and logs suggestions for process improvement.

At the California Department of Transportation (Caltran), engineers have adopted multimedia to speed daily business. The agency is experimenting with a desktop video conferencing system to let district engineers discuss plans and see video images of changes being made to blueprints. The agency has customized a special stand that holds blueprints in position for the camera. The system is expected to change Caltrans' current mode of sending blueprint changes, by courier, back and forth between district offices, since the blueprints are too large to fax. Caltran believes that the cost of the system will be more than offset by the money saved in time and travel.

15.6.   IMPEDIMENTS

A recent (August 1993) Gallup survey of Fortune 1000 companies showed that about 39% were now using multimedia, and that about 10% more will use multimedia next year. However, there are clearly impediments to implementing multimedia applications. Half of the people who responded to a 1993 impediment survey (reported in the 27 September 1993 issue of *Computer Resellers News*) stated that cost was the major impediment. This finding matches a 1991 survey (reported in the 12 August 1991 issue of *Computerworld*). In decreasing order, the 1993 survey found that after cost, the major impediments were: lack of equipment (18%), lack of expertise (12%), costly training (10%), lack of industry standards (8%), management resistance (7%), time (6%) and inadequate applications (4%). Nine percent reported that there were no obstacles.

The 1991 survey results were not markedly different. In 1991, after cost, the important impediment factors were standards, applications, equipment installed, user education, integration, technology, distribution, and development.

Obviously cost is a driving factor. It is the author's impression that cost issue relates to the cost of developing a multimedia application, not the cost of the multimedia workstation. Today, an adequate PC multimedia workstation can be purchased for under $4000, including the CD-ROM player, while an adequate UNIX multimedia workstation can be purchased for under $6000, including the CD-ROM player. In typical technology-cost reduction fashion, these prices should come down by half within the next 18–24 months. However, the cost of producing a multimedia presentation can be several orders of magnitude higher. For example, a small art museum in Purchase, NY is spending more than $300,000 to put their collection of about 300 art objects on a patron-usable multimedia kiosk. This appears to be a typical production cost for a relatively small project – and these costs are not expected to be cut significantly in that same 18–24 month time frame.

The present need for a skilled development team (including content, programming, computer graphic arts, education, and multimedia specialists) suggests that a significant market opportunity exists for multimedia authoring pages that include some level of expert system capability. Today, for example, most presentation packages (like Aldus' Persuasion, for example) include a large number of predefined formats, colour palettes, backgrounds, charting features, and clip art. Some packages help one select colours based on how they will appear on the slide rather than the monitor. There are packages under development which automatically modify the presentation depending on such factors as the country in which the presentation will be made, or the size of the room. The result is that today, someone with little or no graphic arts capability can turn out a very credible slide presentation. Availability of analogous capability in multimedia software, will additional features to facilitate the use of sound and video clips, could significantly reduce the cost of presentations.

15.7.   MARKET FORECASTS

Forecasts of the size of the multimedia market show enormous variations, depending on the forecaster and on what the forecaster may be including in his/her estimates. For example, Ms Meg Whitbread, a senior research analyst for Market Intelligence Research Corporation is quoted in the 27 September 1993 *Computer Resellers News* as follows:

Application revenue alone is expected to rise to $7.2 billion from worldwide sales by the end of 1994, from $5 billion in 1992 . . . in 1995, . . . increase brings sales to $10.9 billion. By 1999 . . . multimedia applications revenue will reach $23.9 billion. Combined sales of multimedia hardware and software . . . will total world-wide revenue of $24 billion by 1999. In 1992, training accounted for 38.7% of multimedia applications sold; business presentations 19.3% . . . and education 11.9%. By 1999 . . . business presentations and education applications . . . most common . . . each capturing 21% of the total applications market.

Our forecasts are somewhat more aggressive. We estimate that all multimedia hardware and software revenue in 1993 will be about $10.2 billion, growing to $25.4 billion by 1995. We estimate that of the totals, about $1.6 billion in 1993 will come from technical applications, growing to $3.1 billion in 1995.

15.8.   SUMMARY

Multimedia is an exciting, challenging, and high growth market and discipline. There still are numerous technical challenges. While hardware and software costs are satisfactory, the cost for producing a professional multimedia presentation is now, and will probably continue in the near-term to be costly, requiring a team of skilled people with complementary capabilities. This suggests that substantial opportunities exist in the services segment of multimedia. One recent multimedia study included the following summary:

1.   It will be a high growth market through 1995, 43.2%.
2.   It will be applications driven.
3.   The main part of the future domestic market will be built around an open system architecture concept.
4.   Strategic alliances, mergers, and acquisitions will play a key role in the future makeup of the multimedia equipment industry.
5.   Price/performance improvements will continue in excess of 50% per year . . . throughout much of the five-year period 1990–1995.
6.   The further development of industry standards is needed to support future growth.

7.   High-end PCs will continue to augment the workstation platforms throughout many application areas.

8.   Entertainment and education/training applications will lead the marketplace . . . 1990–1995.

9.   The consumer end-user group will represent the largest multimedia market segment . . . 1990–1995.

("The US Market for Multimedia Equipment, Systems and Peripherals", #A2383, published by Frost & Sullivan, Summer, 1991.)

About the author

Carl Machover, president of MAC, a computer graphics consultancy, is also an Adjunct Professor at RPI, past-president of NCGA, SID, and Computer Graphics Pioneers, on the editorial boards of many industry publications, and writes and lectures worldwide on all aspects of computer graphics.

Index

W A R N I N G

BY OPENING THIS SEALED PACKAGE YOU ARE AGREEING TO BECOME BOUND BY THE TERMS OF THIS LICENCE AGREEMENT which contains restrictions and limitations of liability.

IF YOU DO NOT AGREE with the terms set out here DO NOT OPEN THE PACKAGE OR BREAK THE SEAL. RETURN THE UNOPENED PACKAGE AND DISKS TO WHERE YOU BOUGHT THEM AND THE PRICE PAID WILL BE REFUNDED TO YOU.

THE MATERIAL CONTAINED IN THIS PACKAGE AND ON THE CD-ROM IS PROTECTED BY COPYRIGHT LAWS. HAVING PAID THE PURCHASE PRICE AND IF YOU AGREE TO THE TERMS OF THIS LICENCE BY BREAKING THE SEALS ON THE DISKS, YOU ARE HEREBY LICENSED BY ACADEMIC PRESS LIMITED TO USE THE MATERIAL UPON AND SUBJECT TO THE FOLLOWING TERMS:

1. The licence is a non-exclusive right to use the material recorded on the disc (which is called the "software" in this Agreement). This licence is granted personally to you for use on a single computer (that is, a single Central Processing Unit).

2. This licence shall continue in force for as long as you abide by its terms and conditions. Any breach of the terms and conditions by you automatically revokes the licence without any need for notification by the copyright owner or its authorised agents.

3. As a licensee of the software you do not own what has been written nor do you own the computer program stored on the disks and it is an express condition of this licence that no right in relation to the software other than the licence set out in this Agreement is given, transferred or assigned to you.

   Ownership of the material contained in any copy of the software made by you (with authorisation or without it) remains the property of the copyright owner and unauthorised copies may also be seized in accord with the provisions of the copyright laws.

4. Copying of the software is expressly forbidden under all circumstances except one. The one exception is that you are permitted to make ONE COPY ONLY of the software on the CD-ROM for security purposes and you are encouraged to do so. This copy is referred to as the back-up copy.

5. You may transfer the software which is on the CD-ROM between computers from time to time but you agree not to use it on more than one computer at any one time and you will not transmit the contents of the CD-ROM electronically to any other. You also agree that you will not, under any circumstances, modify, adapt, translate, reverse engineer, or decompile the software or attempt any of those things.

6. Neither the licence to use the Software nor any back-up copy may be transferred to any other person without the prior written consent of Academic Press Limited which consent shall not be withheld provided the recipient agrees to be bound by the terms of a licence identical to this licence. Likewise, you may not transfer, assign, lend, rent, lease, sell or otherwise dispose of the software in any packaging or upon any carrying medium other than as supplied to you by Academic Press Limited. The back-up copy may not be transferred and must be destroyed if you part with possession of the software. Failure to comply with this clause will constitute a breach of this licence and may also be an infringement of copyright law.

7. It is an express condition of the licence granted to you that you disclaim any and all rights to actions or claims against Academic Press Limited and/or the copyright owner with regard to any loss, injury or damage (whether to person or property and whether consequential, economic or otherwise) where any such loss, injury or damage arises directly or indirectly as a consequence (whether in whole or part):

   a) of the failure of any software contained in these disks to be fit for the purpose it has been sold whether:
      i) as a result of a defect in the software, howsoever caused; or
      ii) any defect in the carrying medium howsoever caused; and/or

   b) any other act or omission of the copyright owner or its authorised agents whatsoever,

   and you agree to indemnify Academic Press Limited and the copyright owner against any and all claims, actions, suits or proceedings brought by any third party in relation to any of the above matters.

8. This agreement is to be read as subject to all local laws which are expressed to prevail over any agreement between parties to the contrary, but only to the extent that any provision in this Agreement is inconsistent with local law and no further.

9. This agreement shall be governed by the laws of the United Kingdom.